DATE DUE

MAY 1 3			
FEB 3			
DEC 1 7 1973			
GAYLORD			PRINTED IN U.S.A.

Protestantism

GREAT RELIGIONS OF MODERN MAN

Richard A. Gard, *General Editor*

BUDDHISM
Edited by Richard A. Gard

CHRISTIANITY: CATHOLICISM
Edited by George Brantl

CHRISTIANITY: PROTESTANTISM
Edited by J. Leslie Dunstan

HINDUISM
Edited by Louis Renou

ISLAM
Edited by John Alden Williams

JUDAISM
Edited by Arthur Hertzberg

Protestantism

EDITED BY

J. Leslie Dunstan

GEORGE BRAZILLER

NEW YORK   1962

284

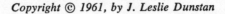

Acknowledgments

The editor wishes to thank the following for permission to reprint the material included in this volume:

ABINGDON PRESS—for selection from Edmund D. Soper, *The Philosophy of the Christian World Mission.* Copyright 1943 by Whitmore & Stone. Used by permission of Abingdon Press.

GEORGE ALLEN & UNWIN LTD.—for selections from W. A. Visser 'tHooft and J. H. Oldham, *The Church and Its Function in Society;*—for selections from Ernst Troeltsch, *The Social Teachings of the Christian Church.*

ALEC R. ALLENSON, INC.—for selections from Stephen Neill, *The Unfinished Task;*—for selection from Sydney Cave, *The Doctrine of the Person of Christ;*—for selection from F. D. Maurice, *The Kingdom of Christ;*—and for selection from Alan Richardson and W. Schweitzer, *Biblical Authority for Today.*

RT. REV. RICHARD BROOK, D.D., M.A.—for selection from Richard Brook, "The Bible," in B. H. Streeter (ed.), *Foundations.*

T. & T. CLARK, PUBLISHERS—for selection from W. A. Curtis, *History of Creeds and Confessions of Faith in Christendom and Beyond,* published by T. & T. Clark, Publishers.

GERALD DUCKWORTH & CO. LTD.—for selections from Sydney Cave, *The Doctrine of the Person of Christ;*—and for selection from Alfred E. Garvie, *The Christian Faith.*

THE EPWORTH PRESS—for selections from Henry Carter, *The Methodist Heritage.*

GOSPEL PUBLISHING HOUSE—for selections from E. S. Williams, *Systematic Theology.*

HARCOURT, BRACE & WORLD, INC.—for selection from Lewis Mumford, *The Condition of Man,* copyright, 1944, by Lewis Mumford.

HARPER & BROTHERS—for selection from J. K. S. Reid, *Authority of Scripture,* copyright by Harper & Brothers, used by permission;—and for selections from Walter M. Horton, *Christian Theology,* copyright by Harper and Brothers, used by permission.

HODDER & STOUGHTON LTD.—for selections from A. E. Garvie, *The Missionary Obligation;*—for selection from Henry Townsend, *The Claims of the Free Churches;*—for selection from John Oman, *The Church and the Divine Order;*—and for selection from V. F. Storr & G. H. Harris, *The Call for Christian Unity.*

THE INTERNATIONAL MISSIONARY COUNCIL—for selection from Norman Goodall, *Missions under the Cross,* published by Edinburgh House Press.

5

INTER-VARSITY FELLOWSHIP—for selection from D. Martyn Lloyd-Jones, *Authority,* published by Inter-Varsity Fellowship.

LUTTERWORTH PRESS—for selections from Hendrik Kraemer, *A Theology of the Laity;*—for selection from Adolph Keller, *Religion and the European Mind;*—and for selections from Stephen Neill, *The Unfinished Task,* copyright 1957, The Lutterworth Press.

THE MACMILLAN COMPANY—for selections from W. Rauschenbusch, *Christianity and the Social Crisis,* copyright, 1907, by The Macmillan Company;—and for selections from Ernst Troeltsch, *The Social Teachings of the Christian Church.*

MACMILLAN & CO. LTD. (London)—for selection from Walter Hobhouse, *The Church and the World;*—from Bernard Lucas, *The Empire of Christ;*—and from Henry B. Swete, *Essays on Some Theological Questions of the Day.*

JOHN MURRAY (PUBLISHERS) Ltd.—for selection from W. R. Inge, *Contentio Veritatis.*

FLEMING H. REVELL COMPANY—for selections from Adolph Keller, *Religion and Revolution.*

CHARLES SCRIBNER'S SONS—for selections from John C. Bennett, *Christian Realism,* pp. 1, 2, 143, 144. Copyright, 1941, by Charles Scribner's Sons.

MARTIN SECKER & WARBURG LTD.—for selection from Lewis Mumford, *The Condition of Man.*

STUDENT CHRISTIAN MOVEMENT PRESS LTD.—for selections from Leonard Hodgson (ed.), *Second World Conference on Faith and Order.*

TRUSTEES FOR WESTMINSTER THEOLOGICAL SEMINARY u/W. J. Gresham Machen—for selections from J. Gresham Machen, *Christianity and Liberalism.*

THE WESTMINSTER PRESS—for selection from Hendrik Kraemer, *A Theology of the Laity.* Copyright © 1959, Hendrik Kraemer. Used by permission.

YALE UNIVERSITY PRESS—for selection from Julius Seeley Bixler, *Conversations with an Unrepentant Liberal.*

Contents

Preface

Protestantism is one of the three main divisions of the universal Christian Church, which together with the Roman Catholic Church and the Orthodox Churches make up one world-wide religion. Protestantism is the most recent of the developments within Christianity, having a relatively short history of slightly more than four centuries; the other two branches of the faith have histories going back to the earliest days of the Christian era. Moreover, compared to the unity which characterizes those other branches, Protestantism is divided within itself among hundreds of separate organizations, some of which deny all relationship to others. The many denominations and sects have differing beliefs and carry on a variety of practices, which give them the appearance of being distinct from one another. There are those who insist, because of the structure which Protestantism has, that it is incorrect to deal with it as a whole.

However, Protestantism rests firmly upon the belief that God deals directly with man as a person, so that salvation is gained "by faith alone." This puts the emphasis upon man's own life as it is lived in relationship to his society and his world. In one sense man becomes the center of his religion. Since men differ from one another, and since circumstances differ from generation to generation and place to place, Protestantism is bound to exist in varied groups. Man, as he is and in his situation, bears a living relationship to God. Therefore, man must express his religious faith in ever-changing forms of thought and action. The dividedness of Protestantism comes about through the very belief upon which it rests. Yet that belief itself makes Protestantism one, regardless of the contentions of its adherents. The basic faith of Protestantism does not change; its outward appearance and form do.

In this volume there is no attempt to deal with the many different groups that have existed and do exist within Protestantism. Nor is any mention made of the distinctive doctrines and types of organization of those groups unless they bear upon the central stream of Protestant development. Those subjects have been omitted, not because they are unimportant, for the opposite is obviously true since men have fought over them and even now refuse to have dealing with one another by reason of them, but because they are the expression of the religious faith rather than the faith itself. And in the limitations imposed by a single volume it was deemed more important to grasp the history of the foundation of Protestantism rather than to deal with matters that grow out of that foundation.

The story of the rise and development of Protestantism is traced through the writings of some representative leaders. Effort has been made to present the various trends that have appeared as Protestantism has lived in intimate contact with a changing world. It is hoped that no injustice has been done to any major line of thought or action within the faith. The citations from the various writers have been organized in sections according to periods of time and different themes. Each section is preceded by an editorial statement which serves to introduce the material that follows. Running all the way through is the belief that Protestantism is a single movement within Christianity which, because of its essential nature,

ever changes as it adjusts to its world, yet never loses
hold on the faith it professes.

For the choice of the citations, their organization, and
the introductory passages, the author alone is responsible.
Without doubt some readers will note what, to them, are
serious omissions and even misrepresentations. Such, however, are matters of personal decision. The author can
only say that, although he is aware of his own limitations
of knowledge and inadequacies of expression, he has tried
faithfully to present the history of the one, united stream
of Protestantism. Work on the volume was done while
the author was in South Asia and traveling through the
Orient. That threw an unusually heavy responsibility
upon the publishers. The author is, therefore, especially
indebted to his editor, who, with patience and care, carried on a lengthy and detailed correspondence, and assumed tasks far beyond the customary ones. Without his
aid, given graciously and freely, this volume would not
be as it is.

J. LESLIE DUNSTAN

Honolulu, Hawaii.
  August, 1961.

Protestantism

CHAPTER ONE

The Rise of Protestant Christianity

Protestant Christianity began with the work of Martin Luther (1483–1546), Ulrich Zwingli (1484–1531), and John Calvin (1509–1564): such is the oft repeated report of history. But if the matter is simply that of listing the names of the men through whose efforts Protestantism was established, this list is not complete enough, for the faith was started by men in countries other than Germany and Switzerland. Nor is it quite correct to say that those who worked in the Scandinavian lands, in France, and in England were acting wholly under the influence or the instigation of Luther or Calvin. Influence there was, without any doubt, but much more was involved besides. The movements which brought Protestantism into existence were many and appear to have had a measure of individual spontaneity about them, even while they were related to the movements started by the earliest reformers.

Jacques Lefèvre (1450–1536) had written commentaries on some books of the Bible before Luther nailed the Ninety-Five Theses to the door of Wittenberg Church, in which he implied his belief in the authority of the Scriptures for religious life. Lefèvre did not realize all that was involved in his ideas until after he had come in touch with Luther's works, but the principles he set forth were those upon which the Protestant faith came to rest. And out of his work and that of the company gathered about him came a stream of Protestant life in France. It is not quite as simple to describe events in England. Yet when Luther's writings reached that land they were read with understanding and appreciation, indicating that men were already prepared in mind and heart for the ideas Luther set forth; and when Henry VIII proclaimed his break with the Papacy a section of the people gave him their approval and support. Patrick Hamilton in Scotland was one among a number of leaders in that land who by their teaching prepared the way for the Reformation. In Scotland, the general outlook on life within which Protestant beliefs had relevance had been accepted by sections of the population even before the overt actions occurred which brought organized churches into existence. In the Scandinavian countries the trade built up by the Hanseatic League and the interchange of ideas which the League made possible created an open route along which the Reformation traveled almost unhindered.

History that concerns itself with events in human affairs dates the onset of Protestantism with precision. But that type of history overlooks the forces which move, often unobserved, beneath the surface of events. The very fact that the Reformation appeared rather widely in Europe within a relatively short space of time indicated the presence of such forces; they must be taken into account in any history of the Protestant faith. Moreover, as is also a commonplace of historical record, there were organized movements and outstanding individuals in the years before Luther, who espoused and upheld principles similar to those of the Reformers. That the movements were, in the main, stamped out and the individuals put to death by the authorities does not alter the significance of their existence. That theirs were abortive efforts while the Reformers' were successful calls for an explanation; but the fact that they appeared is evidence of significant forces at work.

Somewhere in the twelfth century the structure of life in Europe entered upon a period of change and development which has not yet ceased. The development, starting slowly, came to involve all aspects of man's life, and the varied enterprises and trends which composed it were so inter-related that it is impossible to separate them one from another in any kind of accurate description. Economic life changed. Foreign trade which had centered in the cities of the northern Adriatic became centered, with the explorations of the fourteenth and fifteenth centuries, in the towns of northern Europe, not only shifting wealth from one side of the continent to the other, but also bringing into existence a new class of people, men who were independent of support by others, able in their own right to manage their affairs. Politically, the empire which had for all practical purposes unified Europe under the control of Church and ruler began to break up into states and nations which claimed the right to be autonomous. This came about not so much because of the conflict between Church and emperor for supremacy as it did through the assertion by local ruling houses of their own authority in their own realms. The feudalism of the medieval age began gradually to disappear as a changing economy made a different political order possible, and men found a new order desirable. Economics and politics evoked changes in the social order as well. New alignments of people and new relationships evolved to meet the requirements of the new order. Serfs became citizens, and citizens became independent, and independent people undertook enterprises of their own choosing. Nobles became rulers, and rulers realizing the need for contact with their citizens brought into being councilors and parliaments and other similar representative institutions. In the life of the intellect the scholasticism which had put limits upon the extent and method of man's thinking gave way under the impact of a rediscovery of the ancient philosophers and led to the growth of free questioning by scholars, the development of new lines and methods of inquiry, and the establishment of new universities in which the pursuit of classical wisdom was carried forward. At the same time the geographical boundaries, which had kept man's vision and enterprise, in the main, within the limits of continental Europe, were broken; man began to think and to act within the limits of the world itself. Added to all this, man's inventiveness began to be asserted in providing the tools and equipment necessary for his new enterprises. Men experienced a new sense of comfort, security, and fulfillment.

The preceding is a brief, superficial summary of the onset of the modern era. The description is somewhat crude and general. Yet it will serve to recall a story told with careful attention by a number of able scholars. Medieval Europe might be likened to a field surrounded by a high wall within which people moved, in their dealings with one another and in their search for the fulfillment of their desires, along paths that were well traveled, the same roads being used generation after generation for the same ends. Then gradually the walls around the field were broken down, people began to

travel outside the former boundaries and across untrod-
den land, and the old paths began to be overlaid by
feet that disregarded their existence. There was much
confusion in the newness that appeared; some insisted
that the old paths were the only paths along which men
should walk; those who set out in new directions were
not sure of where they were going nor of how they would
get there; yet it was clear that the world that had been
was being changed for a world that was not yet.

When man breaks with his past, it becomes evident
that he is acting on his own authority or with a power
within himself which directs his ways, even though his
deed bears a direct connection to the situation in which
he was living. Man is always within the moving confines
of his own history; but at the same time he can determine that history. The reason is that within himself man
is free spirit. The transition from the medieval to the
modern age came about through such an action of man's
spirit. Man took control of life; he saw himself as a
person in his own right, he grew aware of the mastery
over life that was possible for him, and he began to live
by his own inner power. The modern age began, not
with some event which can be dated specifically, but
within the spirits of men, as men became self-conscious
and alive as persons. Words fail and mislead somewhat
at this point, for to speak of spirit is to speak of the
intangible and the ill-defined. Yet Henry the Navigator,
Vasco da Gama, and Columbus differed from the sea
captains who sailed before their time in that they knew
themselves to be masters over the fears and the knowledge and the experience of seamen up to their day;
their predecessors lived under the authority of that which
had been. And the difference between Colet, Erasmus,

More and the English scholastics who villified and condemned them was that the former allowed the writings
of Scripture and the Greek philosophers to influence all
their thinking, making themselves free of the limiting
dogmas and teachings current at the time, while the
latter clung fast to the authorities they knew. Modern
man came alive in opposing the accepted order of the
day; he insisted on expressing himself as a person.

That was the basic, underlying fact of the coming of
the modern era. Beneath all the changes in the ways of
living, beneath the expansion of European civilization
through exploration and trade and colonization, beneath
the activity of far-ranging minds which searched the
earth and the heavens and writings of the past for new
knowledge and understanding, there were the spirits of
men, spirits awakened to make men know themselves as
persons able to take responsible action of their own
volition and for their own purposes. There is, of course,
the question of how it came about that at the specific
time with which we are concerned the spirits of men
came alive in precisely the way they did; why did this
happen then and not earlier? The cause or causes are
many and complex, and lie hidden beneath the surface
of human affairs. We may, however, note two factors.
First, at about the end of the medieval period Europe
was subjected to the impact of a number of forces,
both from outside and from within its borders, that neces-
sitated positive responses: the attack on Europe by the
Arab world, the rediscovery of the Greek philosophers,
and the degraded state into which the Church had fallen.
Second, for centuries preceding the modern era the
Church had carefully and patiently nurtured the barbarian people who had overthrown the Roman Empire,

bringing to them an orderly existence, a defined moral conscience, and a knowledge of their relationship to God. In this work the Church was carrying on its proper task of spiritual care. The result was to bring to a condition of healthy vitality spirits which had earlier been diffused in primitive waywardness. Suggestions such as these only point the way to the answer to the question which has been raised. It is enough if at this point we see that the answer to the appearance of new spiritual expression must contain an element of spirituality within it.

We are to see, then, the onset of the modern era as coming through a movement of the human spirit. That was the essence of the time and the root of all that occurred. This, however, must be made explicit. Consider man's intellectual life. In the time of scholasticism (tenth century on), men raised questions about life and the meaning of existence as man is bound to do, but the answers to their questions were worked out within the beliefs and principles laid down by the Christian religion. Or, to put the matter in another way, man used his power of reason to explain or define or defend those truths already established by the Church. Man, himself, was not autonomous; his relation to truth was not and could not be direct. But when man's spirit asserted itself in his awareness of himself as a person, man became his own authority and considered his own reason capable of finding truth for itself. When man came to believe that, scholasticism came to an end. Man no longer reasoned within limiting principles, but directed his thinking as he, on his own authority, chose. Or, consider man's political life. There was a time when men accepted without question the rule of kings and lords. Men did as they were ordered to do, put up with the treatment accorded them, even though they grumbled among themselves over their lot, and accepted their state as that which was decreed for them. But when men became conscious of themselves as persons, they rose in protest against the conditions of their living and in the course of time wiped out the existing political order and created a new order in which they were recognized as persons. Men broke with the authority which had determined their living and claimed the right to be their own authority and to make out of life that which they chose. When the spirit of man comes alive man thinks for himself, acts on his own authority, and accepts responsibility for that which he does. He becomes the possessor and molder of his own personality; he puts himself in the position of being master over his own affairs. Those evidences of a new spirit, the evidences of man's freedom from external authority, his trust in his own powers and abilities, appear in the writings of Petrarch (1304–1374).

I love truth and not sects. I am sometimes a peripatetic, a stoic, or an academician, and often none of them; but, always a Christian. To philosophize is to love wisdom; and the true wisdom is Jesus Christ. Let us read the historians, the poets, and the philosophers; but let us have in our own hearts the gospel of Jesus Christ, in which alone is perfect wisdom and perfect happiness.[1]

Petrarch wrote of Robert, King of Naples:

He was the only true king of his time, for I call none kings but those who risk themselves. In him every virtue was united; he was a good master, a good father, and a good husband: religious from principle, courageous from nature, pacific for the good of his people. He was the only prince who loved learning, and encouraged men of learning. He received them with kindness and attended with pleasure to their works. He loved to communicate what he knew, and he blushed not to learn even in his advanced age. One of his favorite sayings was, "we acquire knowledge by giving and receiving."[2]

In a letter, Petrarch wrote to Boccaccio:

I know by experience, how much the knowledge of letters may contribute to produce just opinions; to render a man eloquent; to perfect his manners; and, which is much more important, to defend his religion. If men were not permitted to read poets and heathen writers because they do not speak of Jesus Christ, whom they never knew, how much less ought they to read the works of heretics, who oppose his doctrine; yet this is done with the greatest care by all the defenders of the faith. It is with profane authors as with solid food: it nourishes the man who has a good stomach, and is pernicious only to those who cannot digest it; to the mind that is judicious they are wholesome, but poison to the weak and ignorant. Letters may even render the former man religious, of which we have many examples, and to them they will never be an obstacle to piety. There are many ways of arriving at truth and heaven according to the different necessities of men; surely wisdom may produce as many saints as folly; and we should be careful that we never compare a lazy and blind devotion with an enlightened and industrious piety.[3]

This same new birth of man's spirit was the moving force within Protestantism. There were conditions in the age which stirred men, raising doubts within them as to the adequacy of the authorities under which they lived, and presenting them with subjects for thought to which they had not earlier had ready access. The Church which had been the guide of men's consciences and the preserver of peace within men's spirits had come upon evil days. The leaders of the Church, the papal court, and the clergy of every rank devoted themselves to their own interests with the result that in all too many cases selfishness, love of luxury, nepotism, simony, and immorality had become the marks of the Church. In a lengthy contest between the Church and political rulers for supremacy over the people, intrigue, falsity, duplicity and armed warfare had been used; and the institution which claimed to unite all men in Christ had not only divided men from one another but had become divided in itself at its very center. Thoughtful men throughout Europe had become deeply distressed by the conditions which had developed. Attempts were made to change this state of affairs by the holding of Church councils (Pisa, 1409; Constance, 1410; Basle, 1431); but these were of little avail. Although some matters were dealt with and settled, scarcely any effect was wrought in the evil lives of the clergy, and the basic issue, which only gradually appeared in all its implications, that of the seat of authority over men, was not touched. Men were made doubly aware of the state of the Church by their very inability to bring about any reform. At the same time, there grew up a new interest in the Scriptures and the writings of the leaders of the early Church. Both Scriptures and early Church writings became widely available with the invention of the printing press, and translations were made into the various languages of the people. In this way the story of the origin of the Christian faith, which had been hidden behind rites and festivals and liturgy and myth, became directly available to men. At the very time the authority of the Church appeared fraught with human weakness, a new authority which clearly had a direct power over the existence of the Church became known. There were, then, specific conditions involved in the appearance of Protestantism.

Yet Protestantism, if it is to be understood in its

origin and its historical development, must be seen as a movement which gives form to the awakened spirit of man. There was in Protestantism opposition to the Catholic Church and its activities, and there was a turning for knowledge and guidance to the Holy Scriptures; but those do not account for the appearance of Protestantism. Protests against the condition and conduct of the Church were made within the Church and did not result in a division in the structure of the Church. Church scholars turned to the Scriptures as seriously and as creatively as did men within Protestant ranks; yet their work did not have the same result. Protestantism rested upon the assertion of man's free spirit as the source and authority for his religious life.

Yet even that assessment of the situation does not wholly satisfy. There were also movements in the Church which rested on the spirit of man and his assumption of authority over his religious life. Such movements were pietistic and evangelical: Peter Waldo founded the Poor Men of Lyons (1170); Francis of Assisi (1182–1226) established an order of men pledged to labor in the world for the welfare of others in utter devotion to "the Lord who made Himself poor for us." Later on, after the Franciscans had become infected with the worldly ways of the Church, Joachim of Fiore (1145–1202) led a movement not only to return to the teachings of St. Francis but to go much further and develop a spiritual life apart from the Church. The Brethren of the Common Life were founded by Gerard Groote (1340–1384) in the Netherlands and spread across northern Europe. Societies calling themselves "Friends of God" were organized in various cities; John Tauler (1290–1361) was one of their leaders. These and other similar organizations and groups differed from each other in their teachings and their structure and the work they did; but all of them purposed to find religious life in the personal experience of men rather than through the ministrations of the Church. That is to say, they found the authority for man's relation to God within man and not in the Church. Some of the movements came in conflict with Church authorities, but others existed within the Church without drawing to themselves anything more than criticism by a few of their contemporaries, criticism that went unheeded. Those groups were evidence that a new vitality of the human spirit was making its appearance and taking form among men.

Then there were individuals in Europe who in their preaching and teaching began to express the principles that are involved in man's assertion of his self-awareness and his responsibility before God for his own spiritual welfare. Some of those men were of the clergy and others were of the laity. Some lost their lives when they were called to account by the Church and refused to change the stand they had taken; by their deaths they were simply saying that in their minds their eternal destiny rested in their faithfulness to the truth which God had made known to them rather than in their obedience to the dictates of the Church. Others escaped death either through fortunate twists of events or because the case against them was unclear. But one and all were saying that the Christian religion established a direct relationship between God and man through the spirit of man, so that man was obligated to live by the knowledge which God granted him and not by the guidance of any human institution. In other words, they were men who translated into the sphere of religion the new vitality of man's spirit, which, we have said, was the underlying force bringing the modern era into existence.

In the following quotations appear man's determination to break with the principles of Scholasticism, his desire to find his religious fulfillment for himself, and his increased interest in the Holy Scriptures and the portrayal of Jesus Christ found in them.

Robert Grosteste, Bishop of Lincoln (1175–1253)

From a letter written by Bishop Grosteste to the Pope's representative in England in reply to a request that a prebend be provided for the Pope's nephew in Lincoln, January 26, 1253.

It will be known to your Holiness that I am ready to obey apostolical commands with filial affection, and with all devotion and reverence, but to those things which are opposed to apostolic commands, I, in my zeal for the honour of my parent, am also opposed. By apostolic commands are meant those which are agreeable to the teachings of the Apostles and of Christ Himself, the Lord and Master of the Apostles, whose type and representation is specially borne in the ecclesiastical hierarchy of the Pope. The letter (which you have sent) is not consonant with apostolic sanctity, but utterly at variance and discord with it. . . . The holiness of the Apostolic See can only tend to edification, and not to destruction; for the plenitude of its power consists in its being able to do all things for edification. These "provisions" however, as they are called, are not for edification, but for manifest destruction. They are not, therefore, within the power of the Apostolic See. They owe their inspiration to flesh and blood, which shall not inherit the kingdom of God.[4]

John Huss (1369–1415), Preacher at Bethlehem Chapel, Rector of the University, Prague

From an oration given in defense of Wyclif at the University in 1408.

From the beginning of my studies I have made it a rule, whenever I found a better opinion on any matter, gladly and without a struggle to give up the old one, being well aware that what we know is vastly less than what we do not know.[5]

From an interview with Wenzel Tiem, the legate and agent for the sale of indulgences (1412).

I know well the difference between the apostolic commands and the commands of the Pope. So when I was asked by the legates of John, in the presence of Archbishop Albik, Whether I were willing to obey the apostolic commands? I answered, "I desire with all my heart to obey the apostolic commands." Thereupon the legates, holding apostolic and papal command to be interchangeable, thought that I was willing to preach to the people the campaign against Ladislaus (King of Naples). So the legates said, "He is willing, you see, Lord Archbishop, to obey the commands of our sovereign Pope." So I said to them, "Sirs, understand me. I said that I am willing, with all my heart, to obey apostolic commands, but by apostolic commands I mean the doctrines of the apostles of Christ. So far as the commands of the Pope agree with the commands and doctrines of the apostles, and are after the rule of the law of Christ, so far I am heartily prepared to render them obedience. But if I see anything at variance with this, I shall not obey, even if you kindle the fire for the burning of my body before my eyes."[6]

John Colet, Dean of St. Paul's (1467–1519)

If he be a lawful bishop, he of himself does nothing, but God in him. But if he do attempt anything of *himself,* he is then a breeder of poison. And if he also bring this to the birth, and carry into execution his own will, he is wickedly distilling poison to the destruction of the Church. This has now indeed been done for many years past, and has by this time so increased as to take powerful hold on all members of the Church; so that, unless that Mediator who alone can do so, who created and founded the church out of nothing for Him-

self (therefore does St. Paul often call it a "creature")—
unless, I say, the Mediator Jesus lay to his hand with all
speed, our most disordered church cannot be far from death.
... Men consult not God on what is to be done, by constant
prayer, but take counsel with men, whereby they shake and
overthrow everything. All (as we must own with grief, and
as I write with both grief and tears) seek their own, not the
things which are Jesus Christ's, not heavenly things but
earthly, what will bring them to death, not what will bring
them to life eternal.[7]

Desiderius Erasmus (1466–1536)

As to the Schoolmen, I had rather be a pious divine with
Jerome than invincible with Scotus. Was ever a heretic converted by their subtleties? Let those who like follow the dis-
putations of the Schools: but let him who desires to be instructed rather in piety than in the art of disputation, first
and above all apply himself to the fountainhead—to those
writings which flowed immediately from the fountainhead.
The divine is "invincible" enough who never yields to vice or
gives way to evil passions, even though he may be beaten in
argument. That doctor is abundantly "great" who purely
preaches Christ.[8]

From a letter from Erasmus to Colet.

Not that, valuing as I do all branches of study, I condemn
the studies of these men as such, but that when they are
pursued for themselves alone, unseasoned by more ancient
and elegant literature, they seem to me to be calculated to
make men sciolists and contentious; whether they can make
men wise I leave to others. For they exhaust the mental
powers by a dry and biting subtlety, without infusing any
vigour or spirit into the mind. And, worst of all, theology,
the queen of all science—so richly adorned by ancient elo-
quence—they strip of all her beauty by their incongruous,
mean, and disgusting style. What was once so clear, thanks
to the genius of the old divines, they clog with some subtlety

or other, thus involving everything in obscurity while they try to explain it. It is thus we see that theology, which was once most venerable and full of majesty, now almost dumb, poor, and in rags.

In the meantime we are allured by a never-satiated appetite for strife. One dispute gives rise to another, and with wonderful gravity we fight about straws. Then, lest we should seem to have added nothing to the discoveries of the old divines, we audaciously lay down certain positive rules according to which God has performed his mysteries, when sometimes it might be better for us to believe that a thing was done, leaving the question of how it was done to the omnipotence of God. So, too, for the sake of showing our ingenuity, we sometimes discuss questions which pious ears can hardly bear to hear; as, for instance, when it is asked whether the Almighty could have taken upon Him the nature of the devil or of an ass.

. . . Wherefore, my dear Colet, in having joined battle with this redoubtable race of men for the restoration, in its pristine brightness and dignity, of that old and true theology which they have obscured by their subtleties, you have in very truth engaged in a work in many ways of the highest honour—a work of devotion to the cause of theology, and of the greatest advantage to all students, and especially the students of this flourishing University of Oxford. Still, to speak the truth, it is a work of great difficulty, and one sure to excite ill-will. Your learning and energy will, however, conquer every difficulty, and your magnanimity will easily overlook ill-will.[9]

From the Introduction to "Novum Instrumentum," 1516:

In times like these, when men are pursuing with such zest all branches of knowledge, how is it that the philosophy of Christ should alone be derided by some, neglected by many, treated by the few who do devote themselves to it with coldness, not to say insincerity? Whilst in all other branches of learning the human mind is straining its genius to master all subtleties, and toiling to overcome all difficulties, why is it

that this one philosophy alone is not pursued with equal
earnestness, at least by those who profess to be Christians?
. . . Whatever other philosophers may have been, he alone
is a teacher from heaven; he alone was able to teach certain
and eternal wisdom; he alone taught things pertaining to our
salvation, because he alone is its author; he alone absolutely
practised what he preached, and is able to make good what
he promised. . . . I utterly dissent from those who are un-
willing that the sacred Scriptures should be read by the
unlearned translated into their vulgar tongue, as though Christ
had taught such subtleties that they can scarcely be understood even by a few theologians, or as though the strength of
the Christian religion consisted in men's ignorance of it.
. . . If the footprints of Christ be anywhere shown to us,
we kneel down and adore. Why do we not rather venerate
the living and breathing picture of Him in these books? If
the vesture of Christ be exhibited, where will we not go to
kiss it? Yet were his whole wardrobe exhibited nothing could
represent Christ more vividly and truly than these evangelical
writings. Statues of wood and stone we decorate with gold
and gems for the love of Christ. They only profess to give
us the form of his body; these books present us with a living
image of his most holy mind. Were we to have seen Him
with our own eyes, we should not have had so intimate a
knowledge as they give of Christ, speaking, healing, dying,
rising again, as it were, in our own actual presence.[10]

William Tyndale (1492–1536)

. . . It is right that we obey father and mother, master, lord,
prince, and king, and all the ordinances of the world, bodily
and ghostly, by which God rules us and ministers freely his
benefits unto us all. And that we love them for the benefits
that we receive by them, and fear them for the power they
have over us to punish us, if we trespass the law and good
order. So far yet are the worldly powers or rulers to be obeyed
only, as their commandments repugn not against the commandment of God, and then hold. Wherefore we must have
God's commandment ever in our hearts, and by the higher
law interpret the inferior; that we obey nothing against the

belief of one God, or against the love of God, whereby we
do or leave undone all things for his sake, and that we do
nothing for any man's commandment against the reverence
of the name of God, to make it despised and the less feared
and set by; and that we obey nothing to the hindrance of the
knowledge of the blessed doctrine of God whose servant the
holy day is.

. . . And even so he that trusts in any thing save in God
only and in his Son Jesus Christ, keeps no commandment at
all in the sight of God.

For he that hath trust in any creature, whether in heaven
or in earth, save in God and his Son Jesus, can see no cause
to love God with all his heart, etc. neither to abstain from
dishonouring his name, nor to keep the holy day for the love
of his doctrine, nor to obey lovingly the rulers of this world;
nor any cause to love his neighbor as himself, and to abstain
from hurting him, where he may get profit by him, and save
himself harmless. And in like wise against this law, Love thy
neighbour as thyself, I may obey no worldly power, to do
aught at any man's commandment unto the hurt of my neighbour who has not deserved it, though he be a Turk.

. . . And finally, to know that whatsoever good thing is in
us, that same is the gift of grace, and therefore not of deserving, though many things be given to God through our diligence in working his laws, and chastising our bodies, and in
praying for them, and believing his promises, which else
should not be given us; yet our working deserves not the gifts,
any more than the diligence of a merchant in seeking a good
ship brings the goods safe to land, though such diligence
now and then helps thereto. But when we believe in God, and
then do all that is in our might, and do not tempt him, then
is God true to abide by his promise, and to help us, and
perform alone when our strength is past.

To know these things is to have all the scripture unlocked
and opened before thee, so that if thou wilt go in and read,
thou canst not but understand. . . .

Their [papists] darkness cannot comprehend the light of
scripture, as it is written, John i. The light shineth in darkness, but the darkness could not comprehend it, they turn it

into blind riddles, and read it without understanding, as laymen do our lady's matins, or as it were Merlin's prophecies—their minds are ever upon their heresies. And when they come to a place that soundeth like, there they rest, and wring out wonderful expositions to establish their heresies withal, like the tale of the boy who would fain have eaten of the pasty of lampreys, but durst not until the bells seemed to sing unto him. 'Sit don Jack boy, and eat of the lampreys'—to stablish his wavering conscience! But is it not great blindness to say in the beginning of all together, that the whole scripture is false in the literal sense, and killeth the soul? To prove this their pestilent heresy, they abuse the text of Paul, saying, The letter killeth, because that text was become a riddle unto them, and they understood it not, when Paul, by this word 'letter,' understood the law given by Moses to condemn all consciences, and to rob them of all righteousness, to compel them unto the promises of mercy that are in Christ.

Heresy springs not of the scripture, no more than darkness of the sun; but is a dark cloud that springs out of the blind hearts of hypocrites, and covers the face of the scripture, and blinds their eyes that they cannot behold the bright beams of the scripture.[11]

CHAPTER TWO

The Principles of the Reformation

THREE REFORMERS

The reformers were men whose primary and sole concern was their relationship to God. They were religious men who sought to understand their religious lives in the light of the underlying movement of the age. Some of their contemporaries were moved as they were by the sense that man is and ought to be a free and responsible person; but their interests were more diffuse and varied than those of the reformers. While the humanists, for example, understood the direction the work of the reformers was taking and in some cases gave support to the reformers, their main desire was to win freedom from various kinds of intellectual and political limitation. No one could deny the significance of their efforts, but the humanists were not basically religious men. The reformers were. For them, man's place before God, with all that entailed, was the fundamental fact of life. Events made clear to them that the issue of the age was man's freedom as a person; they dealt with that issue as it involved religion and worked out its resolution in their own lives.

Protestant Christianity arose at a particular time in history as part of a profound development in life itself.

Thus, from one point of view, Protestantism was a product of man's on-going life, and the direct, inextricable connection between the faith and the movement of human affairs is part of the essence of its faith. Where Protestantism loses touch with the times it loses itself. That, however, is only one side of the picture. The Protestant faith is also the product of a tremendous creative act: a bringing into being of a formal expression of the Christian gospel in which man stands as a free, autonomous person before his God. Protestantism insists that man's dependence for his eternal welfare is on God Almighty alone; nothing can come between God and man except a medium through which God works, a medium which cannot become an authority over man, even though God's authority may be transmitted through it. The bringing into being, living being, of a structure within which that understanding of religious life could be manifest was the work of the reformers. They were not simply men of their age; they were men who so trusted God's leading in their own lives that they were able to build that which they had been granted to see. They took the growing spirit of their age, and believing it to be the veritable result of God's dealing with them, they worked out that belief in the implications presented to them. They were creative religious spirits.

The reformers were constructive. As we noted in a previous section, there were reformers in the Church before the days of the Reformation, but those men were intent upon the degraded condition of the Church and were working for a restoration of the Church to its proper state of moral purity and spiritual responsibility. They directed their efforts to the institutions of the existing Church; they did not think of the Church itself in its fundamental structure as being open to question. Savonarola (1452–1498) is an example (even though he was excommunicated by Pope Innocent VI in 1497) and so is William Occam (?–1349?). Those men and others like them held fast to their belief in the Church as divinely established and sought only its reform. Others, however, came to believe that the Church, in its understanding of itself and the authority it held over the lives of men, was in error. Therefore, the efforts of such men were directed to a radical change in the very structure as well as in the life of the Church. The former of these groups of reformers had a definite program. They may not have agreed with each other as to the details of the program, but all of them were specific in their proposals. The latter group, however, while fairly clear as to the negative aspect of their activity (they knew what they wanted changed or removed), were not clear at all as to any positive, constructive program. John Huss, for example, was quite explicit in dealing with some of the evils of the Church leaders; he also set forth some ideas about the nature and make-up of the Church itself (*De Ecclesia*); but he did not set forth a practical program for the implementation of his ideas. There may well be another way of looking at this limitation in the work of other reformers like him, that is, that because they did not gain the support of power which could protect them, they were not put into positions where they were forced to make their ideas explicit. In either case, they did not become leaders of movements that created new orders of Church affairs. They saw the issue of man's freedom and his right of private judgment, but they were not able to put those insights into the context of practical affairs. The reformers from whom the Protestant Church stems were, on the other hand, creatively constructive.

The Reformers were men who had and won the support of other men. That is one way to express the matter; the situation was even more complicated. At the time of the Reformers, leaders in other areas of life had come to see the implications of the free spirit of man. We have referred earlier to the way in which men of education and learning broke with the principles and methods of scholasticism and launched out on lives of independent intellectual enterprises. These men made themselves free from authority and personally responsible in the scholarly field. There were also men— princes, lords, rulers, having authority over areas of Europe and the people within those areas—who threw off the power which the Church had claimed to have over all government and which it had exercised successfully for years, and made decisions on their own. Orders which were sent were disregarded and the local rulers acted as they chose. The new spirit of man was coming to expression in the political realm; men made themselves free and responsible in their governmental positions.

This is illustrated in the lives of the three early Reformers. Elector Frederick of Saxony established the University of Wittenberg. To do so he used the funds which had been collected by the Church from his people for a war against the Turks. The war had not been undertaken, and Frederick had refused to turn over the money he was holding to the Pope; instead he used it in building the University which would add lustre to his otherwise relatively unimportant realm. Moreover, the Elector determined that the University would be a center of liberal studies in opposition to the scholasticism of the Church. Martin Luther joined the faculty of that University, thus in effect putting himself under the care of the Elector. In 1520 a papal bull was issued excommunicating Luther from the Church and ordering Frederick to arrest him and turn him over to Church authorities. Frederick, however, disregarding the excommunication, refused to do anything about putting Luther in the hands of the Church. When subsequently an edict was issued which put Luther under the ban of the Empire, the Elector and other German princes refused to do anything to implement it. When Frederick died in 1524, he was succeeded by his brother John, who continued to protect and defend Luther. In 1530 when the Diet of Augsberg ordered a restoration of the traditional Church throughout the Empire and threatened all who refused to obey with force, the Elector John refused to obey the order and joined with other princes in the formation of what was in effect a league of Protestant rulers. Thus, Martin Luther's religious work was supported by the political rulers who were themselves asserting their own independence from the authority of the Church and the Empire.

The town of Zurich in Switzerland was an independent town, governed by a council of leading citizens. This political arrangement had developed gradually over the years as power had shifted from the royal house to the head of the Benedictine Munster and then to a small group representing the knights and the wealthy trading families, and finally to a much larger group which included representatives of the craft guilds. Late in the fourteenth century the Emperor gave the town complete immunity from responsibility to the Empire: by the end of the fifteenth century all authority had come to rest in the Great Council. And that authority included the management of ecclesiastical affairs. Thus the stage was set for the work of Ulrich Zwingli (1484–1531). Following service at the churches in two other towns during which he had had opportunity for much study and thought and had arrived at certain conclusions as to man's salvation and the manner of worship and church life, Zwingli was made priest at the Great Munster in Zurich. He was then able to have his ideas put into effective operation by gaining for them the approval of the town Council. In 1523, when the Council voted to separate the town from the jurisdiction of the Bishop of Constance, the church in Zurich became a free and independent church. Zwingli gained the support of the Council for his reforming work, which inevitably included moral and practical aspects as well as religious.

The history of the city of Geneva had taken a somewhat different course from that of Zurich. In the eleventh century the Emperor, who was the acknowledged ruler, put the actual conduct of affairs into the hands of the Bishop of the Church. Later, the House of Savoy began to play an increasingly important role in the life of the city because of its importance as a trading center. Church and ruler were working together to manage matters for their own ends. At the same time, the spirit of freedom, which had come to expression in the towns of Zurich, Basel, and Berne, took root in Geneva. The upshot was that in 1526 Geneva became a member of the Swiss Federation and developed a representative form of municipal government. Protestant teachings were brought into the city by William Farel in 1532, and subsequently the citizens voted to make those teachings the basis of their religious faith. This did not settle the matter at once; but after a period of internal struggle marked by much intrigue and open violence, John Calvin was invited by the Council of the city to be their adviser. The events which followed were the result of the harmonious co-operation between the magistrates of the city and Calvin.

The three reformers, then, were able to pursue their constructive work because of the support of the political powers under whom they served. It is quite idle to speculate as to what might have happened at certain points in history if conditions had been different, for conditions are always far too complex to allow for any positive conclusion; yet to raise the question on which such speculation would rest will help to clarify the point at issue. John Huss lost the support of the theological faculty of the University when he engaged in a controversy over the sale of indulgences; and while he claimed that he had such widespread support among the nobles that he did not have to appear before the Council called by the Pope at Constance, the fact is that neither the King of Bohemia nor the King of the Romans nor the nobles protected him when the decision was against him. The question of the possible outcome of the work of Huss, had he been supported by the political powers of his day, remains unanswered. Contrariwise, it is impossible to know what would have happened if the Elector Frederick had turned against Luther and handed him over to the Church. The conjunction of various forces intent on gaining their freedom from external authority would appear to have had a bearing upon the beginning of the Protestant churches.

In their creative work the reformers had to deal with two main subjects: the basic principles, often worked out systematically in beliefs, upon which they rested their enterprises; and the changes they would make in the life and organization of the Church in order to implement their principles. As the reformers speak for themselves these two main elements in their works will be apparent.

Martin Luther (1483–1546)

I first lay down these two propositions, concerning spiritual liberty and servitude.

A Christian man is the most free lord of all, and subject to none; a Christian man is the most dutiful servant of all, and subject to everyone.

. . . Let us examine the subject on a deeper and less simple principle. Man is composed of a twofold nature, a spiritual and a bodily. As regards the spiritual nature, which they name the soul, he is called the spiritual, inward, new man; as regards the bodily nature, which they name the flesh, he is called the fleshly, outward, old man. The Apostle speaks of this: "Though our outward man perish, yet the inward man is renewed day by day" (2 Cor. iv. 16). The result of this diversity is, that in the Scriptures opposing statements are made concerning the same man; the fact being that in the same man these two men are opposed to one another; the flesh lusting against the spirit, and the spirit against the flesh (Gal. v. 17).

JUSTIFICATION BY FAITH

We first approach the subject of the inward man, that we may see by what means a man becomes justified, free, and a true Christian; that is, a spiritual, new, and inward man. It is certain that absolutely none among outward things, under whatever name they may be reckoned, has any weight in producing a state of justification and Christian liberty, nor, on the other hand, an unjustified state and one of slavery. This can be shown by an easy course of argument.

What can it profit the soul that the body should be in good condition, free, and full of life; that it should eat, drink, and act according to its pleasure; when even the most impious slaves of every kind of vice are prosperous in these matters? Again, what harm can ill-health, bondage, hunger, thirst, or any other outward evil, do to the soul, when even the most pious of men, and the freest in the purity of their conscience, are harassed by these things? Neither of these states of things has to do with the liberty or the slavery of the soul.

. . . One thing, and one alone, is necessary for life, justification, and Christian liberty; and that is the most holy word of God, the Gospel of Christ, as He says: "I am the resurrection and the life; he that believeth in me shall not die eternally" (John xi. 25); and also (John viii. 36) "If the Son shall make you free, ye shall be free indeed"; and (Matt. iv. 4), "Man shall not live by bread alone, but by every word that proceedeth out of the mouth of God."

Let us therefore hold it for certain and firmly established, that the soul can do without everything, except the word of God, without which none at all of its wants are provided for. But, having the word, it is rich and wants for nothing; since that is the word of life, of truth, of light, of peace, of justification, of salvation, of joy, of liberty, of wisdom, of virtue, of grace, of glory, and of every good thing.

. . . Hence it is clear that, as the soul needs the word alone for life and justification, so it is justified by faith alone and not by any works. For if it could be justified by any other means, it would have no need of the word, nor consequently of faith.

. . . Since then this faith can reign only in the inward man, as it is said: "With the heart man believeth unto righteousness" (Rom. x. 10); and since it alone justifies, it is evident that by no outward work or labour can the inward man be at all justified, made free, and saved; and that no works whatever have any relation to him. And so, on the other hand, it is solely by impiety and incredulity of heart that he becomes guilty, and a slave of sin, deserving condemnation; not by any outward sin or work. Therefore the first care of every Christian ought to be, to lay aside all reliance on works, and strengthen his faith alone more and more, and by it grow in the knowledge, not of works, but of Christ Jesus, who has suffered and risen again for him; as Peter teaches, when he makes no other work to be a Christian one. Thus Christ, when the Jews asked Him what they should do that they might work the works of God, rejected the multitude of works, with which He saw that they were puffed up, and commanded them one thing only, saying: "This is the work of God, that ye believe in him whom He hath sent, for him hath God the Father sealed" (John vi. 27, 29).

. . . But you ask how it can be the fact that faith alone justifies, and affords without works so great a treasure of good things, when so many works, ceremonies, and laws are prescribed to us in the Scriptures. I answer: before all things bear in mind what I have said, that faith alone without works justifies, sets free, and saves. . . .

. . . From all this you will again understand, why so much importance is attributed to faith, so that it alone can fulfil the law, and justify without any works. For you see that the first commandment, which says, "Thou shalt worship one God only," is fulfilled by faith alone. If you were nothing but good works from the soles of your feet to the crown of your head, you would not be worshipping God, nor fulfilling the first commandment, since it is impossible to worship God, without ascribing to Him the glory of truth and of universal goodness, as it ought in truth to be ascribed. Now this is not done by works, but only by faith of heart. It is not by working, but by believing, that we glorify God and confess Him to be true. On this ground faith is the sole righteousness of a Christian man, and the fulfilling of all the commandments. For to him who fulfils the first, the task of fulfilling all the rest is easy.

GOOD WORKS

. . . And now let us turn to the other part, to the outward man. . . . Although, as I have said, inwardly, and according to the spirit, a man is amply enough justified by faith, having all that he requires to have, except that this very faith and abundance ought to increase from day to day, even till the future life; still he remains in this mortal life upon earth, in which it is necessary that he should rule his own body, and have intercourse with men. Here then works begin; here he must not take his ease; here he must give heed to exercise his body by fastings, watchings, labour, and other moderate discipline, so that it may be subdued to the spirit, and obey and conform itself to the inner man and faith, and not rebel against them nor hinder them, as is its nature to do if it is not kept under. For the inner man, being conformed to God, and created after the image of God through faith, rejoices and delights itself in Christ, in whom such blessings have been conferred on it; and hence has only this task before it, to serve God with joy and for nought in free love.

. . . True then are these two sayings: Good works do not make a good man, but a good man does good works. Bad works do not make a bad man, but a bad man does bad works. Thus it is always necessary that the substance or person should be good before any good works can be done, and that good works should follow and proceed from a good person. As Christ says: "A good tree cannot bring forth evil fruit, neither can a corrupt tree bring forth good fruit" (Matt. vii. 18). Now it is clear that the fruit does not bear the tree, nor does the tree grow on the fruit; but, on the contrary, the trees bear the fruit and the fruit grows on the trees.

. . . Since, then, works justify no man, but a man must be justified before he can do any good work, it is most evident that it is faith alone which, by the mere mercy of God through Christ, and by means of His word, can worthily and sufficiently justify and save the person; and that a Christian man needs no work, no law, for his salvation; for by faith he is free from all law, and in perfect freedom does gratuitously all that he does, seeking nothing either of profit or of salvation—since by the grace of God he is already saved and rich in all things through his faith—but solely that which is well-pleasing to God.

THE CHRISTIAN LIFE

. . . Here is the truly Christian life, here is faith really working by love, when a man applies himself with joy and love to the works of that freest servitude, in which he serves others voluntarily and for nought, himself abundantly satisfied in the fulness and riches of his own faith.

. . . Christ also, when His disciples were asked for the tribute money, asked of Peter, whether the children of a king were not free from taxes. Peter agreed to this; yet Jesus commanded him to go to the sea, saying: "Lest we should offend them, go thou to the sea, and cast a hook, and take up the fish that first cometh up; and when thou hast opened his mouth, thou shalt find a piece of money; that take, and give unto them for me and thee" (Matt. xvii. 27).

This example is very much to our purpose; for here Christ calls Himself and His disciples free men and children of a king, in want of nothing; and yet He voluntarily submits and pays the tax. Just as far then as this work was necessary or useful to Christ for justification or salvation, so far do all His other works or those of His disciples avail for justification. They are really free and subsequent to justification, and only done to serve others and set them an example.

Such are the works which Paul inculcated: that Christians should be subject to principalities and powers, and ready to do every good work (Tit. iii. 1); not that they may be justified by these things, for they are already justified by faith, but that in liberty of spirit they may thus be the servants of others, and subject to powers, obeying their will out of gratuitous love.

Such too ought to have been the works of all colleges, monasteries, and priests; everyone doing the works of his own profession and state of life, not in order to be justified by them, but in order to bring his own body into subjection, as an example to others, who themselves also need to keep under their bodies; and also in order to accommodate himself to the will of others, out of free love. But we must always guard most carefully against any vain confidence or presumption of being justified, gaining merit, or being saved by these works; this being the part of faith alone, as I have so often said.

. . . Finally, for the sake of those to whom nothing can be stated so well but that they misunderstand and distort it, we must add a word, in case they can understand even that. There are very many persons, who, when they hear of this liberty of faith straightway turn it into an occasion of license.

They think that everything is now lawful for them, and do not choose to show themselves free men and Christians in any other way than by their contempt and reprehension of ceremonies, of traditions, of human laws; as if they were Christians merely because they refuse to fast on stated days, or eat flesh when others fast, or omit the customary prayers; scoffing at the precepts of men, but utterly passing over all the rest that belongs to the Christian religion. On the other hand, they are most pertinaciously resisted by those who strive after salvation solely by their observance of and reverence for ceremonies; as if they would be saved merely because they fast on stated days, or abstain from flesh, or make formal prayers; talking loudly of the precepts of the Church and of the Fathers, and not caring a straw about those things which belong to our genuine faith. Both these parties are plainly culpable in that, while they neglect matters which are of weight and necessary for salvation, they contend noisily about such as are without weight and not necessary.

It is not from works that we are set free by the faith of Christ, but from the belief in works, that is, from foolishly presuming to seek justification through works. Faith redeems our consciences, makes them upright and preserves them, since by it we recognize the truth that justification does not depend on our works, although good works neither can nor ought to be wanting to it; just as we cannot exist without food and drink and all the functions of this mortal body. Still it is not on them that our justification is based, but on faith; and yet they ought not on that account to be despised or neglected. Thus in this world we are compelled by the needs of this bodily life; but we are not hereby justified.

. . . Since, then, we cannot live in this world without ceremonies and works; since the hot and inexperienced period of youth has need of being restrained and protected by such bonds; and since everyone is bound to keep under his own body by attention to these things; therefore the minister of Christ must be prudent and faithful in so ruling and teaching the people of Christ in all these matters that no root of bitterness may spring up among them, and so many be defiled, as Paul warned the Hebrews; that is, that they may not lose the faith, and begin to be defiled by a belief in works, as the means of justification. This is a thing which easily happens, and defiles very many, unless faith be constantly inculcated along with works. It is impossible to avoid this evil, when faith is passed over in silence, and only the ordinances of men are taught, as has been done hitherto by the pestilent, impious, and soul-destroying traditions of our pontiffs and opinions of our theologians. An infinite number of souls have been drawn down to hell by these snares, so that you may recognize the work of Antichrist.

. . . Hence in the Christian life ceremonies are to be no otherwise looked upon than builders and workmen look upon those preparations for building or working which are not made with any view of being permanent or anything in themselves, but only because without them there could be no building and no work. When the structure is completed, they are laid aside. Here you see that we do not condemn these preparations, but set the highest value on them; a belief in them we do condemn, because no one thinks that they constitute a real and permanent structure.

. . . We have therefore need to pray that God will lead us, and make us taught of God, that is, ready to learn from God; and will Himself, as He has promised, write His law in our hearts; otherwise there is no hope for us. For unless He himself teach us inwardly this wisdom hidden in a mystery, nature cannot but condemn it and judge it to be heretical. She takes offence at it and it seems folly to her; just as we see that it happened of old in the case of the prophets and apostles; and just as blind and impious pontiffs, with their flatterers, do now in my case and that of those who are like me; upon whom, together with ourselves, may God at length have mercy, and lift up the light of His countenance upon them, that we may know His way upon earth and His saving health among all nations, Who is blessed for evermore.[1]

THE CHURCH: ITS ORDER

It has been devised, that the Pope, bishops, priests and monks are called the Spiritual Estate; princes, lords, artificers and peasants, are the Temporal Estate; which is a very fine, hypocritical device. But let no one be made afraid by it; and that for this reason: That all Christians are truly of the Spiritual Estate, and there is no difference among them, save of office alone. As St. Paul says (I Cor. xii), we are all one body, though each member does its own work, to serve the others. This is because we have one baptism, one gospel, one faith, and are all Christians alike; for baptism, gospel and faith, these alone make Spiritual and Christian people. . . .

As for the unction by a pope or a bishop, tonsure, ordination, consecration, clothes differing from those of laymen—all this may make a hypocrite or an anointed puppet, but never a Christian or a spiritual man. Thus we are all consecrated as priests by baptism, as St. Peter says: "Ye are a royal priesthood, a holy nation" (I Peter ii:9); and in the book of Revelations: "and hast made us unto our God, kings and priests" (Rev. v:10). For, if we had not a higher consecration in us than Pope or bishop can give, no priest could ever be made by the consecration of Pope or bishop; nor could he say the mass, or preach, or absolve. Therefore the bishop's consecration is just as if in the name of the whole congregation he took one person out of the community, each member of which has equal power, and commanded him to exercise this power for the rest; in the same way as if ten brothers, co-heirs as king's sons, were to choose one from among them to rule over their inheritance; they would, all of them, still remain kings and have equal power, although one is ordered to govern.

And to put the matter even more plainly: If a little company of pious Christian laymen were taken prisoners and carried away to a desert, and had not among them a priest consecrated by a bishop, and were there to agree to elect one of them, married or unmarried, and were to order him to baptize, to celebrate the mass, to absolve and to preach; this man would as truly be a priest as if all the bishops and all the Popes had consecrated him. That is why in cases of necessity every man can baptize and absolve, which would not be possible if we were not all priests. This great grace and virtue of baptism and of the Christian Estate, they have almost destroyed and made us forget by their ecclesiastical law. In this way the Christians used to choose their bishops and priests out of the community; these being afterwards confirmed by other bishops, without the pomp that we have now. So was it that St. Augustine, Ambrose, Cyprian, were bishops.

Since then the temporal power is baptized as we are, and has the same faith and gospel, we must allow it to be priest and bishop, and account its office an office that is proper and useful to the Christian community. For whatever issues from baptism may boast that it has been consecrated priest, bishop, and Pope, although it does not beseem everyone to exercise these offices. For, since we are all priests alike, no man may put himself forward, or take upon himself, without our consent and election, to do that which we have all alike power to do. For, if a thing is common to all, no man may take it to himself without the wish and command of the community. And if it should happen that a man were appointed to one of these offices and deposed for abuses, he would be just what he was before. Therefore a priest should be nothing in Christendom but a functionary; as long as he holds his office, he has precedence of others; if he is deprived of it, he is a peasant and a citizen like the rest.

. . . It follows then, that between laymen and priests, princes and bishops, or as they call it, between spiritual and temporal persons, the only real difference is one of office and function, and not of estate; for they are all of the same Spiritual Estate, true priests, bishops and Popes, though their functions are not the same: just as among priests and monks every man has not the same functions. And this St. Paul says (Rom. xii.; I Cor. xii.) and St. Peter (I Peter ii.); ". . . we being many are one body in Christ, and every one members one of another." Christ's body is not double or twofold, one temporal, and the other spiritual. He is one head, and he has one body.

We see then that just as those that we call spiritual, or priests, bishops or Popes, do not differ from other Christians in any other or higher degree, but in that they are to be concerned with the word of God, and the sacraments—that being their work and office—in the same way the temporal authorities hold the sword and the rod in their hands to punish the wicked and to protect the good. A cobbler, a smith, a peasant, every man has the office and function of his calling, and yet all alike are consecrated priests and bishops, and every man in his office must be useful and beneficial to the rest, that so many kinds of work may all be united into one community: just as the members of the body all serve one another.[2]

Here you will ask: "If all who are in the Church are priests, by what character are those, whom we now call priests, to be distinguished from the laity?" I reply: By the use of these words, "priest," "clergy," "spiritual person," "ecclesiastic," an injustice has been done, since they have been transferred from the remaining body of Christians to those few, who are now, by a hurtful custom, called ecclesiastics. For Holy Scripture makes no distinction between them, except that those, who are now boastfully called popes, bishops, and lords, it calls ministers, servants, and stewards, who are to serve the rest in the ministry of the Word, for teaching the faith of Christ and the liberty of believers. For though it is true that we are all equally priests, yet we cannot, nor, if we could, ought we all to minister and teach publicly. Thus Paul says: "Let a man so account of us as of the ministers of Christ, and stewards of the mysteries of God" (I Cor. iv:1).

This bad system has now issued in such a pompous display of power, and such a terrible tyranny, that no earthly government can be compared to it, as if the laity were something else than Christians. Through this perversion of things it has happened that the knowledge of Christian grace, of faith, of liberty, and altogether of Christ, has utterly perished, and has been succeeded by an intolerable bondage to human works and laws; and, according to the Lamentations of Jeremiah, we have become the slaves of the vilest men on earth, who abuse our misery to all the disgraceful and ignominious purposes of their own will.

THE CHURCH: WORD AND SACRAMENTS

Returning to the subject we had begun, I think it is made clear by these considerations that it is not sufficient, nor a Christian course, to preach the works, life, and words of Christ in a historic manner, as facts which it suffices to know

as an example how to frame our life; as do those who are
now held the best preachers; and much less so, to keep silence
altogether on these things, and to teach in their stead the laws
of men and the decrees of the Fathers. There are now not a
few persons who preach and read about Christ with the object
of moving the human affections to sympathise with Christ,
to indignation against the Jews, and other childish and wom-
anish absurdities of that kind.

Now preaching ought to have the object of promoting faith
in Him, so that He may not only be Christ, but a Christ for
you and for me, and that what is said of Him, and what He
is called, may work in us. And this faith is produced and is
maintained by preaching why Christ came, what He has
brought us and given to us, and to what profit and advantage
He is to be received. This is done, when the Christian liberty
which we have from Christ Himself is rightly taught, and we
are shown in what manner all we Christians are kings and
priests, and how we are lords of all things, and may be confident that whatever we do in the presence of God is pleasing
and acceptable to Him.[3]

Concerning the Sacrament of the Altar. To begin,—if we
wish to attain safely and prosperously to the true and free
knowledge of this sacrament, we must take the utmost care
to put aside all that has been added by the zeal or the notions
of men to the primitive and simple institution (such as vest-
ments, ornaments, hymns, prayers, musical instruments,
lamps, and all the pomp of visible things) and must turn our
eyes and our attention only to the pure institution of Christ;
and set nothing else before us but those very words of Christ,
with which He instituted and perfected that sacrament, and
committed it to us. In that word, and absolutely in nothing
else, lies the whole force, nature, and substance of the Mass.
All the rest are human notions, accessory to the word of
Christ; and the Mass can perfectly well subsist and be kept
up without them. Now the words in which Christ instituted
this sacrament are as follows:—While they were at supper
Jesus took bread, and blessed it, and brake it, and gave it to
His disciples, and said: "Take, eat; this is my body which is

given for you." And He took the cup, and gave thanks, and gave it to them, saying: "Drink ye all of this; this cup is the New Testament in my blood, which is shed for you and for many for the remission of sins; do this in remembrance of me."

These words the Apostle Paul (I Cor. xi.) also delivers to us and explains at greater length. On these we must rest, and build ourselves up as on a firm rock, unless we wish to be carried about with every wind of doctrine, as we have hitherto been, through the impious teachings of men who pervert the truth. For in these words nothing has been omitted which pertains to the completeness, use, and profit of this sacrament; and nothing laid down which it is superfluous or unnecessary for us to know. He who passes over these words in his meditations or teachings concerning the mass will teach monstrous impieties; as has been done by those who have made an *opus operatum* and a sacrifice of it.

Let this then stand as a first and infallible truth, that the mass or Sacrament of the Altar is the testament of Christ, which He left behind Him at His death, distributing an inheritance to those who believe in Him. For such are His words: "This cup is the new testament in my blood." Let this truth, I say, stand as an immovable foundation, on which we shall erect all our arguments. You will see how we shall thus overthrow all the impious attacks of men on this sweetest sacrament. The truthful Christ, then, says with truth, that this is the new testament in His blood, shed for us. It is not without cause that I urge this; the matter is no small one, but must be received into the depths of our minds.

If then we enquire what a testament is, we shall also learn what the mass is, what are its uses, advantages, abuses. A testament is certainly a promise made by a man about to die; the idea of a testament implies, first, the death of the testator, and, secondly, the promise of the inheritance and the appointment of an heir. In this way Paul (Rom. iv; Heb. ix) speaks at some length of testaments. We also see this clearly in those words of Christ. Christ testifies of His own death when He says: "This is my body which is given; this is my blood which is shed." He assigns and points out the inheritance, when He

says: "For the remission of sins." And He appoints heirs
when He says: "For you and for many"; that is, for those
who accept and believe the promise of the testator; for it is
faith which makes us heirs, as we shall see.

"You see then that the mass—as we call it—is a promise
of the remission of sins, made to us by God; and such a promise as has been confirmed by the death of the Son of God.
For a promise and a testament only differ in this, that a testament implies the death of the promiser. A testator is a promiser who is about to die; and a promiser is, so to speak, a
testator who is about to live. This testament of Christ was
prefigured in all the promises of God from the beginning of
the world; yea! whatsoever value the ancient promises had
lay in that new promise which was about to be made in
Christ, and on which they depended. Hence the words, "agreement, covenant, testament of the Lord," are constantly employed in the Scriptures; and by these it was implied that
God was about to die. "For where a testament is, there must
also of necessity be the death of the testator" (Heb. ix:16).
God having made a testament, it was necessary that He should
die. Now He could not die, unless He became a man; and
thus in this one word "testament" the incarnation and the
death of Christ are both comprehended.[4]

FAITH

Thus we came to the most perfect promise of all, that of
the New Testament, in which life and salvation are freely
promised in plain words, and are bestowed on those who believe the promise. Christ conspicuously distinguishes this
testament from the old one, by calling it the "New Testament." The old testament given by Moses was a promise, not
of remission of sins, nor of eternal blessings, but of temporal
ones, namely, those of the land of Canaan; and by it no one
could be renewed in spirit and fitted to receive a heavenly
inheritance. Hence it was necessary that, as a figure of Christ,
an unreasoning lamb should be slain, in the blood of which
the same testament was confirmed; thus, as is the blood, so
is the testament; as is the victim, so is the promise. Now
Christ says, "The new testament is my blood," not in an-

other's, but in His own blood, by which grace is promised through the Spirit for the remission of sins, that we may receive the inheritance.

. . . From this you see that nothing else is required for a worthy reception of the Mass than faith, resting with confidence on this promise, believing Christ to be truthful in these words of His, and not doubting that these immeasurable blessings have been bestowed upon us. On this faith a spontaneous and most sweet affection of the heart will speedily follow, by which the spirit of the man is enlarged and enriched; that is, love, bestowed through the Holy Spirit on believers in Christ. Thus the believer is carried away to Christ, that bounteous and beneficent testator, and becomes altogether another and a new man. Who would not weep tears of delight, nay, almost die for joy in Christ, if he believed with unhesitating faith that this inestimable promise of Christ belongs to him? How can he fail to love such a benefactor, who of His own accord offers, promises, and gives the greatest riches and an eternal inheritance to an unworthy sinner, who has deserved very different treatment?[5]

John Calvin (1509–1564)

GOD

By knowledge of God, I intend not merely a notion that there is such a Being, but also an acquaintance with whatever we ought to know concerning him, conducing to his glory and our benefit. For we cannot with propriety say, there is any knowledge of God, where there is no religion or piety. I have no reference here to that species of knowledge, by which men, lost and condemned in themselves, apprehend God the Redeemer in Christ the Mediator; but only to that first and simple knowledge, to which the genuine order of nature would lead us, if Adam had retained his innocence. For though, in the present ruined state of human nature, no man will ever perceive God to be a Father, or the Author of salvation, or in any respect propitious, but as pacified by the mediation of Christ: yet it is one thing to understand that God our Maker supports us by his power, governs us by his providence, nourishes us by his goodness, and follows us with blessings of every kind, and another to embrace the grace of reconciliation proposed to us in Christ. Therefore, since God is first manifested, both in the structure of the world and in the general tenor of Scripture, simply as the Creator, and afterwards reveals himself in the person of Christ as a Redeemer, hence arises a twofold knowledge of him; of which the former is first to be considered, and the other will follow in its proper place. For though our mind cannot conceive of God without ascribing some worship to him, it will not be sufficient without ascribing that he is the only proper object of universal worship and adoration, unless we are also persuaded that he is the fountain of all good, and seek for none but in him.[6]

This, then, is a singular favour, that, in the instructions of the church, God not only uses mute teachers, but even opens his own sacred mouth: not only proclaims that some god ought to be worshipped, but at the same time pronounces himself to be the Being to whom this worship is due; and not only teaches the elect to raise their view to a deity, but also exhibits himself as the object of their contemplation. This method he hath observed towards his church from the beginning: besides those common lessons of instruction, to afford them also his word; which furnishes a more correct and certain criterion to distinguish him from all fictitious deities. And it was undoubtedly by this assistance that Adam, Noah, Abraham, and the rest of the patriarchs, attained to that familiar knowledge which distinguished them from unbelievers. I speak not yet of the peculiar doctrine of faith which illuminated them into the hope of eternal life. For, to pass from death to life, they must have known God, not only as the Creator, but also as the Redeemer: as they certainly obtained both from his word. For that species of knowledge, which related to him as the Creator and Governor of the world, in order preceded the other. To this was afterwards added the other internal knowledge, which alone vivifies dead souls, and apprehends God not only as the Creator of the world and as the sole Author and Arbiter of all events but also as the Redeemer in the person of the Mediator.[7]

SCRIPTURE

Before I proceed any farther, it is proper to introduce some remarks on the authority of scripture, not only to prepare the mind to regard it with due reverence, but also to remove every doubt. For, when it is admitted to be a declaration of the word of God, no man can be so deplorably presumptuous, unless he be also destitute of common sense and of the common feelings of men, as to dare to derogate from the credit due to the speaker. But since we are not favoured with daily oracles from heaven, and since it is only in the scriptures that the Lord hath been pleased to preserve his truth in perpetual remembrance; it obtains the same complete credit and authority with believers, when they are satisfied of its divine origin, as if they heard the very words pronounced by God himself.

. . . Let it be considered, then, as an undeniable truth, that they who have been inwardly taught by the Spirit, feel an entire acquiescence in the scripture, and that it is self-authenticated, carrying with it its own evidence, and ought not to be made the subject of demonstration and arguments from reason; but it obtains the credit which it deserves with us by the testimony of the Spirit. For though it conciliate our reverence by its internal majesty, it never seriously affects us till it is confirmed by the Spirit in our hearts. Therefore, being illuminated by him, we now believe the divine original of the scripture, not from our own judgment or that of others, but we esteem the certainty, that we have received it from God's own mouth by the ministry of men, to be superior to that of any human judgment, and equal to that of an intuitive perception of God himself in it. We seek not arguments or probabilities to support our judgment, but submit our judgments and understandings as to a thing, concerning which it is impossible for us to judge. And that, not like some persons who are in the habit of hastily embracing what they do not understand, which displeases them as soon as they examine it; but because we feel the firmest conviction that we hold an invincible truth: nor like those unhappy men, who surrender their minds captives to superstitions; but because we perceive in it the undoubted energies of the divine power, by which we are attracted and inflamed to an understanding and voluntary obedience, but with a vigour and efficacy superior to any power of any human will or knowledge.[8]

MAN

There is much reason in the old adage which so strongly recommends to man the knowledge of himself. For if it be thought disgraceful to be ignorant of whatever relates to the conduct of human life, ignorance of ourselves is much more shameful, which causes us, in deliberating on subjects of importance, to grope our way in miserable obscurity, or even in total darkness. But in proportion to the utility of this precept ought to be our caution not to make a preposterous use of it as we see some philosophers have done. For while they exhort man to the knowledge of himself, the end they propose is that he may not remain ignorant of his own dignity and excellence: nor do they wish him to contemplate in himself anything but what may swell him with vain confidence, and inflate his pride. But the knowledge of ourselves consists, first, in considering what was bestowed on us at our creation and the favours we continually receive from the divine benignity, that we may know how great the excellence of our nature would have been if it had retained its integrity; yet at the same time, recollecting that we have nothing properly our own, may feel our precarious tenure of all that God hath conferred on us, so as always to place our dependence upon him. Secondly, we should contemplate our miserable condition since the fall of Adam, the sense of which tends to destroy all boasting and confidence, to overwhelm us with shame, and to fill us with real humility. For as God at the beginning formed us after his own image, that he might elevate our minds both to the practice of virtue, and to the contemplation of eternal life; so, to prevent the great excellence of our species, which distinguishes us from the brutes, from being buried in sottish indolence, it is worthy of observation, that the design of our being endued with reason and intelligence is, that leading a holy and virtuous life we may aspire to the mark set before us of a blessed immortality. But we cannot think upon that primeval dignity, without having our attention immediately called to the melancholy spectacle of our disgrace and ignominy, since in the person of the first man we are fallen from our original condition. Hence arises disapprobation and abhorrence of ourselves, and real humility; and we are inflamed with fresh ardour to seek after God, to recover in him those excellencies of which we find ourselves utterly destitute.[9]

And indeed I much approve of that common observation which has been borrowed from Augustine, that the natural talents in man have been corrupted by sin, but that of the supernatural ones he has been wholly deprived. For by the latter are intended both the light of faith and righteousness, which would be sufficient for the attainment of a heavenly life and eternal felicity. Therefore, when he revolted from the divine government, he was at the same time deprived of those supernatural endowments which had been given him for the hope of eternal salvation. Hence it follows, that he is exiled from the kingdom of God, in such a manner that all the affections relating to the happy life of the soul are also extinguished in him, till he recovers them by the grace of regeneration. Such are faith, love to God, charity towards our neighbours, and an attachment to holiness and righteousness. All these things, being restored by Christ, are esteemed adventitious and preternatural; and therefore we conclude that they had been lost. Again: soundness of mind and rectitude of heart were also destroyed; and this is the corruption of the natural talents. For although we retain some portion of understanding and judgment together with the will, yet we cannot say that our mind is perfect and sound, which is oppressed with debility and immersed in profound darkness; and the depravity of our will is sufficiently known. Reason, therefore, by which man distinguishes between good and evil, by which he understands and judges, being a natural talent, it could not be totally destroyed, but is partly debilitated, partly vitiated, so that it exhibits nothing but deformity and ruin. . . . So the will, being inseparable from the nature of man, is not annihilated; but it is fettered by depraved and inordinate desires, so that it cannot aspire after anything that is good.[10]

CHRIST THE REDEEMER

It is a just observation of Augustine, that although heretics profess the name of Christ, yet he is not a foundation to them in common with the pious, but remains exclusively the foundation of the church: because, on a diligent consideration of what belongs to Christ, Christ will be found among them only in name, not in reality. Thus the papists in the present age, although the name of the Son of God, the Redeemer of the world, be frequently in their mouths, yet since they are contented with the mere name, and despoil him of his power and dignity, these words of Paul, "not holding the head," are truly applicable to them. Therefore, that faith may find in Christ a solid ground of salvation, and so may rely on him, it is proper for us to establish this principle, that the office which was assigned to him by the Father consists of three parts. . . . We have before observed, that although God sent prophets one after another in a continual succession, and never left his people destitute of useful instruction, such as was sufficient for salvation; yet the minds of the pious were always persuaded, that the full light of understanding was not to be expected till the advent of the Messiah. . . . Hence the celebrated title of "Messiah" was given to the promised Mediator. But though I confess that he was called the Messiah with particular reference to his kingdom, as I have already shown, yet the prophetical and sacerdotal unctions have their respective places, and must not be neglected by us. . . . We see that he was anointed by the Spirit, to be a preacher and witness of the grace of the Father; and that not in a common manner; for he is distinguished from other teachers, who held a similar office. And here again it must be remarked, that he received this unction, not only for himself that he might perform the office of a teacher, but for his whole body, that the preaching of the gospel might continually be attended with the power of the Spirit. But it remains beyond all doubt, that by this perfection of doctrine which

he has introduced, he has put an end to all prophecies; so
that they who, not contented with the gospel, make any
extraneous addition to it, are guilty of derogating from his
authority. . . . And the tendency of the prophetic dignity in
Christ is, to assure us that all the branches of perfect wisdom
are included in the system of doctrine which he has given us.[11]

KINGDOM OF GOD

I come now to his kingdom, of which it would be useless to
speak without first apprising the reader that it is of a spiritual nature: because thence we may gather what is its use,
and what advantage it confers upon us, and in short all its
power and eternity.

. . . The truth of our observation, that it is impossible to
perceive the nature and advantages of the Kingdom of Christ
unless we know it to be spiritual, is sufficiently evident from
a consideration of the hardship and misery of our condition
in the state of warfare under the cross, in which we have to
continue as long as we live. What advantage then could
accrue to us from being collected under the government of
the heavenly King, if the benefit of it were not to extend beyond the present state? It ought therefore to be known, that
whatever felicity is promised us in Christ, consists not in
external accommodations, such as a life of joy and tranquillity, abundant wealth, security from every injury, and
numerous delights suited to our carnal desires, but that it is
peculiar to the heavenly state. As in the world the prosperous
and desirable state of a nation consists partly in domestic
peace and an abundance of all blessings and every good,
and partly in strong bulwarks to secure it from external
violence: so Christ enriches his people with every thing necessary to the eternal salvation of their souls, and arms them
with strength to enable them to stand invincible against all
the assaults of their spiritual foes. . . .

Here we are briefly taught what advantage results to us
from the kingdom of Christ. For since it is not terrestrial or
carnal, so as to be liable to corruption, but spiritual, it ele-
vates us even to eternal life, that we may patiently pass
through this life in afflictions, hunger, cold, contempt, re-

proaches, and other disagreeable circumstances; contented
with this single assurance, that our King will never desert us,
but will assist our necessities, till having completed the term
of our warfare, we shall be called to be the triumph: for the
rule of his government is, to communicate to us whatever he
has received of the Father. Now since he furnishes and arms
us with his power, adorns us with his beauty and magnifi-
cence, and enriches us with his wealth: hence we derive most
abundant cause for glorying, and even confidence, to enable
us to contend with intrepidity against the devil, sin and death.
In the last place, since we are clothed with his righteousness,
we may boldly rise superior to all the reproaches of the world:
and as he liberally replenishes us with his favours, we ought
on our part to bring forth fruit to his glory.[12]

REPENTANCE AND FAITH

But we must now examine the nature of this faith, by
which all who are the adopted sons of God enter on the possession of the heavenly kingdom: since it is certain that not
every opinion, nor even every persuasion, is equal to the
accomplishment of so great a work. And we ought to be the
more cautious and diligent in our meditations and inquiries
on the genuine property of faith, in proportion to the pernicious tendency of the mistakes of multitudes in the present
age on this subject. For a great part of the world, when they
hear the word faith, conceive it to be nothing more than a
common assent to the evangelical history.

. . . Faith consists, not in ignorance, but in knowledge;
and that, not only of God, but also of the divine will. For,
we do not obtain salvation by our promptitude to embrace as
truth whatever the church may have prescribed, or by our
transferring to her the province of inquiry and of knowledge.
But when we know God to be a propitious Father to us,
through the reconciliation effected by Christ, and that Christ
is given to us for righteousness, sanctification, and life: by
this knowledge, I say, not by renouncing our understanding,
we obtain an entrance into the kingdom of heaven.[13]

It remains for us . . . to explain our position, that repentance consists of two parts: the mortification of the flesh and

the vivification of the spirit. This is clearly expressed by the prophets, although in a simple and homely manner, according to the capacity of a carnal people, when they say, "Depart from evil and do good." . . . For when they call men from the paths of wickedness, they require the total destruction of the flesh, which is full of wickedness and perverseness. It is a thing truly difficult and arduous, to put off ourselves and to depart from the native bias of our minds. Nor must the flesh be considered as entirely dead, unless all that we have of ourselves be destroyed. But since the universal disposition of the flesh is secret "enmity against God," the first step to an obedience of the law is this renunciation of our own nature. They afterwards designate the renovation by its fruits, righteousness, judgment, and mercy. For a punctual performance of these external duties would not be sufficient, unless the mind and heart had previously acquired a disposition of righteousness, judgment, and mercy. This takes place when the Spirit of God hath tinctured our souls with his holiness, and given them such new thoughts and affections, that they may be justly considered as new, or altogether different from what they were before. . . .

Both these branches of repentance are effects of our participation of Christ. For if we truly partake of his death, our old man is crucified by its power, and the body of sin expires, so that the corruption of our former nature loses all its vigour. If we are partakers of his resurrection, we are raised by it to a newness of life, which corresponds with the righteousness of God. In one word, I apprehend repentance to be regeneration, the end of which is the restoration of the divine image within us which was defaced, and almost obliterated, by the transgression of Adam. . . .[14]

THE CHRISTIAN LIFE

We have said that the end of regeneration is, that the life of the faithful may exhibit a symmetry and agreement between the righteousness of God and their obedience; and that thus they may confirm the adoption of which they are accepted as his children. But though this law of God comprehends that newness of life by which his image is restored to us, yet since our tardiness needs much stimulation and assistance, it will be useful to collect from various places of scripture a rule for the reformation of the life, that they who cordially repent may not be bewildered in their pursuits.

. . . This scripture plan, of which we are now treating, consists chiefly in these two things. The first, that a love of righteousness, to which we have otherwise no natural propensity, be instilled and introduced into our hearts: the second, that a rule be prescribed to us to prevent our taking any devious steps in the race of righteousness. . . . It admonishes us that we ought to be holy, because our God is holy. For when we were dispersed like scattered sheep, and lost in the labyrinth of the world, he gathered us together again, that he might associate us to himself. When we hear any mention of our union with God, we should remember that holiness must be the bond of it; not that we attain communion with him by the merit of holiness (since it is rather necessary for us in the first place to adhere to him, in order that, being endued with his holiness, we may follow whither he calls), but because it is a peculiar property of his glory not to have any intercourse with iniquity and uncleanness. Wherefore also it teaches that this is the end of our vocation, which it is requisite for us always to keep in view, if we desire to correspond to the design of God in calling us. For to what purpose was it that we were delivered from the iniquity and pollution of the world, in which we have been immersed, if we permit ourselves to wallow in them as long as we live? Besides, it also admonishes us that, to be numbered among the people of God, we must inhabit the holy city Jerusalem; which, he having consecrated it to himself, cannot without impiety be profaned by impure inhabitants.

. . . And as a farther incitement to us, it shows, that as God the Father hath reconciled us to himself in Christ, so he hath impressed in him an image, to which it is his will that we should be conformed. . . . What can be required more efficacious than this one consideration? indeed, what can be required besides? For if the Lord has adopted us as his sons on this condition, that we exhibit in our life an imitation of Christ, the bond of our adoption; unless we addict and devote ourselves to righteousness, we not only most perfidiously revolt from our Creator, but also abjure him as our Saviour.[15]

Christian liberty, according to my judgment, consists of three parts. The first part is, that the consciences of the faithful, when seeking an assurance of their justification before God, should raise themselves above the law and forget all the righteousness of the law. For since the law, as we have elsewhere demonstrated, leaves no man righteous, either we must be excluded from all hope of justification, or it is necessary for us to be delivered from it, and that so completely as not to have any dependence on works. For he who imagines, that in order to obtain righteousness he must produce any works, however small, can fix no limit or boundary, but renders himself a debtor to the whole law. Avoiding, therefore, all mention of the law, dismissing all thought of our own works, in reference to justification, we must embrace the divine mercy alone, and turning our eyes from ourselves, fix them solely on Christ. For the question is, not how we can be righteous, but how, though unrighteous and unworthy, we can be considered as righteous. And the conscience that desires to attain any certainty respecting this, must give no admission to the law. Nor will this authorize any one to conclude, that the law is of no use to the faithful, whom it still continues to instruct and exhort, and stimulate to duty, although it has no place in their consciences before the tribunal of God. For these two things, being very different, require to be properly and carefully distinguished by us. The whole life of Christians ought to be an exercise of piety, since they are called to sanctifications.

. . . The second part of Christian liberty, which is dependent on the first, is, that their consciences do not observe the law, as being under any legal obligation; but that, being liberated from the yoke of the law, they yield a voluntary obedience to the will of God. For being possessed with perpetual terrors, as long as they remain under the dominion of the law, they will never engage with alacrity and promptitude in the service of God, unless they have previously received this liberty. . . . In short, they who are bound by the yoke of the law are like slaves who have certain daily tasks appointed by their masters. They think they have done nothing, and presume not to enter into the presence of their masters without having finished the work prescribed to them. But children, who are treated by their parents in a more liberal manner, hesitate not to present to them their imperfect and in some respects faulty works, in confidence that their obedience and promptitude of mind will be accepted by them, though they had not performed all that they wished. Such children ought we to be, feeling a certain confidence that our services, however small, rude, and imperfect, will be approved by our most indulgent Father.

. . . The third part of Christian liberty teaches us, that we are bound by no obligation before God respecting external things, which in themselves are indifferent; but that we may indifferently sometimes use, and at other times omit them.

Now since the consciences of the faithful, being privileged with the liberty which we have described, have been delivered by the favour of Christ from all necessary obligation to the observance of those things in which the Lord hath been pleased they should be left free, we conclude that they are exempt from all human authority.[16]

THE CHURCH

From what has been said, I conceive it must now be evident what judgment we ought to form respecting the church, which is visible to our eyes and falls under our knowledge. For we have remarked that the word "church" is used in the sacred scriptures in two senses. Sometimes when they mention the church, they intend that which is really such in the sight of God, into which none are received but those who by adoption and grace are the children of God, and by the sanctification of the Spirit are the true members of Christ. And then it comprehends not only the saints at any one time resident on earth, but all the elect who have lived from the beginning of the world. But the word "church" is frequently used in the scriptures to designate the whole multitude dispersed all over the world, who profess to worship one God and Jesus Christ, who are initiated into his faith by baptism, who testify their unity in true doctrine and charity by a participation of the sacred supper, who consent to the word of the Lord, and preserve the ministry which Christ has instituted for the purpose of preaching it. In this church are included many hypocrites, who have nothing of Christ but the name and appearance; many persons ambitious, avaricious, envious, slanderous, and dissolute in their lives, who are tolerated for a time, either because they cannot be convicted by a legitimate process, or because discipline is not always maintained with sufficient vigour. As it is necessary therefore to believe that church which is invisible to us and known to God alone; so this church which is visible to men, we are commanded to honour, and to maintain communion with it.[17]

We must now treat of the order which it has been the Lord's will to appoint for the government of his church. For although he alone ought to rule and reign in the church, and to have all pre-eminence in it, and this government ought to be exercised and administered solely by his word; yet as he dwells not among us by a visible presence so as to make an audible declaration of his will to us, we have stated that for this purpose he uses the ministry of men whom he employs as his delegates, not to transfer his right and honour to them, but only that he may himself do his work by their lips; just as an artificer makes use of an instrument in the performance of his work. . . .

The Lord therefore has connected his church together, by that which he foresaw would be the strongest bond for the preservation of their union, when he committed the doctrine of eternal life and salvation to men, that by their hands it might be communicated to others. Paul had this in view when he wrote the Ephesians. . . . "And he gave some, apostles; and some, prophets; and some, evangelists; and some, pastors and teachers; for the perfecting of the saints, for the work of the ministry, for the edifying of the body of Christ: till we all come in the unity of the faith, and of the knowledge of the Son of God, unto a perfect man, unto the measure of the stature of the fulness of Christ. . . ." In this passage he shows that the ministry of men, which God employs in his government of the church, is the principal bond which holds the faithful together in one body. He also indicates that the church cannot be preserved in perfect safety, unless it be supported by these means which God has been pleased to appoint for its preservation. Christ, he says, "ascended up far above all heavens, that he might fill all things." And this is the way in which he does it. By means of his ministers, to whom he has committed this office, and on whom he has bestowed grace to discharge it, he dispenses and distributes his gifts to the church, and even affords some manifestation of his own presence, by exerting the power of his Spirit in this his institution, that it may not be vain or ineffectual. Thus is the restoration of the saints effected; thus is the body of Christ edified: thus we grow up unto him who is our Head in all things, and are united with each other: thus we are all brought to the unity of Christ if prophecy flourishes among us, if we receive the apostles, if we despise not the doctrine which is delivered to us.[18]

CHURCH AND THE WORLD

Yet this distinction does not lead us to consider the whole system of civil government as a polluted thing, which has nothing to do with Christian men. Some fanatics, who are pleased with nothing but liberty, or rather licentiousness without any restraint, do indeed boast and vociferate, that since we are dead with Christ to the elements of this world, and being translated into the kingdom of God, sit among the celestials, they think it a degradation to us, and far beneath our dignity, to be occupied with those secular and impure cares which relate to things altogether uninteresting to a Christian man. Of what use, they ask, are laws without judgments and tribunals? But what have judgments to do with a Christian man? And if it be unlawful to kill, of what use are laws and judgments to us? But as we have just suggested that this kind of government is distinct from that spiritual and internal reign of Christ, so it ought to be known that they are in no respect at variance with each other. For that spiritual reign, even now upon earth, commences within us some preludes of the heavenly kingdom, and in this mortal and transitory life affords us some prelibations of immortal and incorruptible blessedness: but this civil government is designed, as long as we live in this world, to cherish and support the external worship of God, to preserve the pure doctrine of religion, to defend the constitution of the church, to regulate our lives in a manner requisite for the society of men, to form our manners to civil justice, to promote our concord with each other, and to establish general peace and tranquillity: all which I confess to be superfluous, if the kingdom of God, as it now exists in us, extinguish the present life. But if it be the will of God, that its order is sufficient to supply the place of all laws; but they foolishly imagine a perfection, which can never be found in any community of men. For since the insolence of the wicked is so great, and their iniquity so obstinate that it can scarcely be restrained by all the severity of the laws, what can we expect they would do, if they found themselves at liberty to perpetrate crimes with impunity, whose outrages even the arm of power cannot altogether prevent?

. . . But for speaking of the exercise of civil polity, there will be another place more suitable. At present we only wish it to be understood, that to entertain a thought of its extermination, is inhuman barbarism; it is equally as necessary to mankind as bread and water, light and air, and far more excellent. For it not only tends to secure the accommodations arising from all these things, that men may breathe, eat, drink, and be sustained in life, though it comprehends all these things while it causes them to live together, yet I say, this is not its only tendency; its objects also are, that idolatry, sacrileges against the name of God, blasphemies against his truth, and other offences against religion may not openly appear and be disseminated among the people; that the public tranquillity may not be disturbed; that every person may enjoy his property without molestation; that men may transact their business together without fraud or injustice; that integrity and modesty may be cultivated between them: in short, that there may be a public form of religion among Christians, and that humanity may be maintained among men. Nor let any one think it strange that I now refer to human polity the charge of the due maintenance of religion, which I may appear to have placed beyond the jurisdiction of men. For I do not allow men to make laws respecting religion and the worship of God now, any more than I did before; though I approve of civil government, which provides that the true religion which is contained in the law of God, be not violated, and polluted by public blasphemies, with impunity.[19]

Ulrich Zwingli (1484–1531)

The following considerations I continually revolved in my mind, till at length the Holy Spirit confirmed in me that which He wrought in me:—

We see, thought I, the whole of mankind striving, their lives long, after the attainment of future bliss, not perhaps directed to the pursuit so much from any natural impulse as from the instinct of self-preservation implanted in us by the Author of our being at our creation; yet the opinions are very various as to how the great end is to be obtained. If we go to the philosophers, we find them disputing on this subject in a manner which makes us turn away from them in disgust. If we seek for a solution of the problem from the Christians, we find here even a greater diversity of opinions than prevails among the heathen, for some are striving to reach the goal in the way of human tradition, and by the elements of this world, i.e., by their own and human opinions, while others are relying entirely on God's grace and promises; both the one and the other, however, are equally urgent that those who come to them for consolation should adopt their sentiments. Let us stand at this point now, where two roads cross, that is, where the opinions of Christians themselves cross. Whither now, I ask, shall I turn? Is the answer given, to men? Then I ask, to whom? To those who, at the origin of Christianity, were held wise, or to those who, shortly before my own time, have given a much greater exhibition of folly than wisdom? It will be said that I ought to follow the old guides, those who deserve the preference as such, as well by their antiquity as by their holy lives. But it may be said farther, even in these one finds much that is foreign to the evangelist and apostles, or that in fact contradicts them. With whom am I now to hold? . . . While I was reflecting on this diversity of opinion in the earthen vessels, and praying to God that He would shew men an outlet to the state of uncertainty it produces, He says, Fool, dost not thou remember "The word of the Lord abideth forever?" hold to this . . . For this cause I put everything aside, and come to the point, that I would rely on no single thing, on no single word, so firmly as on that which comes from the mouth of the Lord. And as I saw poor mortals so far forgetting themselves and God as to make bold to give out their own way as God's, nay, when I saw not a few requiring, in all seriousness, from the simple, that they should set their commands above God's, even though they should be in manifest contradiction to them, I began to weigh with myself, whether there were no means by which one might recognize what was human and what divine. Then the passage occurred to me, "all is clear in the light," in that light, to wit, which says, "I am the light of the world, that lightens every man that cometh into the world"; and again, "believe not every spirit, but try the spirits, whether they be of God." I now began to test every doctrine by this test. Did I see that the touchstone gave back the same colour, or rather, that the doctrine could bear the brightness of the stone, I accepted it; if not I cast it away.[20]

Zwingli expressed his commitments strongly in a Circular Letter (1525):

Dear Sirs and Brethren in the Lord, the Holy Paul cared not alone for those whom he had converted to the faith, but for all the churches, that is, for all the faithful, that no infidelity, error, or scandal, might arise among them. I therefore trust that my present writing to you will not be misinterpreted, on the one hand, because I have heard how you have accepted that true and irresistible Word of God, and have permitted, in the most places, the free preaching of the same, and in the second place, because I am a native of the bishopric of Chur. . . . I beg your worships well to consider how the Papal authority has taken captive the Word of God, and hid it in darkness, whereby the truth has been withheld from us, and an empty semblance presented to us in the place of it, whereby we have been not only cozened out of our worldly goods, but, as there is ground to fear, have had our soul's salvation put in jeopardy. This is the more especially now to be feared, since the truth has been set in the light of day, and yet many, blinded by papistical doctrine, will not yield obedience to it. You see now how it stands with the Popedom, and on the other hand, how glorious and vigorous the truth everywhere displays itself, so that the whole Papal power can effect nothing against it, but has recourse to violence, maltreatment, lies, and bribery, against it, although, God be praised, it has not been able to overcome even the least of those who now, for a considerable time, preach the gospel. Wherefore, it is to be feared that if the civil power do not protect those who proclaim the Word, and who are able to give an account of their doctrine out of that Word, that God will again withdraw His favour from us, and allow us to sink again into our old errors. . . . Wherefore, pious, steadfast, wise and beloved brethren in God, let not yourselves be seduced by those who seek to stir you up by secret lies and calumnies against the Word of God and its preachers, and those who obey it. . . . May the God who hath begun . . . to introduce you into the knowledge of His truth, guide and strengthen you, that we may all appear before Him with joy at the last day. Amen.[21]

THE PRINCIPLES BECOME CONFESSIONS

Following the work of the reformers, confessions, or statements of faith were prepared by certain leaders within the Protestant churches. These were formal, orderly treatises, listing the beliefs the churches held. They were much more than creeds, although they were in effect expansions of one of the historical creeds of the Church with articles or paragraphs added to set forth the particular doctrines of Protestantism. There follow summaries of two of those Confessions, one which has had great influence in the Lutheran churches and the other which has influenced the Calvinistic or Reformed Churches.

The Augsburg Confession was written by Philip Melanchthon in 1530 at the request of certain German princes who had been asked by Charles V, the Emperor, to present a formal statement of the faith of the churches in their domains that had signified their allegiance to the Protestant movement. The Confession was approved by Martin Luther, and was read to a meeting of representatives of church and states held in the city of Augsburg, Bavaria. The Confession was presented over the signatures of seven German princes and the deputies of two free cities.

The Augsburg Confession: a Summary

Of God affirms the Nicene doctrine, explains that "person" means, not a part of quality, but "that which properly subsists."

Of Original Sin teaches that, "since Adam's fall, all men begotten after the common course of nature are born with sin, that is, without the fear of God, without trust in Him, and with fleshly appetite; and that this disease or original fault is truly sin, condemning and bringing eternal death now also upon all that are born again by baptism and the Holy Spirit."

Of the Son of God expands slightly the language of the Apostles' Creed.

Of Justification: "Men cannot be justified before God by their own powers, merits, or works, but are justified freely for

Christ's sake through faith, when they believe that they are received into favour and their sins forgiven for Christ's sake, who by His death hath satisfied for our sins. This faith doth God impute for righteousness before him."

Of New Obedience teaches that "this faith should bring forth good fruits, and that men ought to do the good works commanded of God, because it is God's will, and not for any confidence of meriting justification before God by their works."

The Church "is the congregation of saints in which the Gospel is rightly taught, and the sacraments rightly administered: unto the true unity of the Church it is sufficient to agree concerning the doctrine of the Gospel and the administration of the Sacraments: nor is it necessary that human traditions, rites, or ceremonies instituted by men should be alike everywhere."

Repentance is said to "consist of these two parts:—one is contrition, or terrors stricken into the conscience by the recognition; the other is faith, which is conceived by the Gospel or by absolution, and doth believe that for Christ's sake sins be forgiven, and comforteth the conscience and freeth it from terrors. Then should follow good works, which are fruits of repentance."

Of Ecclesiastical Orders teaches "that those only are to be observed which may be observed without sin, and are profitable for tranquillity and good order in the Church; such as are set holidays, feasts, and such like. Yet concerning such things, men are to be admonished that consciences are not to be burdened as if such service were necessary to salvation. They are also to be admonished that human traditions, instituted to propitiate God, to merit grace, and to make satisfaction for sins, are opposed to the Gospel and the doctrine of faith. Wherefore vows and traditions concerning foods and days, and such like, instituted to merit grace and make satisfaction for sins, are useless and contrary to the Gospel."

Of Civil Affairs teaches that "such civil ordinances as are lawful are good works of God; Christians may lawfully bear civil office, sit in judgements, determine matters by the imperial laws . . . appoint just punishments, engage in just war, act as soldiers, make legal bargains and contracts, hold property, take an oath when the magistrates require, marry a wife or be given in marriage." It condemns the Anabaptists who forbid Christians these civil offices, in as much as "the Gospel teacheth an everlasting righteousness of the heart. . . ." "Christians must necessarily obey their magistrates and laws, save only when they command any sin; for then they must rather obey God than men."

Of Free Will affirms "that man's will hath some liberty to work a civil righteousness, and to choose such things as reason can reach into; but that it hath no power to work the righteousness of God; because the natural man receiveth not the things of the Spirit of God. But this is wrought in the heart when men do receive the Spirit of God through the word."[22]

The Helvetic Confession was written by Henry Bullinger (1504–1575) who was the successor to Ulrich Zwingli in Zurich. Apparently he worked it out to clear his own mind about the beliefs he had come to hold. It was published when the Elector Frederick III asked Bullinger to prepare for his use an exposition of the Reformed Faith. Bullinger sent the Elector the document he had worked out for himself. The Elector had it published. It has been widely used in Reformed Churches.

The Helvetic Confession

We believe and confess that the Canonical Scriptures of the Old and New Testaments are the true Word of God, and have sufficient authority in and of themselves, and not from men: since God himself through them still speaks to us, as

He did to the Fathers, the Prophets, and Apostles. They contain all that is necessary to a saving faith and a holy life; and hence nothing could be added to or taken from them.

From the Scriptures must be derived all true wisdom and piety and the reformation and government of the Churches, the proof of doctrines and the refutation of error. God may illuminate men directly by the Holy Spirit, without the external ministry; yet he has chosen the Scriptures and the preaching of the Word as the usual method of instruction.

We acknowledge only that interpretation as true and correct which is fairly derived from the spirit and language of the Scriptures themselves, in accordance with the circumstances and in harmony with other and plainer passages.

We do not despise the interpretation of the Greek and Latin fathers and the teaching of Councils, but subordinate them to the Scriptures; honouring them as far as they agree with the Scriptures and modestly dissenting from them when they go beyond or against the Scriptures. In matters of faith we can not admit any other judge than God himself, who through his Word tells us what is true and what is false, what is to be followed and what is to be avoided.

God is the only object of worship. And he is to be worshipped in spirit and in truth; and through our only and sufficient Mediator and Advocate Jesus Christ.

Man was created according to the image of God, in true righteousness and holiness, good and upright. But by the instigation of the serpent, and through his own guilt, he fell from goodness and rectitude, and became, with all his offspring, subject to sin, death and various calamities.

Sin is that inborn corruption of man, derived and propagated from our first parents, whereby we are immersed in depraved lusts, averse to goodness and prone to all evil, and unable of ourselves to do or think anything that is good. And as years roll on, we bring forth evil thoughts, words, and deeds, as corrupt trees bring forth corrupt fruits. Therefore we are all by nature under the wrath of God, and subject to just punishment.

The will and moral ability of man must be viewed under a threefold state.

First, before the fall, he had freedom to continue in good-ness or to yield to temptation.

Secondly, after the fall, his understanding was darkened and his will became a slave to sin. But he has not been turned into "a stone or stock"; nor is his will (*voluntas*) a non-will (*noluntas*). He serves sin willingly, not unwillingly (*servit peccato non nolens, sed volens*). In external and worldly mat-ters man retains his freedom even after the fall, under the general providence of God.

Thirdly, in regenerate state, man is free in the true and proper sense of the term. His intellect is enlightened by the Holy Spirit to understand the mysteries and the will of God; and the will is changed by the Spirit and endowed with the power freely to will and to do what is good.

God has from eternity predestinated or freely chosen, of his mere grace, without any respect of men, the saints whom he will save in Christ.

God elected us in Christ and for Christ's sake, so that those who are already implanted in Christ by faith are chosen, but those out of Christ are rejected.

Although God knows who are his, and a "small number of the elect" is spoken of, yet we ought to hope well of all, and not rashly count any one among the reprobate.

We believe and teach the Son of God, our Lord Jesus Christ, was from eternity predestinated by the Father to be the Saviour of the World; that he was begotten of the Father from all eternity in an ineffable manner. Therefore the Son, according to his Divinity, is coequal and cosubstantial with the Father; true God, not merely by name or adoption or by confessing of a dignity.

We also believe and teach that the same eternal Son of God became the Son of Man, of the seed of Abraham and David, not through the will of man (Edionites), but he was conceived by the Holy Ghost and born of the ever Virgin Mary (*ex Maria semper Virgine*), as taught in the gospel history and the Epistles. The body of Christ was therefore neither a mere appearance nor brought down from heaven (the Gnostics Valentinus and Marcion). Moreover his soul was not without reason (Apollinaris), not his flesh without a soul (Eunomius), but he had a rational soul, and a flesh with sense capable of the true suffering.

Hence we acknowledge in one and the same Lord Jesus Christ two natures, a divine and a human, which are conjoined and united in one person without absorption or confusion and mixture.

We believe and teach that Christ, in the same flesh in which he died, rose from the dead and ascended to the right hand of God in the highest heaven, which signifies his elevation to the divine majesty and power, but also a definite place.

In the strict sense of the term the gospel is the glad tidings of salvation by Christ, in whom we have forgiveness, redemption, and everlasting life. Hence the history of Christ recorded by the four Evangelists is justly called the gospel.

Repentance is a change of heart produced in a sinner by the word of the gospel and the Holy Spirit, and includes a knowledge of native and actual depravity, a godly sorrow and hatred of sin, and a determination to live hereafter in virtue and holiness. True repentance is turning to God and all good, and turning away from the devil and all evil. It is the free gift of God, and not the result of our own strength.

We teach that good works proceed from a living faith, through the Holy Spirit, and are done by believers according to the will and rule of the Word of God.

Good works must be done, not to merit thereby eternal life, which is a free gift of God, nor for ostentation or from selfishness, which the Lord rejects, but for the glory of God, to adorn our calling and to show our gratitude to God, and for the good of our neighbour. Although we teach that man is justified by faith of Christ and not by any works, we do not condemn good works. Man is created and regenerated by faith in order to work unceasingly what is good and useful.

Since God willed from the beginning that man should be saved and come to the knowledge of truth, it follows of necessity that there always was, and now is, and shall be to the end of time, a Church or an assembly of believers and a communion of saints, called and gathered from the world, who know and worship the true God in Christ our Saviour, and partake by faith of all the benefits freely offered through

Christ. They are fellow-citizens of the same household of God. To this refers the article in the Creed: "I believe in the holy catholic Church, the communion of saints."

The Church is divided, not in itself, but on account of the diversity of its members. There is a Church militant on earth struggling against the flesh, the world and the devil, and a church triumphant in heaven rejoicing in the presence of the Lord; nevertheless there is a communion between the two. The Church militant is again divided into particular Churches. It was differently constituted among the Patriarchs, then under Moses, then under Christ in the gospel dispensation, but there is only one salvation in the one Messiah, in whom all are united as members of one body, partaking of the same spiritual food and drink. We enjoy a greater degree of light and more perfect liberty.

The Church can have no other head than Christ. He is the one universal pastor of his flock, and has promised his presence to the end of the world. He needs, therefore, no vicar, for this would imply his absence.

The true unity of the Church is not to be sought in ceremonies and rites, but in the truth and in the catholic faith, as laid down in the Scriptures and summed up in the Apostles' Creed. Among the ancients there was a great diversity of rites without dissolving the unity of the Church.

The ministers of the New Testament are called Apostles, prophets, evangelists, bishops, metropolitans, archpresbyters, deacons, and subdeacons, etc. But we are satisfied with the offices instituted by the Apostles for the teaching and governing of the Church.

All ministers are equal in power and commission. Bishops and presbyters were originally the same in office, and governed the church by their united services, mindful of the words of the Lord: "He who will be chief among you, let him be your servant."

The chief duties of the minister are the preaching of the gospel, the administration of the sacraments, the care of the souls, and maintenance of discipline. To do this effectually they must live in the fear of God, pray constantly, study the Scripture diligently, be always watchful, and shine before all by purity of life. In the exercise of discipline, they should remember that the power was given to them for edification and not for destruction.

The sacraments of the Jewish dispensation were circumcision and the paschal lamb; the sacraments of the Christian dispensation are baptism and the Lord's Supper.

The civil magistrate is appointed by God himself for the peace and tranquility of the human race. If opposed to the Church, he can do much harm; if friendly, he can do the Church most useful service.

The duty of the magistrate is to preserve peace and public order; to promote and protect religion and good morals; to govern the people by righteous laws; to punish the offenders against society, such as thieves, murderers, oppressors, blasphemers, and incorrigible heretics (if they are really heretics).

All citizens owe reverence and obedience to the magistrate as the minister of God in all righteous commands, and even their lives when the public safety and welfare require it. Therefore we condemn the despisers of the magistrate, rebels and enemies of the commonwealth and all who openly or artfully refuse to perform their duties as citizens.[23]

The Lutheran and Calvinistic streams in Protestantism were in agreement on certain fundamental beliefs, and those beliefs expressed the freedom and individual responsibility which men had come to know in the Reformation era. The one true God had acted on behalf of man and his salvation by sending His Son, Jesus Christ, to be the Saviour of humanity. Man had to respond to God's action by faith in Christ, and by faith alone. That is, he had to put his life, in free and willing trust, under the supremacy of Jesus Christ. This meant that man had to depend upon the Bible to guide and direct him as the meditating agency of God's authority. Those two beliefs, usually spoken of as "Justification by Faith" and the "Scriptures as the infallible rule of life and practice," were the ground-structure of Protestantism. Man, in his freedom, was to renounce all trust in external authority, whether established in tradition or history or arrived at by his own mind or spirit; he was to trust in Christ alone. The ministry would be made known for him through the Scriptures. Man, thus, had a source of guidance outside himself to which he could turn and the assurance that he could depend upon the deliverance of his own freedom as that was instructed by Christ.

Those two basic beliefs gave rise of necessity to another: the certainty that all men, equally, might work out their individual relationships to God. The two Confessions included sections on the Church and the ministry in the Church. But instead of granting those institutions and persons authority over men, Christian men formed an assembly of believers, with some of their number assigned or called to special tasks among them. The freedom of men puts all men in exactly the same position as individuals before God.

Although the two streams agreed on those basic principles there was a difference in emphasis between them. Philip Schaff stated the matter in this way:

The Lutheran Confession starts from the wants of sinful man and the personal experience of justification by faith alone, and finds, in this Article . . . comfort and peace of conscience, and the strongest stimulus to a godly life. The Reformed Churches (especially the Calvinistic section) start from the absolute sovereignty of God and the supreme authority of his holy Word and endeavour to reconstruct the whole Church on this basis. The one proceeds from anthropology to theology; the other, from theology to anthropology.[24]

This difference affected the histories of the two streams of the church during the years that followed. We should also note that very shortly after the founding of the Protestant churches disagreements over doctrine and practice broke out which kept the churches separated one from the other. At times the feelings between the various parties in the churches became heated, until the conflict took on some of the marks of civil war. We cannot go into the details of that part of the churches' story. It is enough to note that in those disagreements there appeared one characteristic of Protestantism that has continued down to the present. Divisiveness was, humanly speaking, almost inevitable; for when Protestants put the seat of authority in religion within man himself, linking it with man's free spirit, and make it essential for each individual to follow the dictates of his own mind and conscience, illumined and guided by the Scripture, they establish a form of Christian faith in which every difference between people is bound to carry great weight. Since people are different one from another in education, social outlook, emotional make-up and so on, their differences will affect the nature and forms of their religious lives. And this divisiveness appeared soon after the start of Protestantism both within and between the two main streams. The very basic element in life upon which Protestantism rests carries with it the possibility of divisions.

TWO DIVERGENT PROTESTANT MOVEMENTS

While we cannot pursue the subject of the controversies within and between the Lutheran and Reformed faiths, we must take note of two distinct Protestant lines which arose at the time of or shortly after the work of the Reformers. We must notice those lines because they were distinct from the orthodox churches in one or more significant ways.

The Anabaptists

On the one hand, the Anabaptists might be called the right wing group of the Reformation.

The Anabaptists can in no sense be regarded as a unified and cohesive movement. They formed little companies of devout believers scattered all over Germany and allied territories. Some of those companies were knit in a loose kind of federation, but no such organization had any permanency. Among them could be found a variety of religious belief and practice. The number of their sects and their opinions, a contemporary writes, is impossible to know, and no two can be found to agree on all points. Some held millenarian views, others practised a real community of property, and others were characterised by their liberal charity. A good many of them maintained that infant baptism was a meaningless rite, and that entrance into the Church should be a matter of adult decision. It is from this view that they got the name Anabaptists. There were those among them who verged toward extreme religious mania. Tales have come down of women who uttered meaningless prophecies and of those who believed themselves to be Christ or even God. Those, however, were the exceptions rather than the rule. By and large they were earnest religious folk of the underprivileged peasant classes. They allied themselves in spirit with the attack of the Reformers against the presumption and abuses of the Roman Church, but they regarded their constructive efforts with apprehension. With deep religious conviction they believed any true Reformation of the Church must involve the reform of social injustices, although they were divided on the question of the use of force to accomplish these ends.

Furthermore, they stood in clear opposition to the other Protestant parties in their view of the Church. Basic to their thought was the old Donatist conception. The Church was essentially a sect or a number of sects. They denied that it was an institution which had an intimate relation with the world and was organised and upheld by the secular power. Rather did they conceive of it as a number of small associations of believers who had fled from the world. By the purity of their personal life they witnessed to the fact that they renounced its evils, such as warfare, taking oaths in court, and holding political office. Most of them practised passive resistance and believed that the use of the sword was unconditionally forbidden by Christ. Others, of a more radical tendency, resorted to open rebellion to relieve peasant oppression and even "to bring in the Kingdom of God." In either case, the Church was interpreted as a small company of earnest believers who stood in marked contrast to the sin of the world. Either by passive resistance they renounced the world altogether, or else by the use of force they attempted to rectify its abuses and set up the true Kingdom of Christ on earth.

After the ill-fated experiment in Munster, where some of the more extreme Anabaptists tried forcibly to set up the Kingdom of God on earth, they abandoned the policy of using force of arms. They were organised into peaceful and devout groups, whose serious and austere life contrasted with the general tenor of society around them. Under Menno Simons they were established in the Netherlands. From there they spread to England and to America, forming large bodies of dissent from the national and established churches. With champions like Roger Williams in Rhode Island the cause of religious liberty was advanced, and finally the complete separation of the Church from the State effected. At root, this development presupposed the secularisation of the State, which was precipitated by the thinking of the Enlightenment. . . .[25]

Like as a body consisteth of divers parts, and every part hath its own proper work, seeing every part is not a hand, eye, or foot: so it is also in the Church of God: for although every believer is a member of the body of Christ, yet is not every one therefore a teacher, elder, or deacon, but only such who are orderly appointed to such offices. Therefore, also, the administration of the said offices or duties pertaineth only to those that are ordained thereto, and not to every particular common person.

The Holy Baptism is given unto those, in the name of the Father, the Son, and the Holy Ghost, which hear, believe, and with penitent heart receive the doctrines of the Holy Gospel. For such hath the Lord Jesus commanded to be baptized, and no unspeaking children.

The church discipline, or external censures, is also an outward handling among the believers, whereby the impenitent sinner, after Christian admonition and reproof, is severed by reason of his sins, from the communion of the saints for his future good; and the wrath of God is denounced against him until the time of his contrition and reformation.

Worldly authority or magistracy is a necessary ordinance of God, appointed and established for the preservation of the common estate; and of a good, natural, politic life, for the reward of the good and the punishings of the evil, we acknowledge ourselves obnoxious, and bound by the Word of God to fear, honour, and show obedience to the magistrates in all causes not contrary to the Word of the Lord. We are obliged to pray God Almighty for them, and to thank the Lord for good reasonable magistrates, and to yield unto them, without murmuring, beseeming tribute, toll, and tax. This office of the worldly authority the Lord Jesus hath not ordained in his spiritual kingdom, the church of the New Testament, nor adjoined to the offices of his church. Neither hath he called his disciples or followers to be worldly kings, princes, potentates, or magistrates; neither hath he burdened or charged them to assume such offices, or to govern the world in such a worldly manner; much less hath he given a law to the members of his church which is agreeable to such office or government.[26]

The Church of England

On the other hand, there was the Church of England. That the English Reformation has a history all its own, we have had occasion to note earlier in references to Colet, Wycliff, and Tyndale. Here we need to point out that while the movement in England agreed in certain basic principles with the movements on the continent of Europe, it differed significantly in the way it established the relationship between the Church and the State. The following passages describe briefly the events that occurred:

(When) Warham, archbishop of Canterbury died . . . Henry determined to appoint a successor who, upon principle, would oppose Roman usurpations. He therefore . . . chose Cranmer to fill the vacant seat. . . .

When his reluctance in other respects had been overcome, Cranmer stated to the King that he neither could nor would receive the Archbishopric from the pope, whom he considered to have no authority in the realm . . . several civilians of eminence, advised the King that Cranmer should be appointed to office by the King, and suggested that, previously to his consecration he (Cranmer) should solemnly declare his determination, not to act in any manner inconsistent with a minister of Christ or a subject of England.[27]

The parliament assembled at the commencement of 1533 when decisive measures were taken for emancipating the nation from Rome. The pope's supremacy was openly called in question; the earliest result was the taking away of some of the most oppressive and secret proceedings in cases of heresy, and allowing the accused a trial in the open court. The payment of certain taxes to the pope was discontinued, and by various other measures the papal power was entirely set aside in England.

He (Cranmer) proved so evidently and clearly, both by the word of God, and consent of the primitive church, that this usurped power of the pope is mere tyranny, and directly against the law of God, that the issue was the abolishing of that foreign papal power and the expulsion of it out of this realm, by the consent of parliament. . . .

Sinners attain justification by contrition and faith, joined with charity, after such sort and manner as is declared in the sacrament of penance. Not as though our contrition or faith, or any works proceeding thereof, can worthily merit or deserve to attain said justification; for the only mercy and grace of the Father, promised freely unto us for His Son's sake, Jesus Christ, and the merits of his blood and passion, are the only sufficient and worthy causes thereof: and yet notwithstanding to the attaining of the same justification, God requireth to be in us not only inward contrition, perfect faith and charity, certain hope and confidence, with all other spiritual graces and motions, which must necessarily concur in remission of our sins, that is to say, or justification but also he requiteth and commandeth us, that after we are justified, we must also have good works of charity and obedience towards God, in the observing and fulfilling outwardly of his laws and commandments. . . .

As nothing is more destructive to the church than heresies and disputes respecting the doctrines of religion so nothing is more efficacious in gathering together the churches of God, and more powerfully strengthens the flock of Christ, than the uncorrupted doctrine of the Gospel and agreed in opinion. Wherefor I have often desired and still do desire that learned and pious men who pass others in learning and judgment, should meet in some place free from danger, where by mutual deliberation and comparison of their opinions they might consider all the points of Ecclesiastical doctrine, so that by weighty authority they might hand down to posterity work not only rightly setting forth the doctrines themselves but also the manner in which they should be expressed.[28]

In 1563 Queen Elizabeth I called a meeting of Convocation at which a formal statement concerning the doctrine and order of the Church was ratified by both Houses and approved by the Queen. That document is known as the Thirty-Nine Articles of Religion and has remained in use to the present day with only a few changes. In the articles which deal with God, the Trinity, Jesus Christ, sin, salvation, Scripture, justification by faith, and the Sacraments, the document agrees substantially with the Confessions of the continental churches. But in other respects there were differences. Here are the Articles in which the differences appear.

Of the Authority Of the Church. The Church hath power to decree Rites or Ceremonies, and authority in Controversies of Faith: And yet it is not lawful for the Church to ordain anything that is contrary to God's Word written, neither may it so expound one place of Scripture, that it be repugnant to another. Wherefore, although the Church be a witness and a keeper of holy Writ, yet as it ought not to decree anything against the same, so besides the same ought it not to enforce anything to be believed for necessity of Salvation.

Of the Authority Of General Councils. General Councils may not be gathered together without the commandment and will of Princes. And when they be gathered together (forasmuch as they be an assembly of men, whereof all be not governed with the Spirit and Word of God), they may err, and sometimes have erred, even in things pertaining unto God. Wherefore things ordained by them as necessary to salvation have neither strength nor authority, unless it may be declared that they be taken out of the holy Scriptures.

Of the Traditions Of the Church. It is not necessary that traditions and ceremonies be in all places one, and utterly like; for all times they have been divers and may be changed according to the diversities of countries, times and men's manners, so that nothing be ordained against God's Word. Whosoever through his private judgement, willingly and purposely, doth openly break the traditions and ceremonies of the Church, which be not repugnant to the Word of God, and be ordained and approved by common authority, ought to be rebuked openly (that others may fear to do the like) as he that offendeth against the common order of the Church, and hurteth the authority of the Magistrate, and woundeth the consciences of the weak brethren.

Every particular or national Church hath authority to ordain, change and abolish ceremonies or rites of the Church ordained only by man's authority. . . .

Of the Civil Magistrate. The King's Majesty hath the chief power in this Realm of England, and other of his Dominions, unto whom the chief Government of all Estates of this Realm, whether they be Ecclesiastical or Civil, in all causes doth appertain, and is not, nor ought to be, subject to any foreign Jurisdiction.

Where we attribute to the King's Majesty the chief government, by which Titles we understand the minds of some slanderous folks to be offended; we give not to our Princes the ministering either of God's Word, or of the Sacraments, the which thing the Injunctions also lately set forth by Elizabeth our Queen do most plainly testify; but that only prerogative, which we see to have been given always to all godly Princes in Holy Scriptures by God himself; that is, that they should rule all estates and degrees committed to their charge by God, whether they be Ecclesiastical or Temporal, and restrain with the civil sword the stubborn and evildoers.

The Bishop of Rome hath no jurisdiction in this Realm of England.

The laws of the Realm may punish Christian men with death, for heinous and grievous offences.

It is lawful for Christian men, at the commandment of the Magistrate to bear weapons, and serve in the wars.[29]

CHAPTER THREE

Protestantism: Its Inner Life

Protestantism was successfully established in the countries of Northern Europe. There were Protestant movements in Southern Europe, but these grew weak and, for practical purposes, disappeared. In the North, however, Protestant churches had the support of the political powers and drew into their membership large numbers of the rapidly rising middle class, so that in spite of opposition and strong efforts to wipe them out, they continued to exist and to grow in size and strength. The Scandinavian nations, considerable sections of Germany, the northern Netherlands, England, and Scotland became Protestant lands. Though the Roman Catholic Church remained, it often suffered serious disabilities and suspicion. In some places the Protestant churches were established by the action of the rulers, although there was sufficient support by the people to bring about the change without undue opposition. In other places, there was a greater measure of understanding of the Protestant position by the people themselves. But whether the change from Catholicism to Protestantism came about through the authorities in government or through pressure from the people, the shift was made.

The original reformers and their immediate followers were actuated in their work by a profound sense of their understanding of the Christian religion. Within their own lives they themselves had laid hold of their own relationship to God and had worked out that relationship as they felt themselves led to do. The principle of justification by faith was an intellectual statement of that which had been their experience. They knew themselves to have been sinners before God, that is, to have been men who had broken their relationship with God, not only through some acts in their own lives but, much more fundamentally, because as human beings they had been born into and lived in a realm that was established on its own power instead of on its obedience to God. They also knew that by their own efforts they could not gain God's favor nor work themselves back into relationship with God. They believed that God had restored that relationship through Jesus Christ. This was not a belief of the mind, it was an experience which was theirs in the depths of their spirits. The whole structure of their lives, built as it was on their guilt before God, was changed through their faith. They no longer lived as they once had done, but found that they were free men with power to direct their affairs and respond to God's leading as that was mediated to them through the Scripture and the Holy Spirit. Protestantism was, at its inception and in its essence, human experience. Statements about that experience and descriptions of it came afterwards. Confession came out of life.

But when Protestantism spread across Northern Europe and became an established faith in nations and among people, a change took place. The confessions, which were originally testimonies, became tests: a person belonged to the Protestant church by his assent to the statement of belief which a particular branch of the church held. The reformers were men of living faith, their successors were often holders and defenders of creeds or confessions.

But, in Protestantism, no system of orthodoxy can determine a man's faith. The faith is organically related to man's free spirit and thus is forever being forced to test the creeds and confessions which are worked out. Such discussion begins with the very formulation of a confession, for the question must arise as to whether the person who has drawn up the statement has correctly expressed or described the experience out of which it came. In the fifty years which followed the Augsburg Confession, there were more than a dozen serious controversies within the Lutheran churches. An attempt was made to resolve the points at issue by the preparation in 1580 of the "Formula of Concord." But that turned out to be but another theological statement which was added to the others previously in existence.

In the Reformed church more than twenty-five confessions were prepared. While there are certain basic beliefs common to most of them, there are considerable variations among them. And as the Reformed churches spread from country to country, thinkers worked over the confessions which came to them and restated those sections which seemed to them to be inadequate statements.

With the details of this part of the Protestant story we cannot be concerned. Enough to note that there were certain doctrines which were accepted as common to Protestantism: the Trinity, man as sinner, the saving work of Christ, justification by faith. Still, Protestants formulated those doctrines according to their own lights. And there were other doctrines which had much more limited acceptance and many varied forms. Even so, the

significant thing in all this is the question of the role
which a confession plays in Protestantism; and that question, as we shall see, is raised by Protestants on many
occasions and answered in various ways. If Protestantism
rests on the faith of free men, then all else must be
dealt with by that faith.

We are to see, in this section, the manner in which
Protestantism has developed in its knowledge of and
thinking about itself. We shall limit ourselves to a survey
of the seventeenth to the nineteenth centuries. During
those years the churches had to work through the issues
that were created for them by the confessions which
they had inherited from the orthodox period and by the
impact upon their beliefs of the world in which they
existed. For theirs was a world in which all aspects of
human existence developed and changed with great
rapidity.

FAITH AND ITS FORM

The changing attitude toward theological speculation
which was cultivated by Protestantism is reflected in the
following passage:

At the Reformation it might have seemed at first as if the
study of theology were about to return. But in reality an entirely new lesson commenced—the lesson of toleration. Toleration is the very opposite of dogmatism. It implies in reality a confession that there are insoluble problems upon which
even revelation throws but little light. Its tendency is to
modify the early dogmatism by substituting the spirit for the
letter, and practical religion for precise definitions of truth.
This lesson is certainly not yet fully learnt. Our toleration is
at present too often timid, too often rash, sometimes sacri-
ficing valuable religious elements, sometimes fearing its own

plainest conclusions. Yet there can be no question that it is gaining on the minds of all educated men, whether Protestant or Roman Catholic, and is passing from them to be the common property of educated and uneducated alike. There are occasions when the spiritual anarchy which has necessarily followed the Reformation threatens for a moment to bring back some temporary bondage like the Roman Catholic system. But on the whole the steady progress of toleration is unmistakable. The mature mind of our race is beginning to modify and soften the hardness and severity of the principles which its early manhood had elevated into immutable statements of truth. Men are beginning to take a wider view than they did. Physical science, researches into history, a more thorough knowledge of the world they inhabit, have enlarged our philosophy beyond the limits which bounded that of the Church of the Fathers. And all these have an influence, whether we will or no, on our determinations of religious truth. There are found to be more things in heaven and earth than were dreamt of in the patristic theology. God's creation is a new book to be read by the side of His Revelation, and to be interpreted as coming from Him. We can acknowledge the great value of the forms in which the first ages of the Church defined the truth, and yet refuse to be bound by them; we can use them, and yet endeavour to go beyond them, just as they also went beyond the legacy which was left us by the Apostles.[1]

We may summarize the essential issue in Protestant life during the centuries with which we are now concerned in other words. Man is to live by faith—faith in God and God's saving action through Jesus Christ. But this requires that man deal with each aspect of his world that presents itself to challenge him and to force decision from him on the basis of his understanding of God's will for him in that situation. Faith is, actually, man's inner life, granted him by God and informed by God through divine revelation.

In the years of the Reformation some articles of Christian doctrine were confirmed for men in their own experience; other articles of doctrine and certain practices were seen to be inadequate media for expressing man's relationship to God; still others were seen to be opposed to His will. When they had broken with that which seemed false to them, the Reformers created other doctrines and other practices which they believed to be more suitable for the life God had made known to them. Those doctrines and practices were creations out of faith.

But while the confessions worked out by the Reformers and their immediate successors became objective tests of churchly conformity, the principle of Justification by Faith was not forgotten. The Protestant was bound to question any form of imposed authority. Thus it came about that one of the issues Protestantism had to deal with was that of the structure of the faith itself. Was faith imparted directly to man himself? Or, was faith to be known and recognized only within some kind of ordered life, either worked out contemporaneously or else bequeathed to the Church by tradition? Man can quite easily mistake a selfish emotion in his own heart for faith; or he can just as easily lose the life of faith by giving it up for a life of subservience to inherited patterns. How does God deal with man in justifying him through faith? That problem was raised, and to it a number of answers were given.

The Society of Friends

With Friends it is a leading principle, on which they deem it to be in a particular manner their duty to insist, that the operations of the Holy Spirit in the soul are not only immediate and direct, but perceptible; and that we are all furnished with an inward guide or monitor, who makes his voice known to us, and who if faithfully obeyed and closely followed, will infallibly conduct us into true virtue and happiness, because he leads us into a real conformity with the will of God.

I see no reason, where it is so often said in Scripture, the Spirit said, moved, hindered, called, such or such a one, to do or forbear such a thing, that any have to conclude that this was not an inward voice to the ear of the soul, rather than an outward voice to the bodily ear.

Moreover, these divine inward revelations, which were made absolutely necessary for the building up of true faith, neither do nor can ever contradict the outward testimony of the Scriptures, or right and sound reason. Yet from hence it will not follow, that these divine revelations are to be subjected to the test, either of the outward testimony of the Scriptures, or of the natural reason of man, as to a more noble or certain rule and touchstone; for this divine revelation, and inward illumination, is that which is evident and clear of itself, forcing, by its own evidence and clearness, the well-disposed understanding to assent, irresistibly moving the same thereunto, even as the common principles of natural truth do move and incline the mind to a natural assent; as, that the whole is greater than its part; that two contradictions can never both be true, nor both false.

A full and ample account of all the chief principles of the doctrines of Christ is held forth in divers precious declarations, exhortations, and sentences, which, by the moving of God's spirit, were, at several times, and upon sundry occasions, spoken and written unto some churches and their pastors. Nevertheless, because they are known to be only a declaration of the fountain, and not the fountain itself, therefore they are not to be esteemed the principal ground of all truth and knowledge, nor yet the adequate primary rule of faith and manners . . . the spirit is that guide by which the saints are led into all truth; therefore, according to the Scriptures, the Spirit is the first and principal leader.

This most certain doctrine being then received, that there is an evangelical and saving light and grace in all, the universality of the love and mercy of God towards mankind, both in the death of his beloved Son, the Lord Jesus Christ, and in the manifestation of the light in the heart, is established and confirmed, against all the objections of such as deny it. Therefore Christ has tasted death for every man; not only for all kinds of men, but for every man of all kinds.[2]

In theology and religion they are on the extreme border of Protestantant orthodoxy, and reject even a regular ministry and the visible sacraments; yet they strongly believe in the supernatural and constant presence and power of the Holy Spirit. They hold the essentials of the evangelical faith, the divine inspiration and infallibility of the Scripture (though they disparage the letter and the human means of interpretation), the doctrine of the Trinity (in substance, though not in name), the incarnation, the divinity of Christ, the atonement by his blood, the regeneration and sanctification by the Spirit, everlasting life and everlasting punishment. And while they deny the necessity of water baptism and the Lord's Supper as a participation of the elements of bread and wine and regard such rites as a relapse into the religion of forms and shadows, they believe in the inward substance or invisible grace of the sacraments, viz., the baptism of the Spirit and fire, and the vital communion with Christ by faith.[3]

The Methodists

The position of the Methodists in respect to the faith of which they speak differs only slightly from that of the Society of Friends.

I have again and again, with all the plainness I could, declared what our constant doctrines are, whereby we are distinguished only from heathens or nominal christians, not from any that worship God in spirit and in truth.

Our main doctrines, which include all the rest, are three: that of Repentance, of Faith, and of Holiness. The first of these we account as it were, the porch of religion; the next, the door; the third, religion itself.

The faith through which we are saved is "a faith in Christ."

It is "not only an assent to the whole Gospel of Christ, but also a full reliance on the blood of Christ; a trust in the merits of His life, death and resurrection; a recumbency upon Him as our atonement and our life, as given for us and living in us." "None can trust in the merits of Christ, till he has utterly renounced his own."

"Grace is the source, faith the condition, of salvation." Salvation "which is through this faith . . . is a present salvation. It is something attainable, yea, actually attained, on earth, by those who are partakers of this faith." "Ye are saved (to comprise all in one word) from sin . . . saved both from the guilt and from the power of it." "This then is the salvation from sin, and the consequences of sin, both often expressed in the word justification; which, taken in the largest sense, implies a deliverance from guilt and punishment, by the atonement of Christ actually applied to the soul of the sinner now believing in Him, and a deliverance from the whole body of sin, through Christ formed in his heart."[4]

The last and crowning doctrine of Methodism, in which the Quakers likewise preceded it, is Perfectionism. It is regarded as a mighty stimulus to progressive holiness, and forms the counterpart of the doctrine of apostasy, which acts as a warning against backsliding. Methodist perfection is not a sinless perfection or faultlessness, which Wesley denied, but a sort of imperfect perfection, from which it is possible to fall again temporarily or forever. It is entire sanctification or perfect love which every Christian may and ought to attain in this present life. From this state all voluntary transgressions or sinful volitions are excluded, though involuntary infirmities may and do remain; in this state all the normal qualities are possessed and enjoyed in their fullness. As to the attainment of perfection, it comes according to the prevailing view from gradual growth in grace, according to others by a special act of faith.[5]

Yet this understanding of the Christian faith was held within the structure of a well-planned organization.

Methodism is a daughter of the Church of England, and was nursed in the same University of Oxford which, a century later, gave rise to the Tractarian school in the opposite direction towards Rome. The "Holy Club" of the fourteen Oxford students associated for prayer, holy living and working, began with a revival of earnest, ascetic, and ritualistic High-Church-ism, and received the name "Methodists" for its punctual and methodical habits of devotion. . . .[6]

The practical belief of a spiritual operation upon the minds and the hearts of men may be said to constitute the creed of Methodism so far as it is a creed. But as soon as the creed had obtained prevalency, a system developed itself, which is a more complete specimen of organization than any which has been produced in Europe since the days of Loyola. The more this organization is examined, the less it seems to have to do with any spiritual principle; the more evidently it proves itself to be an invention of human policy. This assertion will scarcely be denied by the Wesleyans themselves; though they are stronger than most in asserting the principle of a divine inspiration in individuals, they have pretended less than almost any that their scheme had a divine origin; they attribute it with scarcely any hesitation to the wisdom and sagacity of their founder and of his successors. In one respect only is there a resemblance between the system and that which called it into existence: the spiritual feelings of the Wesleyans led them to overlook national distinctions; the system of the Methodists is essentially extra-national. It is the effort to establish a powerful government in the heart of a nation, which at no point shall impinge upon, or come into contact with, the government of the nation. It differs from the systems of the old dissenting sects in this important point, the limits of each of them are defined by the profession of some peculiar tenet in which they differ from the others, and from the rest of Christendom; that of Wesleyans, professing no tenet which is not recognized or tolerated by the National Church, simply exists to assert their own independence of it, and the importance of such an organization as theirs for the conversion of mankind.[7]

The Independents: Congregationalists

The Independents or Congregationalists represent still another way of handling the issue of the expression of the faith. They held fast to the main doctrines of Calvinism, in contrast to the Quakers, but they insisted upon the complete freedom of the local churches in contrast to the Methodists. That is, they made the sphere of the local church the place wherein man's free spirit was put under control, unlike the Quakers, who allowed the individual freedom for his own inner light, and the Methodists, who established a more widely embracing church order.

The effect of the Congregational polity upon creeds is to weaken the authority of general creeds and to strengthen the authority of particular creeds. The principle of fellowship requires a general creed, but it is reduced to a mere declaration of the common faith prevailing among Congregationalists at a given time, instead of a binding formula of subscription. The principle of independency calls for as many particular creeds as there are congregations. Each congregation, being a complete self-governing body, has the right to frame its own creed, to change it *ad libitum*, and to require assent to it not only from the minister, but from every applicant for membership. Hence there are a great many creeds among American Congregationalists which have purely local authority; but they must be in essential harmony with the prevailing faith of the body, or the congregations professing them forfeit the privileges of fellowship. They must flow from the same system of doctrine, as many little streams flow from the same fountain.

In this multiplication of local creeds Congregationalism far outstrips the practice of the ante-Nicene age, where we find varying yet essentially concordant rules of faith in Jerusalem, Caesarea, Antioch, Aquileja, Carthage, Rome.

With these local creeds are connected "covenants" or

pledges of members to live comfortably to the law of God and the faith and discipline of the church. A covenant is the ethical application of the dogmatic creed.[8]

The Congregational Churches hold it to be the will of Christ that true believers should voluntarily assemble together to observe religious ordinances, to promote mutual edification and holiness, to perpetuate and propagate the gospel in the world, and to advance the glory and worship of God through Jesus Christ; and that each Society of believers, having these objects in view in its formation, is properly a Christian church.

They acknowledge Christ as the only Head of the Church, and the officers of each church, under Him, as ordained to administer His laws impartially to all; and their only appeal, in all questions touching their religious faith and practice, is to the Sacred Scriptures.[9]

The Church of England

The following summarizes briefly the fundamental characteristics and tenets of the Church of England:

It is plain that the foundation-truths of the Reformation—justification by faith, the supremacy and sufficiency of written Scripture, the fallibility of even general councils—are its basis. Yet it is just as plain that in regard of the specific points of theology, which were the root of discord in the Continental Churches, as election, predestination, reprobation, perseverance, and the rest, these Articles speak in a much more moderate tone. . . .

The English Reformers aimed not to create a new, but to reform the historic Church; and therefore they kept the ritual with the episcopate, because they were institutions rooted in the soil. They did not unchurch the bodies of the Continent, which grew under quite other conditions. No theory of an exclusive Anglicanism, as based on the episcopate and general councils, was held by them. Such a view is wholly contradictory to their own Articles. But the historic character of the

Church gave it a positive relation to the past; and they sought to adhere to primitive usage as the basis of historic unity.

They kept the ancient Apostles' Creed and the Nicene in the forefront of the service, the sacramental offices, the festivals and fasts relating to Christ or Apostles, with whatever they thought pure. Such a work could not be perfect, and it is false either to think it so or to judge it save by its time.[10]

The Anglican tradition has displayed unique genius in attempting to hold in delicate balance the positive insights of both Catholicism and Protestantism. Although the emphasis has shifted from time to time, Anglicanism perseveres in holding to both. The result is such frequent tension that Anglicanism is recognized as probably the most dialectical form of Christianity.

In this connection, it will be useful to include a statement from a leader of the Oxford Movement, which originated early in the nineteenth century. A number of questions were involved in the movement, but primarily those who were responsible for its origin were concerned to ground man's faith firmly within the historical Church. They did not want to depart from the basic beliefs of the Reformation, but were convinced that their belief must be rooted in the church established by God in history. John Henry Newman, from whose works the following quotation is taken, is judged one of the founders of the movement although, without doubt, he gave voice to the thinking of many within the Church of England.

While I was engaged in writing my work upon the Arians (1883) . . . the great Reform Agitation was going on around me. The Whigs had come into power; Lord Grey had told the Bishops to set their house in order, and some of the prelates had been insulted and threatened in the streets of London. The vital question was, how were we to keep the Church from being liberalized? There was such apathy on the subject in some quarters, such imbecile alarm in others; the true principle of churchmanship seemed so radically decayed, and there was such distraction in the councils of the Clergy. Blomfield, the Bishop of London of the day, an active and open-hearted man, had been for years engaged in diluting the high orthodoxy of the Church by the introduction of members of the Evangelical body into places of influence and trust. He had deeply offended men who agreed in opinion with myself, by an off-hand saying (as it was reported) that belief in the Apostolical succession had gone out with the non-jurors. . . . I felt affection for my own Church, but not tenderness; I felt dismay at her prospects, anger and scorn at her do-nothing perplexity. I thought that if Liberalism once got a footing within her, it was sure of victory in the event. I saw that Reformation principles were powerless to rescue her. As to leaving her, the thought never crossed my imagination; still I ever kept before me that there was something greater than the Established Church, and that was the Church Catholic and Apostolic, set up from the beginning, of which she was but the local presence and the organ. She was nothing unless she was this. She must be dealt with strongly, or she would be lost. There was need of a second Reformation.

First was the principle of dogma: my battle was with liberalism; by liberalism I mean the anti-dogmatic principle and its developments. . . . From the age of fifteen, dogma has been the fundamental principle of my religion: I know no other religion, and cannot enter into the idea of any other sort of religion; religion, as a mere sentiment, is to me a dream and mockery.

I had the consciousness that I was employed in that work which I had been dreaming about, and which I felt to be so momentous and inspiring. I had a supreme confidence in our cause; we were upholding that primitive Christianity, which was delivered for all time by the early teachers of the Church, and which was registered and attested in the Anglican formularies and by the Anglican divines. That ancient religion had well nigh faded away out of the land, through the political changes of the last 150 years, and it must be restored. It would be in fact a second Reformation:—a better Reformation, for it would be a return not to the sixteenth century, but to the seventeenth.[11]

As these variations were worked out in history by Protestants a number of other elements in human life became involved. For example, there was the matter of a man's relationship and his responsibility to his nation. This included man's understanding of the place of the nation in the economy of God and thus of the connection, if any, between nation and church. Or again, there was the matter of man's belief about church tradition and the significance that it had, either as a whole or in part, for his spiritual welfare. Yet, important though such matters were, they were caught up in that which was more fundamental: the faith through which man was justified. And the issue was as to whether that faith was held within the spirit of individual man, so that man could depend upon the guidance of his own inner self as being the leading of God for him, or whether there needed to be some check upon each individual. That the Protestant churches came at once to a clear and undoubted resolution of this issue is obviously not so. But Protestantism raised the issue. It lifted man's awareness of his own free spirit into the heart of his religious faith; it made man know that when he in his freedom faces the authority of Almighty God, he must understand his situation and conduct himself so as to do full justice to the place where he lives. And this issue, which is not a rational one, but is rooted in life itself, has remained and, if we may dare a word of prophecy, will remain as long as man lives. The Protestant faith keeps that issue before man and makes him responsible for living in it and with it.

One inevitable result of this has been the splintering of Protestantism into a large number of groups and sects which have each maintained their uniqueness. From one point of view this part of Protestant history has been destructive; but from another point of view it must be seen as a positive and, therefore, essential expression of the principles upon which Protestantism rests. The difficulty may be deplored, but the reality in the development cannot be forgotten. And the difficulty cannot be overcome at the expense of the reality. This issue, inherent and clearly observable at the start of the Reformation, was made explicit during subsequent years.

FAITH AND REASON

Another issue which appeared during the centuries with which we are dealing was the relation between man's reason and his religious faith. As we shall see, the Protestant churches became involved in the matter because of the conflicts which became apparent between the formulations of their beliefs and the knowledge which men acquired through the power and work of their own minds. As we noted earlier, one of the results of the awareness and development of freedom was the break with scholastic theology; man made his own reason autonomous and authoritative. He advanced in his knowledge of the world and his own life and, consequently, in his ability to order his ways more satisfactorily for himself and to manage his world for his own benefit; he gained an orderly understanding of nature, history, and human beings. It was inevitable, then, that man would relate his self-acquired knowledge to his religious beliefs. We must see how he dealt with this relationship as it bore upon some of the basic principles of Protestantism.

All tended to give to their confessions a large measure of authority. The test of a Christian was taken to be his adherence to the proper doctrines. But with the development of man's understanding of his world and the process of reason by which he gained that understanding a conflict arose between the conclusions of reason and the doctrines of faith. If reason determined that man was a natural creature limited only by ignorance and lack of experience, while religion taught that he was a sinner, there had to be a decision as to which description was correct. Man had to resolve the apparent discrepancies between his reason and his religion.

The Power of Reason over Faith

The growth and gradual diffusion through all religious thinking of the supremacy of reason: this, which is rather a principle, or a mode of thinking, than a doctrine, may be properly enough called Rationalism. This term is used in this country with so much laxity that it is impossible to define the sense in which it is generally intended. But it is often taken to mean a system opposed to revealed religion imported into this country from Germany at the beginning of the present century. A person, however, who surveys the course of English theology during the eighteenth century will have no difficulty in recognising that throughout all discussions, underneath all controversies, and common to all parties, lies the assumption of the supremacy of reason in matters of religion.

Rationalism was not an anti-Christian sect outside the Church making war against religion. It was a habit of thought, under the conditions of which all alike tried to make good the peculiar opinions they might happen to cherish. The Churchman differed from the Socinian, and the Socinian from the Deist, as to the number of articles in his creed; but all alike consented to test their belief by the rational evidence for it. Whether given doctrines or miracles were conformable to reason or not was disputed between the defence and the assault; but that all doctrines were to stand or fall by that criterion was not questioned. The principles and the priority of natural religion formed the common hypothesis on the ground of which the disputants argued whether anything, and what, had been subsequently communicated to man in a supernatural way. The line between those who believed much and those who believed little cannot be sharply drawn.

Rationalism, which is the common character of all the writers of this time, is a method rather than a principle from which they reason. They would, however, all have consented in statements such as the following: (Bishop Gibson, *Second Pastoral Letter*, 1730) "Those among us who have laboured of late years to set up reason against revelation would make it pass for an established truth, that if you will embrace revelation you must of course quit your reason, which, if it were true, would doubtless be a strong prejudice against revelation. But so far is this from being true, that it is universally acknowledged that revelation itself is to stand or fall by the test of reason, or, in other words, according as reason finds the evidences of its coming from God to be or not to be sufficient and conclusive, and the matter of it to contradict or not contradict the natural notions which reason gives us of the being and attributes of God."

Prideaux (Humphrey, Dean of Norwich), *Letter to the Deists,* 1748. "Let what is written in all the books of the N.T. be tried by that which is the touchstone of all religions, I mean that religion of nature and reason which God has written in the hearts of every one of us from the first creation; and if it varies from it in any one particular, if it prescribes any one thing which may in the minutest circumstances thereof be contrary to its righteousness, I will then acknowledge this to be an argument against us, strong enough to overthrow the whole cause, and make all things else that can be said for it totally ineffectual for its support."

Tillotson (Archbishop of Canterbury), *Sermons.* "All our reasonings about revelation are necessarily gathered by our natural notions about religion, and therefore he who sincerely desires to do the will of God is not apt to be imposed on by vain pretences of divine revelation; but if any doctrine be proposed to him which is pretended to come from God, he measures it by those sure and steady notions which he has of the divine nature and perfections; he will consider the nature and tendency of it, or whether it be a doctrine according to godliness, such as is agreeable to the divine nature and perfections, and tends to make us like unto God, if it be not, though an angel should bring it, he would not receive it."

The received theology of the day taught on this point the doctrine of Locke, as clearly stated by himself. "Reason is natural revelation whereby the eternal Father of light and fountain of all knowledge communicated to mankind that portion of truth which he has laid within the reach of their natural faculties; revelation is natural reason enlarged by a new set of discoveries communicated by God immediately, which reason vouches the truth of, by the testimony and proofs it gives, that they come from God. So that he that takes away reason to make way for revelation, puts out the light of both, and does much the same as if he would persuade a man to put out his eyes the better to receive the remote light of an invisible star by a telescope" (*Essay*, IV, 19, iv).[12]

I was yesterday in company with a great many Clergymen, it being our Bishops primary Visitation; where the Complaint was general, of the Coldness and Indifference, with which People received the speculative Point of Christianity, and all its holy Rites; for which formerly they had shewn so great a zeal. This Coldness they chiefly imputed to those Low Churchmen who lay the main stress on Natural Religion; and withall so magnify the Doctrine of Sincerity, as in effect to place all Religions on a level, where the Professors are alike sincere. The Promoters of these Notions, as well as these Notions themselves, were expos'd with warmth; how justly, I will not determine, till we have talk'd the matter over with our usual Freedom: For which reason, I have made you this early Visit, and Would be glad to know the Sentiments of so good a judge, on these two important Points; viz. Sincerity, and Natural Religion.

I thank you for this Favour, and shall freely tell you, I so little agree with those Gentlemen in relation to Sincerity, that I think a sincere examination into religious matter can't be too much press'd; this being the only way to discover true Christianity. The Apostles thought themselves oblig'd, in making Proselytes, to recommend an impartial Search; they both desir'd, and requir'd Men to judge for themselves, to prove all things, etc. This they thought necessary, in order to renounce a Religion, which the Force of Education had impress'd on their Minds and embrace another directly contrary to the Notions and Prejudices they had imbib'd. Nay, even those very Men, who most ridicule the Doctrine of Sincerity, never fail on other Occasions to assert, that Infidelity is owing to the want of a sincere Examination; and that whosoever impartially considers Christianity, must be convinc'd of its Truth. And I might add, That could we suppose a sincere Examination wou'd not always produce this Effect, yet must it always make Men acceptable to God, since that is all God can require; all that it is in their power to do for the Discovery of his Will. These, in short, are my sentiments as to this point; and as to the other, I think, too great a stress can't be laid on Natural Religion; which, as I take it, differs not from Reveal'd, but in the manner of its being communicated: The one being the Internal, as the other the External Revelation of the same unchangeable will of a Being, who is alike at all times infinitely wise and good.

The greater stress you lay on Reason, the more you extol Revelation; which being design'd to exalt and perfect our rational Nature, must be itself highly reasonable.

I grant you this is the Design of Religion; but have not the Ecclesiasticks in most Places entirely defeated this Design, and so far debas'd Human Nature, as to render it unsociable, fierce and cruel? Have they not made external Revelation the Pretence of filling the Christian World with Animosity, Hatred, Persecution, Ruin and Destruction; in order to get an absolute Dominion over the Consciences, Properties and Persons of the Laity? But passing this over, if the Perfection of any Nature, whether human, angelical, or divine, consists in being govern'd by the Law of its Nature; and ours, in acting that Part, for which we were created; by observing all those Duties, which are founded on the Relation we stand in to God and one another; can Revelation any otherwise help to perfect Human Nature, but as it induces Men to live up to this Law of their Nature: And if this Law is the test of the Perfection of any written Law; must not that be the most perfect Law, by which the Perfection of all others is to be try'd?

If nothing but Reasoning can improve Reason, and no Book can improve my Reason in any point, but as it gives me convincing Proofs of its Reasonableness; a Revelation, that will not suffer us to judge for its Dictates by our Reason, is so far from improving Reason, that it forbids the Use of it; and reasoning Faculties unexercis'd, will have as little Force, as unexercis'd limbs; he that is always carry'd, will at length be unable to go; And if the Holy Ghost, as Bishop Taylor says, works by heightening, and improving our natural Faculties; it can only be by using Means as will improve them, in proposing Reasons and Arguments to convince our Understanding; which can only be improv'd, by studying the Nature and Reason of Things: I apply'd my Heart (says the wisest of Men) to know, and to search and to seek out wisdom, and the Reason of Things (*Eccles.* 7:25).

So that the Holy Ghost can't deal with Men as rational Creatures, but by proposing Arguments to convince their Understandings, and influence their wills, in the same manner as if propos'd by other Agents; for to go beyond this, would be making impressions on Men, as a Seal does on Wax; to the confounding of their Reason, and their Liberty in choosing; and the Man would then be merely passive, and the Action would be the Action of another Being acting upon this; for which he could be no way accountable: but if the Holy Ghost does not act thus, and Revelation itself be not arbitrary; must it not be founded on the Reason of Things? And consequently to a Republication, or Restoration of the Religion of Nature?[13]

The Truth of Christianity Supported by Reason

In response to the claim of reason to have authority over faith, two responses were made: The proposition itself was accepted as valid and then strong efforts were made to present evidence for the truth of Christianity that would be convincing to man's reason.

The sterner genius of Protestantism required definition, argument, and proof, where the ancient church had been content to impress by the claims of authority, veneration, and prescription, and thus left the conception, truth, to take the form of a mere impression of devotional feeling or exalted imagination.

Protestantism sought something more definite and substantial, and its demands were seconded and supported, more especially by the spirit of metaphysical reasoning which so widely extended itself in the 17th century, even into the domains of theology; and divines, stirred up by the allegations of the Deists, aimed at formal refutations of their objections, by drawing out the idea and the proofs of revelation into systematic propositions supported by logical arguments. In that and the subsequent period the same general style of argument on these topics prevailed among the advocates of the Christian cause. The appeal was mainly to the miracles of the Gospels, and here it was contended we want merely the same testimony of eye-witnesses which would suffice to substantiate any ordinary matter of fact; accordingly, the narratives were to be traced to writers at the time, who were either themselves eye-witnesses, or recorded the testimony of those who were so, and the direct transmission of the evidence being thus established, everything was held to be demonstrated. If any antecedent question was raised, a brief reference to the Divine Omnipotence to work the miracles, and to the Divine goodness to vouchsafe the revelation and confirm it by such proofs, was all that could be required to silence sceptical cavils.

It is true, indeed, that some consideration of the internal

evidence derived from the excellence of the doctrines and morality of the Gospel was allowed to enter the discussion, but it formed only a subordinate branch of the evidences of Christianity. The main and essential point was always the consideration of external facts, and the attestations of testimony offered in support of them. Assuming Christianity to be essentially connected with certain outward and sensible events, the main thing to be inquired into and established, was the historical evidence of those events, and the genuineness of the records of them; if this were satisfactorily made out, then it was considered the object was accomplished. The external facts simply substantiated, the intrinsic doctrines and declarations of the Gospel must by necessary consequence be Divine truths.[14]

One of the earlier approaches of Protestantism to the justification by reason of the truth of Christianity is outlined in the following selection:

Sir,

In Answer to yours of the Third Instant, I much condole with you your unhappy circumstances of being placed amongst such Company, where, as you say, you continually hear the Sacred Scriptures, and the Histories therein contain'd, particularly of Moses and of Christ, and all Reveal'd Religion turn'd into Ridicule by Men who set up for Sense and Reason. And they say, That all these pretences to Revelation are Cheats, and ever have been among Pagans, Jews, Mahometans and Christians: That they are all alike Impositions of Cunning and Designing Men, upon the Credulity, at first, of simple and Unthinking People; till, their Numbers encreasing, their Delusions grew Popular came at last to be Establish'd by Laws; and then the force of Education and Custom gives a Byass to the Judgments of after Ages, till such Deceits come really to be Believ'd, being receiv'd upon Trust from the Ages foregoing, without examining into the Original and Bottom of them. Which these our modern Men of Sense (as they desire to be esteem'd) say, That they only do, that they

only have their Judgment freed from the slavish Authority
of Precedents and Laws, in Matters of Truth, which, they
say, sought only to be decided by Reason: Tho' by a prudent
Complyance with Popularity and Laws, they preserve themselves from Outrage and Legal Penalties; for none of their
Complexion are addicted to sufferings or Martyrdom.

Now, Sir, that which you desire from me, is, some short
Topic of Reason, if such can be found, whereby, without
running to Authorities, and the intricate Mazes of Learning,
which breed long Disputes, and which these Men of Reason
deny by Wholesale, tho' they can give no Reason for it, only
suppose that Authors have been Trump'd upon us, Interpo-
lated and Corrupted, so that no stress can be laid upon them,
tho' it cannot be shewn wherein they are so Corrupted; which,
in Reason, ought to lie upon them to Prove, who Alledge it;
otherwise it is not only a Precarious, but a guilty Plea: And
the more, that they refrain not to Quote Books on their side,
for whose Authority there are no Better, or not so Good
Grounds. However, you say it makes your Disputes endless,
and they go away with Noise and Glamour, and a Boast,
That there is nothing, at least nothing Certain, to be said on
the Christian side.

Therefore you are desirous to find some One Topic of Reason, which should Demonstrate the Truth of the Christian Religion; and at the same time, Distinguish it from the Im-
postures of Mahomet, and the Old Pagan World: That our
Deists may be brought to this Test, and be either oblig'd to
Renounce their Reason, and the common Reason of Mankind, or to submit to the clear Proof, from Reason, of the
Christian Religion, which must be such Proof, as no Imposture can pretend to, otherwise it cannot prove the Christian
Religion not to be an Imposture. And, whether such a Proof,
one single Proof (to avoid Confusion), is not to be found out,
you desire to know from me. . . .

And you say, that you cannot imagine but there must be
such a Proof, because every Truth is in it self Clear, and One:
and therefore that One Reason for it, if it be the true Reason,
must be sufficient: And, if sufficient, it is better than Many;
for Multiplicity confounds, especially to weak Judgments.

Sir, you have impos'd an hard Task upon me; I wish I could perform it: For tho' Every Truth is One, yet our Sight is so feeble, that we cannot (always) come to it Directly, but by many Inference, and laying of things together.

I think that in the Case before us, there is such a Proof as you require; and I will set it down as Short and Plain as I Can.

First then I suppose, that the Truth of the Doctrine of CHRIST Will be sufficiently Evinced, if the Matters of Fact, which are Recorded of him in the Gospels be True; for His Miracles, if True, do vouch the Truth of what he delivered.

The same is to be said as to Moses. If he brought the Children of Israel through the Red-Sea, in that Miraculous manner, which is related in Exodus, and did such other wonderful things as are there told of him it must necessarily follow, that he was sent from GOD; These being the strongest Proofs we can desire, and which every Deist will confess he cou'd acquiese in, if he saw them with his Eyes. Therefore the stress of this Cause will depend upon the proof of these Matters of Fact.

1. And the Method I will take, is, First, to lay down such Rules, as to the Truth of Matters of fact, in General, that where they ALL meet, such Matters of Fact cannot be False. And then, Secondly to shew that all these Rules do meet in the Matters of Fact of Moses, and of Christ; and that they do not meet in the Matters of Fact of Mahomet, of the Heathen Deities, or can possibly meet in any Imposture whatsoever.

2. The Rules are these: 1st. That the Matter of Fact be such as that Men's outward Senses, their Eyes and Ears, may be Judges of it. 2. That it be done publickly in the face of the world. 3. That not only publick monuments be kept up in memory of it, but some outward actions to be performed. 4. That such monuments and such actions or observances be instituted, and do commence from the time that the matter of fact was done. . . .

Therefore from what has been said, the cause is Summ'd up Shortly in this, That tho' we cannot see what was done before our Time, yet by the Marks which I have laid down concerning the Certainty of Matters of Fact done before our Time, we may be as much Assur'd of the Truth of 'em as if we saw them with our Eyes; because whatever Matter of Fact has all the Four Marks before mention'd, could never have been invented and Received but upon the Conviction of the outward Senses of all those who did Receive it, as before is Demonstrated. And therefore this Topick which I have Chosen, does stand upon the Conviction even of Men's outward Senses. And since you have Confin'd me to one Topick, I have not insisted upon the others, which I have only Nam'd.

And now it lies upon the Deists, if they wou'd appear as Men of Reason to shew some Matter of Fact of former Ages, which they allow to be True, that has greater Evidences of its Truth, than the Matters of Fact of Moses and of Christ: Otherwise they cannot, with any shew of Reason, Reject the one and yet Admit of the other.[15]

Reason and Faith Separated

The proposition which led to the conclusion that reason has validity in one realm of human experience and religion has validity in another was shown to have completely overlooked the real nature of religion.

In advancing beyond these conclusions to the doctrines of revelation, we must recognise both the due claims of science to decide on points properly belonging to the world of matter, and the independence of such considerations which characterizes the disclosure of spiritual truth as such.

All reason and science conspire to the confession that beyond the domain of physical causation and the possible conceptions of intellect or knowledge, there lies open the boundless region of spiritual things, which is the sole dominion of faith. And while intellect and philosophy are compelled to disown the recognition of anything in the world of matter at variance with the principle of the laws of matter—the universal order and indissoluble unity of physical causes—they are the more ready to admit the higher claims of divine mysteries in the invisible and spiritual world. Advancing knowledge, while it asserts the dominion of science in physical things, confirms that of faith in spiritual; we thus neither impugn the generalizations of philosophy, nor allow them to invade the dominion of faith, and admit that what is not a subject for a problem may hold its place in a creed.

In an evidential point of view it has been admitted by some of the most candid divines that the appeal to miracles, however important in the early stages of the Gospel, has become less material in later times, and others have even expressly pointed to this as the reason why they have been withdrawn; whilst at the present day the most earnest advocates of evangelical faith admit that outward marvels are needless to spiritual conviction, and triumph in the greater moral miracle of a converted and regenerate soul.

They echo the declaration of St. Chrysostom: "If you are a believer as you ought to be, and love Christ as you ought to love him, you have no need of miracles, for these are given to unbelievers."

Matters of clear and positive fact, investigated on critical grounds and supported by exact evidence, are properly matters of knowledge, not of faith. It is rather in points of less definite character that any exercise of faith can take place; it is rather with matters of religious belief belonging to a higher and less conceivable class of truths, with the mysterious things of the unseen world, that faith owns a connexion, and more readily associates itself with spiritual ideas, than with external evidence, or physical events: and it is generally admitted that many points of important religious instruction, even conveyed under the form of fictions (as in the instances of doctrines inculcated through parables) are more congenial to the spirit of faith than any relations of historical events could be.

The more knowledge advances, the more it has been, and will be, acknowledged that Christianity, as a real religion, must be viewed apart from connexion with physical things.[16]

The rise of this modern naturalistic liberalism has not come by chance, but has been occasioned by important changes which have recently taken place in the conditions of life. The past one hundred years have witnessed the beginning of a new era in human history, which may conceivably be regretted but certainly cannot be ignored, by the most obstinate conservatism. Modern inventions and the industrialism that has been built upon them have given us in many respects a new world to live in; we can no more remove ourselves from that world than we can escape from the atmosphere that we breathe.

But such changes in the material conditions of life do not stand alone; they have been produced by mighty changes in the human mind, as in their turn they themselves give rise to further spiritual changes. The industrial world of today has been produced not by blind forces of nature but by the conscious activity of the human spirit; it has been produced by the achievements of science. The outstanding feature of recent history is an enormous widening of human knowledge, which has gone hand in hand with such perfection of the instrument of investigation that scarcely any limits can be assigned to future progress in the material realm.

In such an age, it is obvious that every inheritance from the past must be subject to searching criticism; and as a matter of fact some convictions of the human mind have crumbled to pieces in the test. Indeed, dependence of any institution upon the past is now sometimes even regarded as furnishing a presumption, not in favour of it, but against it; so many convictions have had to be abandoned that men have sometimes come to believe that all convictions must go.

If such an attitude be justifiable, then no institution is faced by a stronger hostile presumption than the institution of the Christian religion, for no institution has based itself more squarely upon the authority of a by-gone age. . . . Christianity during many centuries has appealed for the truth of its claim, not merely and not even primarily to current experience, but to certain ancient books the more recent of which was written nineteen hundred years ago. Inevitably the question arises whether (those books) can ever be normative for men of the present day; in other words, whether first-century religion can ever stand in company with twentieth-century science.

It is this problem which modern liberalism attempts to solve. Admitting that scientific objections may arise against the particularities of the Christian religion—against the Christian doctrines of the Person of Christ and of redemption through His death and resurrection—the liberal theologian seeks to rescue certain of the general principles of religion, of which these particularities are thought to be mere temporary symbols, and these general principles he regards as constituting "the essence of Christianity."

. . . But it appears that what the liberal theologian has retained after abandoning to the enemy one Christian doctrine after another is not Christianity at all, but a religion which is so entirely different from Christianity as to belong to a distinct category . . . we shall be interested in showing that despite the liberal use of traditional phraseology modern liberalism not only is a different religion from Christianity of the New Testament which is in conflict with science, but the supposed Christianity of the modern Liberal Church, and that the real city of God, and that city alone, has defenses which are capable of warding off the assaults of modern unbelief.[17]

REASON AND THE PROTESTANT PRINCIPLES

The discussion of the relative authority of reason and the doctrines of faith in religious life was carried on not only as a general issue, giving rise to the question of the role of natural religion in living, but it became specific as it dealt with the various doctrines themselves. Man began to subject the various items in the confession of his church to the test of his reason. The results which followed from this were not conclusive, although various fairly well-defined positions were worked out. We now survey this development in Protestantism.

Justification by Faith

Of a light speaking to his conscience, and warning him of the evil he had done, and of the temptations within and without which were tempting him to forsake it, Luther knew as much as any Quaker could have told him. But the thought of such a light, instead of giving him peace, was the cause of all his tumult and confusion. It spoke to him of a Being of absolute power and wisdom and righteousness, between whom and himself there was no sympathy. It bade him seek, by all means, to be reconciled to that Being, and account all trials and sufferings light, if so be they might but give a promise, now or hereafter, of such a blessing. But it told him also of a strict, irreversible law, from which there could be no departure, no dispensation; and the recollection of which made every effort to heal the breach between him and his Maker a new witness to him that it was perpetual. Then came the dream of a possible deliverance from the curse of this law, brought to him in words which he had heard from his infancy, but to which till then he had been unable to attach any meaning. He had been told of a Mediator between the Creator and his creatures; of his having offered a sacrifice for men; of their being united with or grafted into him; of their possessing a righteousness in him which they had not in themselves.

The written word of God seemed to him, from beginning to end, to be witnessing that a man is justified by faith; no school phrases being used to express the idea, but every act of affiance in a divine Person who had revealed himself to man as the object of his trust and confidence being an exemplification of it. He could thus see the meaning of St. Paul's assertion that Abraham was justified by faith. He trusted in God's promise and word, and that made him a godly and righteous man. All the psalms, in like manner, were nothing but acts of faith and affiance, whereby a man, crushed down with all kinds of evils, inward and outward, rose up and claimed that relation to God which his covenant had given him, and shook off the sins into which he had fallen through forgetting it. Still these, properly speaking, were acts of trust in a Mediator; they were recognitions of one to whom the suppliant himself was related, who was a bond between him and the absolute God, in whom alone he could dare to call upon him. Therefore all these justifications were foretastes and anticipations of that justification which the Son of God made for all who would trust in him, when, having offered up his body as a sacrifice, he rose again from the dead. To announce this work as accomplished; to tell men that they became righteous by believing it, and so entering into union with their Lord and Master—this was, Luther believed, the great end of St. Paul's life. He believed also that it was his own appointed office.[18]

Justification by faith includes two principal matters combined; that the transgressor, believing, has a righteousness generated in him, which is not built upon under the law, by his own practice; and that something has been done to compensate the law, violated by his past offences, and save it in honour, when his sin is forgiven.

As to the former, the righteousness ingenerated, the manner is sufficiently indicated, when it is called the righteousness that is of God by faith, unto and upon such only as believe; because, as we just now said, speaking of salvation, it is only by faith that the soul is so trusted to, and deposited in, the supernatural grace of God, as to be invested with His righteousness, or assimilated to it. Besides, it will be observed that this is called justification, partly because the natural laws of retributive justice, which are penally chastising the sinner, holding him fast in the meshes of inextricable disorder and woe, can be controverted, or turned aside, only by a power supernatural and divine.

As to the latter point concerned, the implied compensation to law, in the supposed free justification, it is not that something is done to be a spectacle before unknown worlds, or something to square up a legal account of pains and penalties, according to some small scheme of bookkeeping philosophy, but it is simply this: that, as there must be two stages of discipline to carry on the world viz., letter and spirit, law and grace—the introduction of pardon, or the universal and free remission of sins, must be so prepared, as not to do away with the law stage that is precedent, but must let them both exist together to act concurrently on the world. And this is done by the obedience of Christ, obedience unto death. Who can say or think that God yields up His law, in the forgiveness of sins, when the word incarnate, having it on him as a bond of love, the same that our human sin has broken, renders up His life to it, and bows to the awful passion of the cross, that He may fulfil its requirements. Magnified and made honourable by such a contribution or respect, no free remission or removal of penalties running against us can be felt to shake its authority.[19]

We cannot get a clear view of this reconciliation by taking a single instance of religious experience, and setting our cognitive faculty to reflect on it and analyse it. We may see that the sense of guilt implies in some vague outline the ideas of a broken moral order and an offended God; but such logical inference does not give us any assurance as to the reality of existences corresponding to these ideas. The exertion of the cognitive faculty in the search for truth leads us to an impasse. The only existence we know as real is our own, and it is by drawing upon ourselves that we give reality to our ideas. After all, in considering religion we have not to do merely with the cognitive faculty but also with the will: the gist of the Christian life consists in the reconciliation of the human will with the Divine—the control of the human will as it expresses itself in action; and in this mode of statement the severance between our subjective ideas and the real existences outside us does not arise as a sharply set opposition which we cannot satisfactorily bridge. The human will is conscious of itself as an activity; it knows itself not only as existing, but as doing; there is certitude in its feeling of its own doings; and this certitude is extended in varying degrees to other existences. In his moral consciousness man feels that he accepts some aim, or frames it for himself, and strives to realise it. He is aware of obstacles which balk him, and which are real to him, just because they hamper and thwart him; he is certain of the existence of an external world. He may be aware, too, of a Power which co-operated with him, not as an external agent but as a spiritual influence; which convicts him of evil when his aims are sordid and self-seeking, but which strengthens his purpose when it is something that he lays down for all intelligences as well as for himself. He may recognise a "not ourselves that makes for righteousness" in the world, because he is certain of a Power that makes for righteousness in his own internal life.

Devout literature, in which various phases of the Christian consciousness are set forth fully and explicitly, testifies to two points on which it is worth while to lay stress—on the one hand, the certainty of reconciliation as attainable; on the other, the sense of frequent failure to maintain this harmonious relationship. There is a process of reconciliation going on, but a process that is not fully accomplished. The attempt to universalise one's action may be occasional, and it may become habitual. As the moral law is thought of as a law for all intelligences, so when I act rightly, I act from the standpoint of the universal will; but still it is my action, there is no force that overmasters the personal will, but rather a personal desire to come into accord with the Universal Will —to think and to do what is pleasing to God. "We have to choose whether we shall make ourselves the end of our action and the centre on which it turns, or whether we shall seek an aim and a centre outside and above ourselves. Every generous action, every effort to get out of ourselves, however rudimentary it may be, is an acceptance and affirmation of God, and at the same time a step towards the light." And in this universalising of his will and activities there is no loss of his individual personal life; it is not merged in the Universal with which it is reconciled.[20]

The Holy Scriptures

It ought now to be clearer where and in what Luther finds the authority of Scripture. He brings subject and object into a living relationship. Authority does not reside in the object, with the subject obliged to play a passive role. Nor does it reside wholly within the subject as such, so that it becomes just what each individual cares to make of it. The charge that he makes of Scripture a "wax nose" Luther hotly rebuts, declaring that it is the heretics and not he who are thus guilty. The fact is, as Kohler says, that for the understanding of Scripture and the recognition of its authority object and subject have to be held together. This coming together takes place in the stillness (*Stillehalten*) of the individual before the Word. But this stillness is not on the one hand a "sacred vacancy of mind," nor any ready-made equipment which the individual must himself supply (such as for example the *ratio*, which is indeed used by Luther in understanding Scripture, but in a merely formal and not a substantial way). It is rather the waiting of the believer upon God. Luther thus propounds a new conception of authority. It is not the same authority that is now differently disposed between the possible claimants and distributed to give each a fair share. The authority which Scripture possesses is one which is objectively grounded in a book which speaks of Jesus Christ. This authority, however, it establishes within the heart into which Christ enters, or (which is much the same thing) upon which the Holy Spirit works, to create the faith in which it is both recognized and obeyed. In the last resort, the authority of Scripture is not its own possession held by independent right. For Luther, Scripture is not the Word, but only witness to the Word, and it is from Him whom it conveys that it derives the authority it enjoys.

When the co-operation of the Church in establishing the authority of Scripture is repudiated, Holy Scripture is left on its own, and it becomes urgently necessary to enquire concerning the ground or sanction of its authority. Orthodoxy found the answer, as Luther and Calvin did not, in crediting Scripture independently with much the same kind of external authority as it had formerly derived from the sanction of the Church. Scripture regarded as in this sense authoritative is then equipped with various other attributes by which its authority is exalted, but at the same time also stiffened and hardened.[21]

To the plain man the Bible is no longer the Book of Books. On investigation we shall find that the plain man is wrong, but at first sight there is much to be said for his point of view. He is no critic and has no time for critical studies, but he had learnt that the Bible is not infallible in its statements of fact, in its ethical teaching or even in its theology. He knows what modern science has to say with regard to the creation narratives in Genesis, and he is vaguely aware that similar stories are to be found in Babylonian mythology. And in many other places, chiefly perhaps in the stories of patriarchs and of the early monarchy, he suspects that there is a large element of folk-lore and tradition, and he has not the means of finding out what element of historicity the narratives contain. Consequently, he is invaded by a general sense of insecurity, and believing that many of its statements are untrue, he not unnaturally asks how the Bible can be regarded as in any real sense inspired, or, indeed, as having any particular value.

Moreover, he is not really interested in "the kings of Israel and Judah." Why should he read these old stories and legends, even supposing that they are true? Still less is he interested in the ceremonial enactments of Leviticus or in the symbolism of such books as Daniel and Revelation, which he does not the least understand. He has always been taught that the chief value of the teaching of the prophets lay in their miraculous predictive powers, and now that he is told that the old "argument from prophecy" is discredited, nothing seems to remain. He perceives, too, that the ethical standpoint of some of the Biblical writers is relatively crude. He cannot but condemn, for example, the treacherous act of Jael which is singled out for special praise in the Song of Deborah. What, he asks, is he to gain by reading such stories as these? And he sees almost as little reason why he should read the New Testament. He already knows, in broad outline, the story of the life of Christ. Why should he read it again? Is the Gospel narrative really trustworthy in all its details? And what is he to make of the Pauline Epistles with their elaborate and obscure arguments? . . .

Accordingly the question we have to ask is whether this

value of the Bible in the past was due to some inherent quality which the Bible itself possesses or to that conception of
it as verbally inspired and infallible which has been held up
to our own time and is now seen to be untenable, whether,
in fact it was due to what the Bible is or to what it has
wrongly been supposed to be. . . .

The essence of the answer lies in the fact, which modern
scholarship has enabled us to recognise in its full significance,
that the Bible is God's book because it is in a unique and
universal sense Man's book. It is the record of and the vehicle
for transmitting a great human experience, an experience of
God, of human need, and of God's response to that need.
The authors, the editors, the compilers of the various books
and of their literary sources are now seen to be men of flesh
and blood, linked to us by the possession of a common
humanity. They are not, as men had almost come to think,
like the dolls of a ventriloquist, or like children repeating
from memory a lesson they have learned but not understood,
quoting catch-words and phrases which are not a part of
themselves and find no answer within their own experience;
but they are living men, sharing our joys and our sorrows,
our hopes and our aspirations, our needs and our fears, facing
the problems and perplexities of life, "the old misgivings"
and "the crooked questions" which are the common heritage
of humanity, saying what they feel and know, and speaking
with the conviction which is born of personal experience. It
is because we have a real kinship with them that we are
irresistibly drawn to them and that their power survives "deep
in the general heart of man."[22]

The discussion of some of the most important among the
problems which historical criticism raises as to the Gospels
leads us finally to the question what is at the present time,
and what in the future is likely to be, the effect of historical
criticism on Christian belief.

Yet without controversy the student of Christian doctrine
is profoundly affected by the recognition of the validity of
the principles of historical criticism.

Our acceptance of them must be no mere otiose assent: it

must be real and practical. It seems to me to involve three chief consequences.

1. It quickens the desire for truth as opposed to an easy contentment with traditional ways of thinking. The loyal seeker after truth is sure to meet with perplexities and trials of faith; he may even be saddened by what at first appear to be losses. That it is possible that he will find some readjustments and some restatements needful, cannot beforehand be absolutely and categorically denied. But I at least believe that in the end he will hold in reassured possession all that is deepest and most fundamental in the orthodoxy of the past.

2. It will, I believe, be more and more clearly seen that, in regard to the events of our Lord's life on earth recorded in the Gospels, there is a wide difference between the amount and the nature of the evidence available in the several cases, and a corresponding difference between the degrees of certitude or (to speak strictly) of historical probability which can be attained. All evidence is not the same evidence. All belief is not the same belief. Christianity is an historical religion; and therefore, as in the natural order, so in the world of faith there must needs be twilight as well as noontide splendour. Inability to rank all articles of the Creed on the same level in regard to historical evidence is not equivalent to the denial of any.

3. The thoughtful Christian will recognise more clearly than in past days that he lives his religious life by faith, not by sight, not by that demonstrated certainty which in the intellectual sphere corresponds to sight. He will also be content to admit that round his central beliefs there lies a margin of admittedly open questions. The cry "all or nothing" is the confession of despair.[23]

The Church is not tied then by any existing definitions. We cannot make any exact claim upon any one's belief in regard to inspiration, simply because we have no authoritative definition to bring to bear upon him. Those of us who believe most in the inspiration of the Church, will see a Divine

Providence in this absence of dogma, because we shall perceive that only now is the state of knowledge such as admits of the questions being legitimately raised.

But if we thus plead that theology may leave the field open for free discussion of these questions which Biblical criticism has recently been raising, we shall probably be bidden to "remember Tübingen," and not be over-trustful of a criticism which at least exhibits in some of its most prominent representatives a great deal of arbitrariness, of love of "new views" for their own sake, and a great lack of that reverence and spiritual insight which is at least as much needed for understanding the books of the Bible, as accurate knowledge and fair investigation. To this the present writer would be disposed to reply that, if the Christian Church has been enabled to defeat the critical attack, so far as it threatened destruction to the historical basis of the New Testament, it has not been by foreclosing the question with an appeal to dogma, but by facing in fair and frank discussion the problems raised. A similar treatment of Old Testament problems will enable us to distinguish between what is reasonable and reverent, and what is high-handed and irreligious in contemporary criticism whether German, French, or English. Even in regard to what makes prima facie a reasonable claim, we do not prejudice the decision by declaring the field open: in all probability there will always remain more than one school of legitimate opinion on the subject: indeed the purpose of the latter part of this essay has not been to inquire how much we can without irrationality believe inspiration to involve; but rather, how much may legitimately and without real loss be conceded. For, without doubt, if consistently with entire loyalty to our Lord and His Church, we can regard as open the questions specified above, we are removing great obstacles from the path to belief of many who certainly wish to believe and do not exhibit any undue scepticism. Nor does there appear to be any real danger that the criticism of the Old Testament will ultimately diminish our reverence for it. In the case of the New Testament certainly we are justified in feeling that modern investigation has resulted in immensely augmenting our understanding of the different books, and

has distinctly fortified and enriched our sense of their inspiration. Why then should we hesitate to believe that further
study will similarly enrich our sense that "God in divers
portions and divers manners spake of old times unto the
fathers," and that the Inspiration of Holy Scriptures will
always be recognised as the most conspicuous of the modes
in which the Holy Spirit has mercifully wrought for the illumination and encouragement of our race?[24]

Jesus Christ

For him (Luther), as for Athanasius, the Divinity of Christ
was not just a doctrine of the Church. It was the one guarantee of men's salvation. Thus, in his larger Catechism, he
declared: "We could never recognise the Father's grace and
mercy except for our Lord Christ, who is a mirror of His
Father's heart." And in his exposition of the second article
of the Apostles' Creed, in the same Catechism, he writes,
"Now, when it is asked: what dost thou believe in this second
article concerning Jesus Christ? answer most briefly thus: I
believe that Jesus Christ, the true Son of God, has become
my Lord. And what do the words to become thy Lord mean?
They mean that He has redeemed me from sin, from the
devil, from death and all misfortunes . . . So the main point
of this article is, that the little word Lord, taken in its
simplest sense, means as much as Redeemer; that is, He who
led us back from the devil to God, from death to life, from
sin to righteousness, and holds us safe."

For speculations about God's nature, such as the School-
men, the "Sophists," indulged in, Luther had only aversion.
"True Christian divinity," he writes in his commentary on
Galatians, "commandeth us not to search out the nature of
God, but to know His will set out to us in Christ." "Know
that there is no other God but this man Christ Jesus."
"Embrace Him and cleave to Him with thy whole heart."
"Look on this man Jesus Christ, who setteth Himself out to
be a mediator, and saith "come unto Me all ye that labour
and are heavy laden and I will refresh you." Thus doing thou
shalt see the love, goodness and sweetness of God; thou shalt

see His wisdom, power and majesty, sweetened and tempered to thy capacity.[25]

Let us then ask ourselves, What is the truth, in the spiritual order, which it is intended to protect by the doctrines of the virgin birth, resurrection, and ascension? The answer is plain: it is the identification of the man Christ Jesus with the Word of God.

The historical fact of a supremely important religious movement in the first century A.D. is not disputed, nor can it be denied that the first Christians believed that it had its source in Christ. But is it certain that the Christ of the Church is not merely an idealised figure, to whom was attributed (in perfectly good faith) all that the religious consciousness of the age found to be most worthy of a Divine Being? The scepticism with which the story of the Incarnation is often regarded by thoughtful people must not be condemned as a perverse refusal to accept a narrative which is unusually well attested, still less as a judicial blindness. In almost all other cases the historian is able to test his materials by some external criterion of probability.

But in the case of the Incarnation we have nothing with which to compare it; the only external criterion to which we can appeal is the judgment of the Christian Church, as to what it "behoved" the Son of God to do and suffer; and this is a matter on which human beings cannot speak with authority and are not likely to agree. The historian of Christianity has to take account of events of an unique kind, which are no better attested than many other narratives which are rejected without hesitation, because they contradict "Laws" which we assume to be uniform. . . .

It is from no wish to ask a hearing for unprofitable speculations that I think it right to say that doubts of this kind cannot be dispelled with the completeness which all Christians would desire. In dealing with the past, be content with something less than certainty. The whole of history is beyond all question honeycombed with false statements which must go for ever uncorrected; even the simplest event or conversation is seldom described with any approach to accuracy by those who have seen or heard it a few minutes before. It is therefore barely honest to assert, as some have done, that, on the historical evidence only, either the discourses of Christ, or His miracles, or His resurrection on the third day after His crucifixion are absolutely certain. The evidence may be as good as possible; it is not possible for it to be good enough to justify such a statement as this.

Can we then appeal to intuition or inward experience to reinforce, or even guarantee, the historical evidence? Unquestionably an intense conviction of the fact of an Incarnation in the person of Jesus has been for nearly two thousand years a normal result or concomitant of earnest personal religion. This fact is valid evidence for mystics, who believe that growth in grace is accompanied by a progressive enlightenment of the understanding, which may even be compared to the acquisition of a new sense. But even for them it does not amount to proof; for the holiest saint is still far from having reached the height whence all things can be seen in their true proportions. And it will be objected, (a) that such evidence is valid only for those who have this experience—intuitions are not transferable; and (b) that the mythopoetic tendency of the religious consciousness is so pronounced as to throw suspicion upon its affirmations, even when they are supported by historical evidence. We are driven back to the question: Is the demand for a local and temporal Incarnation based on the nature of things, or on the temporary needs of a still only half-developed spiritual sense? This is a question which obviously we cannot answer, since we cannot stand outside our environment.[26]

The religious problem of the day, however, is to bring back the realisation of the Human Christ. Men of the most different opinions are urging upon the Christian Church the need of laying aside all accretions and presenting the Christ of the original Gospel to the world. The doctrine of the Divine Christ has, in the opinion of many, removed the man Jesus so far from us that they desire to see Him divested of all that to them appears supernatural whether related in the Gospel narrative or attributed to Him by the reverence of His fol-

lowers. They feel, in fact, that a Christ who neither claimed
Divinity nor wrought wonders would better satisfy the needs
of mankind; but they confess they find it most difficult to
depict accurately this purely Human Christ. Those who reverence His Person, but cannot receive all that the creed of
Christendom teaches concerning Him, are put to constant
shifts in their attempts to describe Him. So many passages
have to be explained away as not belonging to the original
Gospels, so many words and actions of His have to be apol-
ogised for, that every attempt to tell the story of Jesus Christ
from the standpoint of appreciative rationalism fails to com-
mend itself to a candid mind. We are as it were driven by
the investigation of the Human Christ to acknowledge that
He must be also Divine. . . .

When, however, we speak of Christ as the Word of God,
we are brought, not to a conclusion, but to a vista of fresh
problems; and if, after considering the unique influence of
our Lord on mankind in the past, we are led to acknowledge
Him to be the manifestation of the Divine Logos, it is necessary to enquire what we mean by so tremendous a statement.

It has been said indeed with perfect truth that Jesus has
taken His place in history as Man and not as God, and the
realisation of this, never more vivid than at the present time,
makes some look to the historical rather than to the Divine
Christ. But as has been pointed out, the difficulties of accepting a Christ, who is no more than human are almost in-
superable. As the reality of the Christ seems to fade away
when He is regarded only as a manifestation of Divinity, so
the results of His life become inexplicable when we refuse to
see Divinity in His Manhood.

A remarkable result of modern criticism is that, at the very
time when the Human Christ is most earnestly sought for,
the historic figure of Jesus is threatened with being relegated
to the realm of myth. Few indeed of those competent to discuss the question have denied that Jesus of Nazareth is an
historical character, but the sayings of Jesus have been declared to be but four, and these taken apart from any context
are purely negative in character; whilst several of the more

moderate critics refuse to look for any words of His outside the Sermon on the Mount.

Though the tendency of the present day seems to be in favour of accepting the main outlines of the Gospel as they are generally received, the above views cannot be altogether disregarded. To the historian they appear to be even more incredible than they are to the literary critic, since the less that is known of Christ in the Gospels the harder it is to give an adequate reason for what has happened since the Incarnation.

The teaching alike of St. Paul and St. John, illustrated by the testimony of history, leads us to the acknowledgement that Christ is more than a great personality who played His part in the world long ago. We are, it would seem, compelled to confess that the Christ of these great teachers is in some respects more majestic than the beautiful conception of Him as transmitted to us by the Synoptic Gospels. . . .

We seem, however, to be in danger of being placed in a dilemma. On the one side we are directed solely to the historic Jesus and challenged to face the limitations of an age little versed in the field of scientific criticism. On the other we may be tempted so to fix our gaze on the transcendental Christ of St. Paul and the Fourth Gospel as to neglect the gracious Figure of the Synoptists. The alternative may even be to choose between a Christ altogether Human and one altogether Divine. . . . But neither alternative can be accepted to the exclusion of the other. The instinct which leads men in all religious revivals back to the historic Christ of the Synoptists is indeed a sound one; for in a certain sense, the Figure of our Lord taking upon Himself the form of a servant, and the glorified Christ of a later age are equally Divine. If we fail to recognise this, the reason lies in our own inability to realise that the essence of the Kingdom of God consists not only of a glorified Monarch in heavenly state, but also a King tending, guarding, helping, toiling on with His subjects.[27]

The importance of Christianity lies here. It is a law of human history that principles and tendencies which are really universal, should at first make their appearance in an individual form, as if bound up with the passing existence of a particular nation or even of a single man. The general idea needs, so to speak, to be embodied or incarnated, to be "made flesh and dwell among men" in all the fulness of realisation in a finite individuality before it can be known and appreciated in its universal meaning. So the life of Jesus, "however otherwise we may conceive it," remains "to us the typical expression of religious feeling; for it brings the consciousness of finitude into a perfect unity with the consciousness of the infinite, it reconciles the monotheistic ideas of the evil that is in the world and of the transcendence of God, with the pantheistic idea of the immanence of God both in man and in nature. Jesus Christ, we may say, first discovered man's true relation to God and lived in it. From no other life, even in the imperfect records of it that have come down to us, do we get the same impression of reconciliation with self and God, of conscious union with a divine Spirit, manifesting itself immediately in self-conquest and devotion to the service of humanity.

Thus "Christianity was simply the universal principle of religion, coming to self-consciousness in the nation which was ripest for the expression of it," and the significance of Jesus is to be sought not in Himself, but in the idea that He embodied. By him, as by no other individual before, the pure idea of a divine humanity was apprehended and made into the great principle of life; and, consequently, in so far as that idea can be realised in an individual—and it was a necessity of feeling and imagination that it should be regarded as so realised—in no other way could it find so pure an embodiment. Nay, we may add that, so long as it was regarded as embodied in him only in the same sense in which it flowed out from him to others, so long the primacy attributed to Christ could not obscure the truth. It only furnished it with a typical expression, whereby the movements of the feelings and the imagination were kept in harmony with that of the intelligence.[28]

With these quotations as a background we may summarize the thinking of the Church about the person and work of Jesus Christ. That thinking tried to unite in a coherent whole the belief that Jesus Christ was the Saviour of mankind and the knowledge of man's own power to save himself from the limitations of his existence, knowledge which had been gained through scientific studies and the experiences of advancing civilization. The Church could not deny the traditional doctrine about Christ without denying the very basis of its own existence; and the Church could not deny the conclusions reached by objective study without being guilty of a lack of intellectual integrity. Yet, in the form in which the doctrine of Christ had been transmitted to the Church, there were statements that were contradictory to man's new knowledge of himself.

For example, there was the record of the life of Jesus Christ in the Bible. That record contained accounts of events which, in light of the facts of the natural order which were known, could not possibly have happened. Children are not born to virgins, angels do not bring messages to people, men do not walk on water, people who die do not return to life, and so on. The story of Jesus Christ was filled with what men had learned were impossibilities; therefore, the story could not be a literal account of actual happenings. When the New Testament was written, men may have been naïve enough to believe the things that were said about Jesus, and they may have seen no contradiction between the reports and their knowledge of the world, but now all was otherwise. The Church had to bring its thinking about Jesus Christ into harmony with the wisdom men had gained through their studies.

Or again, traditionally the Church had believed that Jesus Christ was God's Son sent into the world to save men, and that apart from Him there was no salvation possible. Those beliefs had to come to terms with some rather serious questions. What did the Church mean by claiming that Christ was God's Son? How could that assertion be interpreted in understandable terms? The possibility of some mysterious process of divine generation was ruled out, for that turned God into a kind of magician hidden away beyond the human realm, who occasionally injected Himself into human affairs. The early Church may have had a meaning for its doctrine of Christ, but in light of man's new knowledge some other meaning had to be found. Similarly with the idea of Christ as Saviour. The Church may once have thought of Christ lifting men out of limitations and dangers and evil, and giving them lives of security and peace, but that would no longer serve. Men were able to remove their own limitations and to wipe out evil. Once men prayed to God when disease afflicted them; now they cured the disease and attacked its cause. Men are their own saviours; and since they are saviours by using their own powers of mind and spirit, it is obvious that God intended them to be saviours. What role, then, does Jesus Christ play in the work of man's salvation?

In some such fashion the doctrine of Jesus Christ which the Church held was called in question. There were some in the Church who refused to deal with the issue. They were scattered throughout the various divisions of Protestantism at first, but slowly they drew together into separate groups marked by their distinctive position. They held that the record of Jesus' life in the Bible was an accurate historical account and that Christ was the one and only Saviour. They defended the record by pointing out that Jesus Christ was divine and therefore was not subject to the laws of the natural world under which ordinary human beings existed. Indeed, the very evidence for Christ's Saviourhood was in His willingness to appear in the guise of man and to submit to the limitations of human existence. He was born, He ate and slept, and He died. In those experiences He was as all men, yet He was not bound by those limitations. He could do things men could not do, and after His death could appear alive again. The record testified to His divinity.

And the same groups in the Church asserted Christ's Saviourhood on the ground of His own sayings and the experience of men through the centuries. They were quite willing to grant that men had learned how to make their own lives more comfortable and secure and had discovered ways of dealing with the world so that their own interests were furthered. Indeed, they enthusiastically participated in the various enterprises which were enlarging the scope of man's living. But they denied that those efforts could save man. Salvation was of the soul; and that took place only through a firm, unshakable faith in Jesus Christ, the Christ whose earthly career was told in the Bible.

Not all who held to the traditional doctrine of Christ bothered to defend their position. Many of them, even though they were caught up in the intellectual climate of the time, never saw the issue that was involved. But whether apologetic support was given to the position or not, the doctrine of the Christ transmitted from the past was held without change.

Others within the Church, and they were in the majority, worked to bring the doctrine of Christ into harmony with the scientific understanding of the world and man. The doctrine asserted the divinity of Christ. Christ was divine in the absolute perfection of His life. He lived in the same human setting as all men; in His character and His attitudes and His behavior He was as all men ought to be. He was true life at its highest and best. There could never be any finer life for there is nothing beyond the perfect. Religion, all religion, has known and taught that God is spirit, which means that God is the reality of life itself. Men in the past have had to guess what God is like for they have had only the evidence of their own lives to guide them. While some of their insights have been remarkably accurate, men could not be certain. But in Jesus Christ the divine was clear for all to see. He was the ultimate reality of life, the truth men should know, and the way they should go. God was in Christ; that was what men understood.

As for the record of Jesus' life, with its collection of strange actions and impossible deeds, that had to be used with discretion. The men who put that record together were not aware of the real nature of the universe so they could tell the stories about Jesus which they included in the Gospels without being troubled by their incongruity. Modern man can read those stories for what they were, tales told to prove the supreme power of Jesus' earthly life, and man can find through those stories the portrait of a perfect man whose being was love. That this was the real point of the record is shown by the account of Jesus' death, repeated with remarkable agreement by the four writers of the Gospels. For Jesus Christ died because He deliberately chose to live out the wholeness of His personal character in the face of an opposition that set out to destroy Him. He was killed as a martyr to perfection. And in the resurrection there is the portrayal of the fact that while man may try to wipe out the reality of God in his midst, all his efforts to that end are bound to fail. The perfection of love is eternal.

What then did it mean to say that Jesus Christ is Saviour? The answer to that rests upon an obvious fact of human living. Human history shows what might be called the power of living goodness. A good man, that is, a man who incarnates within himself the kind of life which men either know or sense they ought to live, has a wide and often hidden influence. Again and again through the centuries as human affairs have disintegrated into confusion and conflict, individuals have appeared who in themselves rose above the conditions of their time. They committed themselves to the goodness they knew. Their contemporaries may have paid little attention to them; they may even have put them to death. But the influence of the lives of those good men molded the ways of subsequent generations and brought peace and harmony to their societies.

In that sense Jesus Christ is Saviour. Since He is perfect man, He is the final and complete Saviour. Men whose ways are evil or whose lives are caught in limitations and disabilities and handicaps are changed when they get to know Him. He throws light upon all human weakness and He shows that such weakness is not and need not be determinative of man's character. By the very impact of Himself He calls men to be like Him. And since His perfection was within the structure of a simple, relatively undeveloped society no man can ever say that because of the conditions under which he lives perfection is impossible for him. And no man, having once come in contact with Jesus Christ, can ever escape the power of His influence; either man is molded in himself by that

influence or he is confirmed in the evil of his ways until
that destroys him. The effect which Christ has is quite
irresistible for good or ill depending upon the response
men make. Men cannot escape the necessity of reacting
to the reality of Christ once they hear about Him.

Such was the interpretation given to the traditional
doctrine of the person and work of Christ. The doctrine
was not denied in any of its essential points: Christ was
the divine Son of God; Christ was the Saviour of men.
Those statements were defined in language and with ideas
comfortable to the thought patterns of the age. In the
minds of those who made them, the new explanations did
not change the meaning of the doctrine at all, they
simply removed some of the illogical and unrealistic
accretions put on by uneducated minds and brought
into prominence the basic truths which had been covered
up. Jesus Christ was as the Church had always claimed
Him to be, and His power over the lives of men was
undimmed.

The Doctrine of Man

The doctrine of man which the Church held as it entered the modern era had been worked out through the
preceding centuries. That doctrine was based upon the
Scriptures, and had been given its theological form as
man's experience had cast light upon the Biblical statements. Briefly, the doctrine was: a) man had been created by God at a specific time, through a specific Divine
action, and in a specific place; b) man at creation was
perfect in spirit, living in selfless communion with God;
c) man had disobeyed God's will for him and had acted
on his own self-centered authority; d) through that action
man had lost the simple openness of his relationship to

God, his place in a realm of perfection, and the purity of his own soul; e) because of this action of the first man all men are sinners, deniers of God, and lost in a world apart from God; and f) man is wholly dependent upon God for release from his sinfulness and restoration to a relationship with God. The formulation of the doctrine varied somewhat among different sections of the Church, but in its essential features it was the same everywhere. Pelagius had denied the doctrine, teaching that the nature of man had not been corrupted by the fall, and he had gained some supporters. But the Church had concluded that Pelagius was wrong on the ground of the Biblical teaching and man's experience.

During the centuries with which we are concerned here the Church had to face the conclusions about man reached by scientists and students of human history. Those men found no evidence to support the Biblical account of man's origin, with its age of perfection and its sudden fall into a state of evil. Instead, the whole natural order appeared to operate under the control of a process of evolution, various forms of life developing through an unceasing adjustment to the everchanging universe. From archaeological findings men learned that they had been subject to that same evolving process both in their physical beings and their social life; and they learned that the process had been going on for untold numbers of years which stretched far back into unrecorded history. Individuals had developed from rather crude beings scarcely more than animals to persons of culture and refinement and learning; society had developed from simple forms of family unity to large, inclusive structures of nations. The changes that were involved had taken place through an interaction of natural evolution and man's free will. These scientific conclusions raised some serious questions about the traditional doctrine of man held by the Church.

As we have noted earlier in dealing with other doctrines, there were those in the Church who refused to make any adjustment to the findings of the intellectual leaders. That which the Bible and Church tradition said about man was true, and all contradictory statements were false. Of that there could be no mistake, for the Bible was the Word of God, and God did not make known that which was not so. The defenders of the tradition found it difficult at times to maintain their position in the face of the evidence produced by the scholars, but because the doctrine involved so many aspects they were able to shift the point of argument whenever they appeared to suffer defeat. And in the assertion that man was a sinner they possessed a position which appeared, on the ground of the observable character of life, to be quite unassailable. In the final analysis the traditionalists did not defend the position they held. They accepted the gibes of their contemporaries and insisted that the received doctrine was accurate.

But in the main the Church worked to come to terms with the conclusions of science. In doing so the Church had to deal with a number of issues.

There was the Biblical story of creation. The Church conceded that this was not an account of that which actually occurred. There was no Garden of Eden; Adam was not a being brought into existence suddenly by a creative act of the Divine, nor was Eve formed to be his companion; there was no voluble serpent to beguile the innocent pair into disobeying Divine orders; and the disobedient couple were not driven from the Garden to labor for their own livelihood in a harsh and difficult world. The whole record was a tale told by people who enjoyed spinning out imaginary answers to questions they asked about themselves. They knew nothing of the knowledge men had recently gained and thus could be quite unrestrained in the stories they told. But their work, interesting though it was, just was not historically true.

Yet there were two points in that ancient tale that were unassailable. Man lived in a world that was filled with evil; man was aware of his condition. That is, although man is evil, he can envision a life of peace and happiness. The fact of evil is clear. Human experience everywhere is marred by it. Yet man sees another possibility for himself and has already begun to work for the achievement of that possibility. The Biblical tale may have been spun out of man's imagination, yet within it was the setting forth of these two facts. In the Garden of Eden is a picture of what life should be like; and in the story of the fall is a description of man as he is and the reason why he is as he is. Writers in the Church were not as explicit as that, but such were the implications of their work.

Man is a sinner and is, simply because of his place in humanity, involved in sin from the very hour of his birth. That was the doctrine of the Church. And men agreed that the doctrine was true, although they gave their own interpretation to it. Sin, it was pointed out, is a word that has both ethical and religious connotations. Sin is an ethical word because it points to man's actions. Man is a sinner because he denies the good he knows. Non-religious writers dealt with the same phenomenon, and called it "moral evil." They were correct. Sin and moral evil are the same thing. An immoral act is a sin, and vice versa. Man is both immoral and a sinner. The terms are interchangeable. However, the word "sin" has a wider setting than the term used by the philosophers. Moral evil points to a specified social context; sin is a term with universal reference, that is, a theological term.

Furthermore, the world of humanity is a sphere of moral evil. Over the years and across the world men have acted wrongly, and the total structure of life has become infected by evil. At the very start of man's story, as far as that can be uncovered, he acted contrary to his best insights and to the reality of his true self, and his behavior has wrought harm on his society. And all men, since they are born into that society, cannot escape from its nature nor from the power of its influence upon them. Man now acts immorally because that is the kind of person his world has made him. In that sense man is a sinner. And the teaching that all men are sinners through their place in humanity is true. The Genesis story of man's character is not factual history, but the account of man's denial of God's command and its effect upon the whole human race is substantially correct. Man is a sinner in the very structure of his moral existence.

How, then, can man escape from this state of sinfulness? The traditional doctrine said that man was quite unable to rid himself of sin, so that his only hope was in the forgiveness and grace of God. God would free man from sin. In light of the work of the intellectual leaders of the time the Church worked out a restatement of this part of the doctrine that appeared to do justice to the newly gained knowledge. Man, the church pointed out, seeks self-satisfaction, self-expression, self-fulfillment. He knows himself to be a person in his own right. God cares for him and desires him to be fully and truly a complete personality. But man has made a mistake in the manner of his seeking. He did not really know, as he developed self-consciousness, how he ought to seek; and when he did learn something of the direction he ought to take, he often did not follow it. In his seeking he made himself the center. He tried to find fulfillment through self-assertion, instead of seeing that since he was a social being, formed to be a member of a group, he had to seek through a life devoted to the well-being of all. Man is a sinner because of ignorance and selfishness. In the earliest days of his history man erred in his behavior, so that now he is estranged by the very forces by which he lives.

Yet this sinful state is not unchangeable. Ignorance and selfishness can be removed and by their removal the state of humanity can be improved. Indeed, that is precisely what has been happening. Education has begun to free man from his ignorance, and the Christian Church has begun to make clear to man his inability to achieve the ends he desires through selfishness, and the more appropriate ways of acting. Evidence indicates that already an advance has taken place. Evil is not as widespread nor as destructive as it once was, nor does sin exert as strong a hold upon men. The teaching that by his nature man is condemned to everlasting bondage by evil is incorrect for it contradicts the actual testimony of man's experience. It is true that up to the present no individual has been brought to a state of perfect uprightness, and no society has reached the state of perfect civilization; yet an amazing development has taken place. Men once lacked even the rudimentary knowledge for satisfactory living and were so self-centered that the social organization they achieved was scarcely more than their own families. Through their experience over the centuries and the knowledge they have gained men have created new and more fulfilling ways and have gradually evolved larger and more inclusive social organizations. And this development which is clearly apparent to all who thoughtfully read the record of history can continue if man will give his attention and strength to it.

History shows that, in the past, two forces have been at work. One was the power of natural evolution. This worked in the sphere of man's moral life just as it did in his physical life. A choice made by man produced its own results, and the results of many choices produced a change in the human situation, and that change in its turn produced the necessity of new choices. The connectedness of action and result was built into the very structure of things, making the milieu in which man exists. This is the interdependence of all humanity. It is not a static unchangeable mass within which man plays out his days; it is an ever developing pattern which is part of man himself and which makes man what he becomes.

The other force is man's own freedom of spirit. Man's choices are basically his own, made through the power of his own will. They are, of course, within the possibilities man can see and are influenced by the circumstances in which they are made, yet nevertheless they are tokens of man's freedom. Because of this, the history of humanity is a story of ups and down, of eras during which man seemed to grow toward a more perfect fulfillment of himself, and eras during which exactly the reverse seemed to take place. However, this only serves to confirm the description of man which the Church worked out. When man made his choices out of ignorance or out of self-centeredness, his society deteriorated and his own development was stopped; when his choices were made out of knowledge and unselfishness society developed in a way that was productive of finer and more complete personalities. The two forces, natural evolution and man's free spirit, working together, wrote the tale of man's history.

The religious word "sin" was a perfectly legitimate word, for it pointed to that which is true of man. Man does act out of ignorance and selfishness; man is a sinner. And what is more, man is born into a whole structure of sin. The Biblical teaching that through Adam all men sinned, although it is obviously a mythological form of expression, points to that which is true. The Church must hold on to the traditional word. But sin is not ineradicable; it is not a reality of man's basic nature. Sin is caused. To the extent, then, that man wills to learn and to be unselfish sin will be removed. The Church worked out that new statement of human possibilities.

Moreover, said the Church, such is clearly the purpose of God. That purpose is expressed in the process of evolution. Fearful souls may be troubled by the thought that the doctrine of evolution implies that man is caught in some kind of mechanistic order which turns him out on its own mold, but that is not true. Evolution is of God's creation. And it clearly shows God's care for all men and His intention for them. Man is the crown, the ultimate achievement, if such language is allowable, of the whole evolutionary process. This is clear of man the individual, and it is equally clear of society. Moreover, in light of the doctrine of evolution man's history appears, not as a kind of fortuitous, relatively meaningless sequence of events, but as a total, inter-related structure working for the welfare and the development of man. The very nature of the world as man has come to know it, shows that its function is the creation and the training of a true person.

Then God has taken one further step in man's behalf. He has set in the midst of humanity a person of spiritual perfection. That is, he has portrayed the end toward which all history can and should lead. Men do not need to grope and experiment after the way to the finest life, learning only by their own choices. They can see the example God has provided for them. By following that example man can move forward toward a better world. The whole universe, with the forces at work in it, and the life of Jesus Christ the perfect man, is designed to overcome man's sin and to lead him to the fullness of life which is his proper end.

The Church

The doctrine of the Church was not a matter of deep interest during the period of time with which we are concerned here. One basic issue had been dealt with at the time of the Reformation, and the understanding that had been reached then, that the Church was made up of those who through faith had been saved, had been held through the years that followed. The Church had a place in God's work of salvation, but it was not the instrument of that salvation. The teaching that outside the Church there was no salvation was not correct, for the power of salvation was with God alone acting through Jesus Christ. Such was, in the main, all that needed to be said. Other matters of theological and practical interest occupied the immediate attention of the Church. Yet in the writings of the time certain points were made.

The Church was a society of men. It was an organization or an institution men joined, to which they had certain obligations, and within which they found satisfaction for their spiritual needs. God might save man in any way He chose and through whatever circumstances He used, just as He saved Paul on the road to Damascus; but once having been saved, man had to make his way into the Church. There had to be a Church, a visible group of Christian people, and all Christians had to be in that group. The group was absolutely essential, spiritually and morally, and the Christian, for his own spiritual and moral welfare, had to belong to it.

The Church was a voluntary society. Individuals were not born into the Church. There was discussion over whether a child of church people was different from a child of non-church people; more was involved in the discussion than the doctrine of the Church and the discussion did not last very long. Men were clear that they had to choose to belong to the Church. Their choice rested upon the action of God in their behalf, but they had to acknowledge that action and show their acknowledgment by asking for a place in the Church. Some carried out the implications of this by limiting the sacrament of baptism to those who had attained the age of discretion and thus were in a position to ask for church membership on their own decision. Those who continued to practice infant baptism were quite clear that the ceremony did not make the children members of the Church. The Church was a society of those who had chosen to join and had been accepted on good grounds by those already members.

In the Church the primary activity was the worship of God. Men needed to worship for their spiritual welfare. In addition, there was within the Church a common life of cooperation, mutual assistance, and fellowship in love. Church members made the rules under which the society carried on it affairs, using the Scriptures as their inspiration and guide. And the members could change the rules at will. In like fashion the members could decide upon the varied activities they would carry on within the Church and could participate in those activities or not just as they chose. The Church was seen to be a training place for a life of unselfish working with others, and a demonstration in the midst of humanity of the kind of existence all men ought to achieve. Always the voluntary nature of the Church had to be safeguarded. The authority of God was spiritual and moral; man's freedom had always to be respected.

The one point which aroused a bit of interest at the time was that of the relation between Jesus Christ and the Church. The positions which were taken were in harmony with the beliefs about Jesus Christ which were held. The Church was sure that in some way or other it had its existence because of Jesus Christ; the issue was how. Those at one extreme believed that Christ through His death and resurrection had given new life to men. The Holy Spirit had come, and the Church was formed by and with the Spirit. Men in the Church possessed the new life of the Spirit and were thus participators in a common existence. The Church was built around the life of Jesus Christ; He was the life of the Church. At the other extreme were those who emphasized the action of God saving individual men. The Church was a number of such saved individuals united in a group. Again, Jesus Christ was the foundation of the Church, but in quite a different way than in the former way of thinking. According to one idea men were united to one another by the Spirit of Christ, while according to the other men who were reborn through the Spirit of Christ were united in fellowship one with another. In both Jesus Christ formed the Church.

Basically, there was one characteristic in the thinking about the Church which was indicative of the general outlook of the era. Men had thought of the Church as an institution established by divine action and maintained by divinely appointed tradition; the Church was not something with which men could tamper and over which they could take any control. Men were to live under the authority of the Church for that authority was the very rule of Almighty God. In the centuries with which we are concerned here man came to an understanding of his own power and his own authority; he claimed and took control over his own affairs. And that which he did over a wide range of his interests and activities he did in the Church. In the new thinking man did about the Church, he came to emphasize his own part in the formation of the institution and its program. Man held to the traditional belief that the Church was built upon Jesus Christ, but he wove that belief into a pattern of thought which gave weight to his own work in its visible structure.

CHAPTER FOUR

Protestantism and the World

Since Protestantism established itself on the foundation of a direct relationship between God and the freedom of man, a relationship that was worked out through God's saving action in Jesus Christ on the one side and the faith of man on the other, it was inevitable that the new Christian movement had to work out a connection between itself and other human institutions. During the medieval age the Church was the controlling power in Europe. There were structures by which men found the necessities of existence, maintained their common life, and sustained a generally accepted pattern of moral behavior. But over all these structures and giving force to them was the Church with its various institutions—the governing hierarchy, the churches with their priests, the schools, the monasteries, and the orders. While the statement needs careful limitation, it is correct to say that in a real sense the Church and man's life were one: Church teaching, sacraments, influence, and direct control penetrated the totality of existence. Toward the end of that age, a serious conflict arose between the Church and the political rulers, a conflict in which the rulers claimed their freedom from ecclesiastical control. But that conflict was only a sign of the developing human force which was rooted in Protestantism.

Protestantism, however, when it separated from the Catholic Church, altered profoundly the relationship which had existed between the Church and the life of men. Yet that change in relationship was not simply the result of the action of a group of men who out of an inner conviction asserted their own understanding of the Christian faith. Even if that had been all that was involved, the problem of the connection between the new movement and contemporary society would have been difficult enough. Much more was involved. The reformers and the reformed church had, of necessity, to establish themselves in society; as we have noted earlier, they did so with the support of some of the political leaders and of the new middle class. But they also had to work out their judgment of and their connection with the varied elements in the new age.

We have insisted that Protestantism was and is the stream of Christian Church life that has put at its center the freedom of man and the purpose of the personal living God to deal with man in his freedom. As such, Protestantism was but one expression of man's living; it sent him to create new political forms, to develop new ways of carrying on his economic affairs, and to reorder his social existence. The modern age is the age of freedom, the age in which human orders are never fixed but are always subject to change by the will of those who possess the power. Protestantism had to find itself in the midst of this new world and had to work out, not only its place in the structures of humanity, but also its thinking about that place, its justification and its functions.

When an institution possesses fixed form or forms that allow for gradual modification within a settled pattern; that is, when an institution and faith itself become almost synonymous, then the relation between that institution and its contemporary world can be worked out with relative ease, for it is worked out from a stable position. But when an institution is a gathering by faith alone, then the problem of its relationship to its world is complex, for that relationship must change as the world changes. And when both the world and religion build on the reality of man's freedom, the problem of their relationship becomes tremendously complex.

The modern age has produced a variety of political forms, and has, in effect, wiped out the monarchical structures of earlier years, replacing them with structures that give all men an opportunity to share in their own government. It has developed an economic order based on industry and mechanization, completely changing the method and place of agriculture; it has brought into existence a society which is more or less fluid, thus undermining the fixed classes or orders in which men were confined; and it has spread to all peoples of the earth the developments which occurred in the West. As someone remarked: while once the Western World was a unity through the Christian Church, now the whole world is a unity through the machine and the idea of man's freedom. Protestantism has had to work out its life while all this has been taking place; and its working out has had to be in terms of those developments in which it was inextricably involved.

Thus Protestantism is always open to the charge of being either too pragmatic or too idealistic; and both charges are based in truth. Protestantism is sure to reflect the day-by-day living expression of those who are its adherents, for they are the ones who, precisely where they are, must live by faith; the results of their serious response to God must be pragmatic. Contrariwise, Protestants, because their minds are ever fixed on the Holy Scriptures, so that the claims which their faith makes upon them are always made specific as the words of Scripture touch their common life, again and again understand those claims in utterly idealistic terms. And this alternation or contradiction appears throughout the history of Protestantism.

In surveying the development in this aspect of Protestantism it is important to remember that the missionary enterprise which Protestant people have undertaken, the social gospel which has held a place of prominence in Protestant pulpits, and the efforts for the eradication of social ills which have emerged among Protestants are all part of the essential life of Protestantism. However often Protestants may have insisted that missions and social action are inherent ingredients of the Christian faith, the fact remains that both enterprises have developed within Protestantism as it has sought to work out its relation to its world. Protestantism has evolved through its history in its knowledge of itself, that is in its theology; similarly, it has evolved in the relations it has worked out with its world and in its understanding of the significance of these relationships.

THE AGE OF THE REFORMERS

The Reformation movement began on all sides with a return to Christ; for the belief that man is justified by the merits of Jesus Christ and not by obedience to a complex system of ecclesiastical regulations was by no means originated by or confined to the German reformers. Even the Jesuits, the most formidable of the reactionaries, owed their initial success to the way they led their followers back to the contemplation of the Saviour. . . .

No branch indeed of the Western Church can be refused the honour of having assisted in the progress of humane ideas, and non-Christians have participated largely in the work of diffusing the modern spirit of kindness; but the credit of the inception of the movement belongs without doubt to that form of Protestantism which is distinguished by the importance it attaches to the doctrine of the Atonement. No part of the Christian system has found less favour than this among the educated classes of our day, and many thoughtful minds have revolted against its apparent presentation of an unworthy conception of Divine justice. It has even been asserted that the thought of Christ's sufferings being a part of the Divine scheme of Salvation has in a measure sanctioned cruelty among Christians. But history shows that the thought of Christ on the Cross has been more potent than anything else in arousing a compassion for suffering and indignation at injustice. Early Puritanism, which occupied itself chiefly with such questions as the election of the saved by the Father and left but little room for the work of the Son, was doubtless hard and unsympathetic. But the later Evangelicalism, which saw in the death of Christ the means of free salvation for fallen humanity, caused its adherents to take the front rank as champions of the weak, the feeling roused by their form of belief in the Atonement being summed up in the lines

Thou hast done this for me:
What shall I do for Thee?[1]

In all the greatest forward movements of humanity, religion has been one of the driving forces. The dead weight of hoary institutions and the resistance of the caked and incrusted customs and ideas of the past are so great that unless the dormant energies of the people are awakened by moral enthusiasm and religious faith, the old triumphs over the new. "Mighty Truth is yet mightier man-child" come to the hour of birth, but there is no strength to bring forth.

But in turn the greatest forward movements in religion have always taken place under the call of a great historical situation. Religious movements of the first magnitude are seldom purely religious in their origin and character. It is when nations throb with patriotic fervor, with social indignation, with the keen joy of new intellectual light, with the vastness and fear of untried conditions, when "the energy sublime of a century bursts full-blossomed on the thorny stem of Time," that religion, too, will rise to a new epoch in its existence.[2]

John Calvin was never a monk. He had lived in cities, had studied at universities and knew the ways of the common people. Rejecting the submissiveness of medieval Christianity, the chief end of man, according to Calvin, was to consecrate his active will in the service of his Master. Calvin reformed theology and ethical ideals by compelling men to think of their personal responsibility in the light of the majesty and sovereignty of God. Under the profound conviction of God's personal demands upon their time and labour, the followers of Calvin conceived their duty in the terms of activity and exertion; a call to establish righteousness in the earth and to overthrow the strongholds of wickedness. This theology which gave men steady and iron nerve, this relentless logic of the divine sovereignty, led Carlyle to say that Calvinism had created all the heroes. . . .

In contrast to the Reformers the Anabaptists affirmed freedom of the will and complete moral responsibility; the individual interpretation of Scriptures; that the State was ordained of God and ought to be obeyed unless its laws offended the conscience; they denied its supremacy in religious matters; they were Separatists and rejected the State establishment of the Church; they affirmed universal toleration. They were passivists. In Moravia they had large communal settlements, but many did not favour such settlements and taught that wealth and property were a personal stewardship to be rendered to God. They opposed usury and lent money without interest. . . .

Long before Luther walked out of his cell the storm in Germany had been brewing. The peasants had lacked leaders who could voice their grievances, but with the rise of Luther it seemed that he had been sent to deliver them from feudal bondage. True, he was no political revolutionary, but he had attacked the landlords, the Church and the wealthy merchant class, until the peasants were encouraged to submit to him their programme of reform. The Twelve Articles of the peasants of Upper Swabia indicate the reasonableness of their demands: it is said that Hubmaier contributed to the form of these articles which were: the right to choose their own pastors; they will pay the tithe of corn for the support of the preacher of the pure gospel, but they refuse to pay the tithe of a head of cattle any longer; they will no longer submit to villainage which is incompatible with the Gospel; they demand their share of fish and game on the estate; they ask for the restoration of the woods which the landlords had stolen and enclosed; they insist on a reduction of oppressive service; they ask for reasonable wages, a fair rent; the abolition of unjust punishment; the restoration of common land which unless granted they will take back from the landlords; the abolition of death duties as a merciless oppression of widows and orphans; the last article agrees to forego any of the above demands which cannot be reconciled with God's Word.

These Articles are moderate and clearly derive from Luther's teaching. The peasants were ready to reason with their masters and submit their demands to arbitration; they disclaimed the use of force except as the last resort of resolute men. As the movement spread to other areas the aims became more revolutionary even to the threat of establishing a republic. When their demands were rejected by the princes and the Church, the peasants began in 1525 to burn churches, sack monasteries, and attack the castles of the rulers and the bishops: "Hatred of the Church and its degenerate hierarchy is, in fact, a notable feature of the rising."

Several of Luther's former friends and fellow-workers had shown sympathy with the aims of the peasants; but when the latter consulted Luther and hoped to win his support and leadership, he wrote his *Exhortation to Peace in Response to the Twelve Articles of the Peasants in Swabia*.

He also denounced his former friends who were becoming more alienated from him and who had urged the peasants to revolt; at the same time he rebuked the violence of the peasants as a defiance of the law of God. However tortuous their existence might be, they must submit to wicked as to beneficent rulers: "suffering, suffering, cross, cross—this is the Christian's right and no other." The Gospel, he said, had nothing to do with temporal things nor did it condone such methods as they had adopted to abolish their feudal miseries: had not Abraham, the patriarch, practised slavery? Had not Paul taught slaves to be obedient to their masters? It is not surprising that the peasants began to despise Luther. If their feudal lords were avaricious and inhuman, why should they passively submit? At one and the same time Luther was countenancing tyranny and advising a fatalistic submission to it. Hence the peasants were ready to follow the advice of Luther's former friends and fight it out to the finish. To such a decision Luther's answer was his outburst: *Against the Robber and Murdering Bands of the Peasants*. He now charged them with doing the devil's work, and he urged the German princes "to strike, throttle, stab, secretly or openly, whoever can, and remember that there is nothing more poisonous, more hurtful, more devilish than a rebellious man. . . . I believe there is no longer a devil in hell. They have all taken possession of the peasants." Luther advised the princes "to wield the sword without mercy." He had previously denounced the princes as scoundrels; now they are ministers of God and martyrs if they are slain by the rebels. By such means was the rising crushed.[3]

THE CHURCH AND THE STATE

That the Church should be no mere creature of the State, should be able to act in the world, expressing its conviction and making plain its requirements, being a living manifestation of a true inward fellowship, was a great advance upon the quiescent Erastianism into which Lutheranism was falling. Not only has this teaching of Calvin been a leaven of quite incalculable influence in the Church, it has been an enormous social force as well, working for constitutional government in the State as well as in the Church. That such government is, as Sohm argues, Pagan and not Christian, is surely inconsistent with the historical fact that no Christian nation, with the possible exception of Russia, has failed to develop a constitution and find some measure of true freedom in it, and no non-Christian nation, with the exception of a few attempts in recent years directly under the influence of Christian example, has even tried such a thing. For its effective working, men emancipated from mere subjection to law and ready to die for freedom to follow their own consciences are necessary.

But this recognition of Calvinism as a vast historical force, keeping alive in Protestantism a sense of the Church as no mere creature of the State and making for such freedom in the State as now admits almost unfettered liberty of thought and action, need not hinder us from recognising the defects in its temper.

First of all, we must remember that it wrought with the old conception of the nation as Christianity with the two swords. Calvin taught that the Church is God's kingdom and different from the civil authority, but even in the days when the authorities were against Protestantism, he held that it was the duty of the magistrate to see that no idolatry, no injury to the divine name should exist. Later, he maintained that, while the authorities are to use their own judgment, that is, to determine whether what the ministers of the word submit to them is truly God's word or not, they are to be guided by the word, strengthen the hands of those who teach it, and not to hinder the free judgment of the Church regarding what is against God's honour. Here the danger of the Church ruling the State and becoming a theocracy is manifest, and the criticism is probably right that the system never is found in its purity except where it is compelled to develop itself in opposition to the power of the State.

To Hooker, every nation professing Christianity is a Church. The Church and the State are merely two aspects of the same society, which has as much right to determine how men shall worship as how they shall pay taxes. The authority of the Church, which it is mere insolence in the individual to question, is in the last issue the authority of the Queen. Whatsoever government a nation, in the capacity of a Church, appoints for itself is right. Though episcopal government is ancient and almost universal, he refuses to oppose Cartwright's divine right of presbyters with a divine right of bishops. Geneva may govern her Church by presbyters so long as it is merely what is thought convenient for itself, and not "tendered unto the people as things everlastingly by the law of the Lord of lords." The Scripture has authority in matters of salvation, but the organisation of Churches is left to reason, which, in this case, means the national legislator. . . .

This view of the Church as resting on the common Christian conscience had also its effect on the Puritan view of the State. The sphere of the State was no longer everything not demonstrably wrong, but only that which was demonstrably right. The non-essential was the sphere of liberty not of law, because it was the sphere in which every elect soul must be guided of God. In business, for example, the Puritan asked freedom, not on any ground of individual competition, but that he might, as a chosen vessel, live his common life and exercise his stewardship over the goods God had given him, as God required. No doubt the leaven of the past intolerance and reliance upon the secular arm still wrought in him, but there was also the leaven of the new spirit of Christian liberty, with regard to which the only regret is that it had so imperfectly prevailed to this day.[4]

. . . Protestant theory lent itself to an exaggerated nationalism, and insularity, by which Christendom has been divided into separate compartments with little or no inter-communication or mutual understanding. Nationalism led on easily and naturally into Erastianism, as the religious community in each nation found itself unequal to the assertion of its spiritual independence; and Erastianism chilled religious life, not in England only, but in Germany, in Holland and in Scandinavian countries. And when once the vital conviction of the unity of the divine society had disappeared, individualism or congregationalism could run riot. . . . The Church is still faced by the old problem of the things of Caesar and the things of God; and while experience has taught her that she can no longer cling to the mediaeval principle of enforced conformity and absolute coextensiveness with the World, she has not yet substituted for it any clear principle of discipleship, but seems to halt between different opinions in the determination of her relations with the World. Yet never had the World greater need of the Church. And the Church, we believe, is still "the Spirit-bearing body"; and the Spirit of the Lord, which should be the pledge of liberty, proceeds from Him who is not a God of confusion, but of peace.[5]

JOHN WESLEY ATTACKS SOCIAL EVILS

In the sermon on "Scriptural Christianity," preached in 1744 at St. Mary's, Oxford, before the University, John Wesley considered Christianity "under three distinct views"; as beginning to exist in individuals; as spreading from one to another; and as covering the earth. True to his doctrinal position he showed that the individual to whom "God was the desire of his eyes, and the joy of his heart . . . " could not but love his brother also; and "not in word only, but in deed and truth." The affection of this lover of God would embrace "all mankind for His sake." When, therefore, Christianity in its beginnings spread from person to person Christians laboured "to do good to all men," calling them to repent, and reasoning with them of temperance, and righteousness, or justice, that is "of the virtues opposite to their reigning sins." This brought him to envisage the ultimate triumph of Christ's gospel. . . .

In his descriptive letter to Vincent Perronet, John Wesley explains how, after discussion with the Stewards (presumably of the Society in London), plans were made for the distribution of relief to the poor and visitation of the sick. He goes on to name other social services to people in need; his own medicinal services to persons "ill of chronical distempers," in which he was assisted by "an apothecary and an experienced surgeon"; temporary provision for some who

"had none who took care to provide for them," chiefly feeble
aged widows; an experiment in schooling by which "near
sixty children . . . learned reading, writing, and arithmetic
swiftly, and at the same time they were diligently instructed
in the sound principles of religion"; and a loan fund from
which Methodists in sharp distress could borrow up to twenty
shillings (later, up to five pounds) on repayment within three
months."

The *Journal* for 1741 gives a vivid picture of Methodism,
in its beginnings, making Christian fellowship real:

> I reminded the United Society that many of our brethren
> and sisters had not needful food; many were destitute of
> convenient clothing; many were out of business, and that
> without their own fault; and many sick and ready to
> perish; that I had done what in me lay to feed the hun-
> gry, to clothe the naked, to employ the poor, and to visit
> the sick; but was not, alone, sufficient for these things,
> and therefore desired all whose hearts were as my heart:
>
> 1. To bring what clothes each could spare, to be dis-
> tributed among those that wanted them most.
> 2. To give weekly a penny, or what they could afford,
> for the relief of the poor and sick.
>
> My design, I told them, is to employ, for the present,
> all the women who are out of business, and desire it, in
> knitting. To these we will first give the common price
> for what work they do; and then add, according as they
> need.
>
> Twelve persons are appointed to inspect these, and to visit
> and provide things needful for the sick. Each of these is to
> visit all the sick within their district, every other day; and to
> meet on Tuesday evening, to give an account of what they
> have done, and consult what can be done farther.[6]

PROTESTANTISM AND THE INDUSTRIAL REVOLUTION

In the aggressive position which, after the eighteenth century had culminated in the French Revolution, the older spiritual forces again adopted towards the modern world, and in which they, with the union of ideological and practical politico-social powers, advanced victoriously against the new world, the restoration of Prussian-German Lutheranism was one of the most important events in social history. It united with the reactionary movement the monarchical ideas of agrarian patriarchalism, of the militaristic love of power; it gave an ideal to the political Restoration and its ethical support. For this reason, then, it in turn was supported by the social and political forces of reaction, by all the means of power at their disposal. Finally, Lutheranism of this type hallowed the realistic sense of power, and the ethical virtues of obedience, reverence, and respect for authority, which are indispensable to Prussian militarism. Thus Christianity and a conservative political attitude became identified with each other, as well as piety and love of power, purity of doctrine, and the glorification of war and the aristocratic standpoint. . . .

Lutheranism naturally does little towards building up a new social structure. In the main its efforts are confined to the philanthropic activity of the Home Mission Movement: otherwise its tendency is to alleviate but not to re-create. Wherever the Christian social ethic and social policy strikes out in another direction we may be sure that other influences are at work than those of genuine Lutheranism.

Thus there arose a current—definite, particularly powerful, and influential—of the bourgeois capitalistic spirit, which was pre-eminently typical of the bourgeois way of life in general. This was the predominance of labour and of the "calling," of industry for its own sake, a process of objectifying work and the results of work, which was only possible where work was exalted by means of an ascetic vocational ethic of that kind, into the sphere of that which is necessary in itself. . . . Calvinism, which in its early days included a good many groups of the aristocracy, was at first indifferent to social questions, but in the course of the political development in various countries it became bourgeois; this social transformation, however, was entirely in line with certain elements in its spirit. . . .

The significant point which is important even to-day for our subject is this: that in these Christian circles, and in them alone, was it possible to combine modern economic activity with Christian thought, and indeed, that down to the present day it is possible to do this with a clear conscience. . . . Seen in this light, the significance of this new Calvinistic form of Christianity for the whole modern development, and especially for the position of Protestantism within it, becomes plain. It is the only form of Christian social doctrine which accepts the basis of the modern economic situation without reserve. The reason for this does not lie in any supposed "greater insight" into the essence of the economic processes, but in the fact that here the super-idealistic and Pietistic hindrances in the fundamental ethical idea have fallen away, which would have otherwise hindered or restrained this development; because, on the contrary, the Calvinistic ethic contains energies which directly further this economic development.

Whether a Christian ethic of this kind, contrasted with that of Catholicism and of Lutheranism, is entirely an advantage, whether it is not tinged rather strongly with the spirit of "business" and the avidity of a materialistic outlook on life, is another question. The main point is that it is peculiar to the leading modern nations, or at least to majority groups amongst them, and that it here effects an adjustment to the modern economic world which has not been achieved by the Christian piety of other nations.

The Christian element in this Calvinistic justification of Capitalism would, however, be greatly misunderstood if one did not at the same time remember the limits with which the real Christian idea of love here also surrounds the ethic of industry, and which have continued to exert a beneficent influence right down to the present day, wherever, in all capitalistic labour, the main Calvinistic ideas have remained vitally alive. Labour is asceticism, an asceticism which is absolutely necessary. Profit is the sign of the blessing of God on the faithful exercise of one's calling. But labour and profit were never intended for purely personal interest. The capitalist is always a steward of the gifts of God, whose duty it is to increase his capital and utilize it for the good of Society as a whole, retaining for himself only that amount which is necessary to provide for his own needs. All surplus wealth should be used for works of public utility, and especially for purposes of ecclesiastical philanthropy. Thus the Genevese assessed themselves to the furthest possible limit for special cases of need, and gave regularly in support of the local poor as well as for the numerous refugees. The charitable activity of the Church which was exercised by the board of deacons was part of the requirement of the Church-order instituted by God, was organized with great energy, and, with the aid of voluntary gifts which were often amazingly large, it was able to cope with the demands made upon it. This is the origin of the practice known among us through the example of American millionaires—in which even men who have become quite indifferent to religion will give a large portion of their profits for public purposes. The actual theory and practice of money and interest has also been determined by this spirit of philanthropy.

The great English system of legislation which deals with the poor, with workmen and with wages—in the guild-professional sense and, above all, with respect to education for work—bore traces of its spirit. In opposition to the "Manchester" conception of the State and of economics, Carlyle deliberately asserted the old Puritan ideas. The Christian Socialism of the English people at the present day is essentially of Calvinistic origin, and the activity of the American churches is often of a Christian Socialist kind directed against the abuses of Capitalism. In Switzerland, in the Netherlands, in England, and in America there are to-day Socialist clergy, whereas within the sphere of Lutheranism such a phenomenon is regarded as an offence against the sacred foundation of the Divine order, as taking part in purely secular matters, as a reprehensible revolutionary spirit, and a human intervention in the order of Providence; among us social heresies are more dangerous and more objectionable than doctrinal heresies. The meaning of that is, however, that Calvinism is in closer agreement with modern tendencies of social life than Lutheranism, or than Catholicism, which, at least in the Latin lands of its origin, likewise holds these heresies at arms length. This also is the basis of that intense self-consciousness of Calvinism, the sense that it is the only form of Christianity adapted to modern life, because, on the one hand, it is able to justify modern forms of economic production before the tribunal of conscience, and because, on the other hand, by means of Christian Socialism, it strives to rectify the abuses of the system when they occur. It is very conscious of representing "modern Christianity"—not because it is in touch with modern theological thought (for its theological tendency inclines to conservatism, and it is only its overwhelmingly practical character which leads to dogmatism being relegated to a secondary position), but because it is in harmony with the political and economic way of life, and understands how to further and yet to define its problems, whereas it considers that Lutheranism is philosophically diseased, unpractical, and remote from the problems of ordinary life.[7]

THE TWO EMERGING PRINCIPLES

We are met at the outset by two widely differing conceptions of the mode and direction in which Christianity acts as a regenerating influence on the life of mankind. On the one side, Christianity is identified with civilization, and the function of the Church is regarded as simply the gathering up, from age to age, of the higher aspirations of mankind: her call is to enter into, to sympathize with, and to perpetuate whatever is pure, noble, and of good report, in laws and institutions, in art, music, and poetry, in industry and commerce, as well as in the moral and religious usages and beliefs of mankind. Christianity is thus not a higher order, standing over against and correcting a lower, but is itself the product or rather the natural outgrowth of the progressive moral consciousness of mankind. The value of this mode of thought is in emphasizing the sacredness of secular interests and duties, and in its protest against dividing the field of conscience, and assigning to the one part a greater sanctity than to the other. "As our salvation depends as certainly upon our behaviour in things relating to civil life, as in things relating to the service of God, it follows that they are both equally matters of conscience and salvation." Its weakness lies in its not sufficiently recognising one decisive fact of human nature, the fact of sin. No one, as it seems to us, looking at human nature, in himself or others, with clear, open, unprejudiced eyes, can doubt the existence of sin, its corrupting influence on the whole nature, and yet its fundamental unnaturalness. But if states and societies are as the individuals who compose them, then any theory of society must rest on a theory of man; and the theory of man is imperfect unless it recognises the fact of sin.

On the other hand, the recoil from secularism, or the overwhelming sense of the power and destructiveness of sin in the lives of men and of societies, leads others to draw sharp the distinction between things sacred and things secular. The order of things, it is said, of which the Incarnation is the starting-point, is admittedly higher than that secular order which existed before it, and which even now surrounds it as darkness encompasses light. Let us put on one side political life, local and national interests, all that sphere of mixed social relations, which is so imperfect, so full of fierce passions, of strife, envy, and ambition, so productive of distractions and entanglements. Let us concentrate our own thoughts on sin, and devote our own lives to its remedy. Let us at least keep our own hands clean, and use for our own discipline that narrower sphere which is sufficient. No doubt individuals will find their vocation in some such attitude as this; and for some it may be wise to abstain from political and social interest, in order thus to strengthen their influence in other directions. But we are not now considering the call of individual Christians, but the attitude of the Christian Church as a whole: and it would be easy to accumulate references to show that the leading minds of Christendom have declined to recognise, except in cases of special vocation, as the duty of Christians, the abdication of responsibility for the problems, the entanglements, the more or less secular issues of the ordinary social life of mankind. Christianity, in the words of a modern writer, has both to deliver humanity from its limitations, and to bring it to a true knowledge of itself.[8]

THE CHURCH SEES THE IMPLICATIONS
OF ITS PRINCIPLES

Human nature is the raw material for the Christian character. The spirit of Christ working in the human spirit is to elevate the aims, ennoble the motives, and intensify the affections. This process is never complete. The Christian is always but in the making.

In the same way human society is the raw material for Christian society. The spirit of Christ is to hallow all the natural relations of men and give them a divine significance and value. This process, too, is never complete. The kingdom of God is always but coming.

The situation is changed when the individual presents not only the obstacles of raw human nature, a will sluggish to good, a preference for pleasure rather than duty, and the clogging influence of evil habits, but a spirit and principles consciously hostile to the influence of Christianity, and sets defiant pride and selfishness against the gentleness and unselfishness urged by the spirit of Jesus.

In the same way the situation is changed when the social relations are dominated by a principle essentially hostile to the social conceptions of Christ. Then the condition is not that of a stubborn raw material yielding slowly to the higher fashioning force, but of two antagonistic spirits grappling for the mastery. The more such a hostile principle dominates secular society, the more difficult will be the task of the Church when it tries to bring the Christ-spirit to victorious ascendency.

Christianity bases all human relations on love, which is the equalizing and society-making impulse. The Golden Rule makes the swift instincts of self-preservation a rule by which we are to divine what we owe to our neighbor. Anything incompatible with love would stand indicted. Christ's way to greatness is through preeminent social service. Self-development is desirable because it helps us to serve the better. So far as the influence of the Christian spirit goes, it bows the egoism of the individual to the service of the community. It bids a man live his life for the kingdom of God. . . .

The individualistic philosophy was worked out at the end of the eighteenth century in order to cut away the artificial restraints inherited from a bygone period of industry. The noblest thinkers enthusiastically believed that the unfettered operation of self-love would result in happy conditions for all. Experience has proved this a ghastly mistake. Scientific thought and practical statesmanship have abandoned the policy of unrestrained competition. The more enlightened business men, too, view it with moral uneasiness and a certain shame. The selfish hardness of business life is to them a sad fact, but they feel they must play the game according to the rules of the game. Yet as long as competitive commerce continues and is the source of profit in the business world, competitive selfishness will be defended as the true law of life.

As soon as the competitive philosophy of life encounters an opposing philosophy in socialism, it is angrily insistent on its own righteousness. The same is the case when any attempt is made to urge the Christian law of life as obligatory for business as well as private life. "Don't mix business and religion." "Business is business." These common maxims express the consciousness that there is a radical divergence between the two domains of life, and that the Christian rules of conduct would forbid many common transactions of business and make success in it impossible. Thus life is cut into two halves, each governed by a law opposed to that of the other, and the law of Christ is denied even the opportunity to gain control of business. When a man lives a respectable and religious life in one part of the city and a life of vice in another part, he is said to live a double life. That is the heart-breaking condition forced upon Christian business men by the antagonism of Christianity and competitive commerce. They have to try to do what Christ declares impossible: to serve God and mammon. It is no wonder that many try to maintain their faith in their own integrity of character by denying that business life is antagonistic to Christianity at all. But the rest of the community judge differently. The moral sincerity of the most prominent members of the Churches is impugned by the public, which has little sympathy with the tragic situation in which Christian business men find themselves. This deeply affects the moral prestige of the Churches in the community. They are forced into the defensive instead of challenging the community to a higher standard of morals.

When two moral principles are thus forced into practical antagonism in daily life, the question is which will be the stronger. If the Church cannot Christianize commerce, commerce will commercialize the Church. When the churches buy and sell, they follow the usual methods and often drive hard bargains. When they hire and dismiss their employees, they are coming more and more to use the methods of the labor market. In the teaching of the Church those elements of the ethics of Jesus which are in antagonism to commercial life are toned down or unconsciously dropped out of sight. The Sermon on the Mount, in which Jesus clearly defines the points of difference between his ethics and the current morality, is always praised reverently, but rarely taken seriously. Its edge is either blunted by an alleviating exegesis, or it is asserted that it is intended for the millennium and not for the present social life. Thus the principles of commerce affect the moral practice of the Church and silence its moral teachings in so far as they are antagonistic to business morality. . . .

This is the stake of the Church in the social crisis. If one vast domain of life is dominated by principles antagonstic to the ethics of Christianity, it will inculcate habits and generate ideas which will undermine the law of Christ in all other domains of life and even deny the theoretical validity of it. If the Church has not faith enough in the Christian law to assert its sovereignty over all relations of society, men will deny that it is a good and practicable law at all. If the Church cannot conquer business, business will conquer the Church.[9]

CONCLUSION AT THE END OF THE
NINETEENTH CENTURY

What is the significance of Christianity for the solution of the social problem of the present day? This social problem is vast and complicated. It includes the problem of the capitalist economic period and of the industrial proletariat created by it; and of the growth of militaristic and bureaucratic giant states; of the enormous increase in population, which affects colonial and world policy, of the mechanical technique, which produces enormous masses of material and links up and mobilizes the whole world for purposes of trade, but which also treats men and labour like machines.

We only need to formulate this question thus in order to recognize as its most important reply that this problem is entirely new, a problem with which Christian-Social work has never been confronted until now.

In the face of the vast and serious nature of this problem the radical ideals of social reformers of the Chiliastic sects seem like child's play and childish fantasies; admirable and noble, no doubt, but Utopian even in their modern form of a Christian Socialism which dreams of a radical social transformation of the world. From the very outset mysticism declined to make any attempt to find a solution of the problem; in all this confusion it only discerns how impossible it is for the world to give the peace which passes all understanding.

All the Christian churches—the Lutheran Church least of all, however—are evolving schemes for the alleviation of all this distress which weighs on our hearts and minds like a perpetual menace, and each church does its part eagerly and unselfishly. But in all this the churches are only returning in essentials to the old and great main types of their social philosophy, which they are trying to mobilize afresh for the titanic struggles of the present day. Now, as we have seen, there are only two great main types of social philosophy which have attained comprehensive historical significance and influence. The first is the social philosophy of mediaeval Catholicism which is based on the family, guild, and class, which was able to combine a relative dependence on the struggle for existence, the establishment of all fellowship upon personal relations of authority and reverence, the relatively simple economic forms and needs of the pre-capitalistic period, the remains of old solidarities in conditions which involved being bound to the soil or involved in the fortunes of some ancient family, with the Christian ethos of the personal value of the individual and of the universal fellowship of love within the ecclesiastical organization of life. The second is the social philosophy of Ascetic Protestantism, which developed out of that kind of Calvinism which was tinged with a Free Church, Pietistic outlook, and also out of those ascetic sects which had almost broken with the churches altogether, which is inwardly related to modern Utilitarianism and Rationalism, with diligence in one's calling and the glorification of work for its own sake, with political democracy and Liberalism, with the freedom of the individual and all-dominating idea of the social group, which, however, knows how to neutralize the ethically dangerous consequences of modern life by the religious ideas of the responsibility of the individual, and of the duty of love, both of the individual and of the community, through the taboo on luxury, mammon, and love of pleasure, and finally through heroism in serving the cause of Christ all over the world.

Other Christian-Social ideals which developed alongside of these two main types were unable to make any impression on the hard mass of social realities; against this rock they fling themselves in vain to-day.

Both these powerful types of social philosophy, however, in spite of their great and enduring achievements, have now spent their force. So far as Catholicism of the patriarchal guild type is concerned, its failure is due to the fact that it is almost a sheer impossibility to realize its aims at the present day; a further cause of failure is the fact that these ideals cannot be carried out in practice, owing to the weakened religious forces of Catholicism; this also produces other results which are almost intolerable. Ascetic Protestantism, however, which had attempted to establish the rule of Christ over society by a rational method, controlled by the ruling idea of religion, finds to its dismay that the results of its theory have long ago slipped away from its control, and that they have cast aside as useless all the original restrictions and landmarks, whether religious, intellectual, or metaphysical. On the other hand, by its cool austerity, its restraint and its concrete outlook, its proselytizing zeal, and its inartistic and Puritan characteristics, it is opposed to all the instincts of modern civilization; from the purely religious standpoint also its tendency to legalism and Pharisaism, to feverish activity and a mechanical outlook, is very far from being in complete agreement with the deepest Christian ideas.

Under these circumstances our inquiry leads to the conclusion that all Christian-Social work is in a problematic condition. It is problematic in general because the power of thought to overcome brutal reality is always an obscure and difficult question; it is problematic in particular because the main historic forms of the Christian doctrine of society and of social development are to-day, for various reasons, impotent in face of the tasks by which they are confronted.

If the present social situation is to be controlled by Christian principles, thoughts will be necessary which have not yet been thought, and which will correspond to this new situation as the older forms met the need of the social situation in earlier ages. These ideas will have to evolve out of the inner impulse of Christian thought, and out of its vital expression at the present time, and not exclusively out of the New Testament, in precisely the same way as both those great main types of Christian-Social philosophy were evolved out of the Christian thought of their own day, and not solely from the New Testament. And when they have been created and expressed, they will meet the fate which always awaits every fresh creation of religious and ethical thought: they will render indispensable services and they will develop profound energies, but they will never fully realize their actual ideal intention within the sphere of our earthly struggle and conflict.

As little as any other power in this world will they create the Kingdom of God upon earth as a completed social ethical organism. One of the most serious and important truths which emerge as a result of this inquiry is this: every idea is still faced by brutal facts, and all upward movement is checked and hindered by interior and exterior difficulties. Nowhere does there exist an absolute Christian ethic, which only awaits discovery; all that we can do is to learn to control the world-situation in its successive phases just as the earlier Christian ethic did in its own way. There is also no absolute ethical transformation of material nature or of human nature; all that does exist is a constant wrestling with the problems which they raise. Thus the Christian ethic of the present day and of the future will also only be an adjustment to the world-situation, and it will only desire to achieve that which is practically possible. This is the cause of that ceaseless tension which drives man onward yet gives him the sense that he can never realize his ethical ideal. Only doctrinaire idealists or religious fanatics can fail to recognize these facts. Faith is the source of energy in the struggle of life, but life still remains a battle which is continually renewed upon ever new fronts. For every threatening abyss which is closed, another yawning gulf appears. The truth is—and this is the conclusion of the whole matter—the Kingdom of God is within us. But we must let our light shine before men in confident and untiring labour that they may see our good works and praise our Father in Heaven. The final ends of all humanity are hidden within His Hands.[10]

CHAPTER FIVE

Protestantism and Evangelism

In this section we review the way Protestantism has understood its tasks or purpose in the world. This understanding rests upon principles and beliefs that have been surveyed in previous sections, so that as in earlier sections, the intimate and inseparable connection between the thought and action of the Protestant Churches and the age in which they live will be clear. For example, the missionary enterprise of the churches was but part of the movement of European civilization into other parts of the world. Men crossed the seas to establish trading centers and colonies, and to engage in activities that would enhance their economic welfare and that of their nations. The reports they brought back of conditions they found as well as the enlarged vision of mankind which their enterprise spread among men produced a reaction among church men, a reaction made up of a concern for the spiritual welfare of the people about whom they had heard and a desire to share in the adventures inspired by the inner drives of the new age.

At the same time the missionary enterprise belonged within the continuing life of the churches themselves and was molded by the understanding which the churches had of their own nature. A Protestant church which saw itself as part of a national life, so that it was just one facet of the state organization—that institution charged with the special responsibility for the spiritual welfare of all the citizens and thus always having a most intimate and direct involvement with the agencies of government—would see a missionary enterprise in light of its own character; while a church which saw itself as a company of people saved by the action of God from the midst of a lost humanity would in like fashion see its missionary obligation from the standpoint of its own essential nature.

What was true of the missionary enterprise was also true of evangelism, the work of presenting the Christian gospel to people living in the western lands in the neighborhood of the churches. If the State and the Church are one, then the task of the Church in keeping all citizens active in their religious duties and obligations is defined for it; while if the Church as a company of saints looks out upon godless neighbors, then its task of winning converts to the faith is similarly defined.

Much has been made of the fact that the Protestant churches did not begin to engage in missionary activity in other parts of the world until two or three centuries after their founding. The reason is usually said to be that the churches were so busily engaged in defending themselves against the powers that sought to wipe them out and were so completely absorbed in the task of defining themselves that they had neither the interest nor the strength for any larger efforts. And doubtless there was some truth in that contention, but it is far from being all that can be said. As we have seen, the Reformation Churches were national churches, and national churches see themselves in a particular way with limited responsibilities which do not extend beyond the borders of the nation in which they are set. It has been reported that Martin Luther dismissed with scorn the suggestion that the church should send spokesmen to non-Christian peoples.

Two points may be made. We have insisted that Protestantism is that branch of the Christian faith which ties man directly to the current affairs of his daily life. As his faith finds expression in living, living affects his understanding of the faith. In light of this it follows that Protestant churches would not have been involved in missions until Protestant people were involved with non-Christian peoples. Further, as we have noted, in its early years Protestantism took the form of state churches so that these early Protestant churches would be concerned only for the people of their own lands as long as this idea prevailed. There is no reason, then, why the early reformers should have been interested in missions: the peoples of their lands were not involved in overseas expeditions, and they saw the church as a state institution. On the same ground, there is reason why in the case of the English and the Dutch, the early trading companies formed by those people should have provided Christian chaplains to minister to their citizens in other lands and every reason why the early colonists to the American shores should have sought to convert the natives to their faith. The understanding of the Church and extra-ecclesiastical developments were determinative in both cases.

We look first at the developments of missions.

PROTESTANTISM AND MISSIONS

The Old Missionary Society, "For the Propagation of the Gospel in Foreign Parts," founded in 1702, had special reference to the American colonies. But only when the "con-

secrated cobbler," William Carey, in 1792 founded the
Baptist Missionary Society, and himself went to India did
organized Christianity start upon the modern conquest of
the world, and really proclaim the international character of
Christianity. This international character attached itself to
the whole Evangelical philanthrophy. The London Missionary Society was founded in 1795, the Scottish Church Society
in 1795, the Church Missionary Society in 1799, the London
Jews' Society in 1808, the General Baptist Missionary Society
in 1813, and in the same year the Wesleyan Missionary
Society. The same spirit prompted the founding of the Bible
Society in 1804. These Societies were, of course, primarily
for spreading the Gospel as that was variously formulated
in the different parties of the great movement. But true to
the traditions of the various branches at home the missionary
activity was humanitarian in the best sense of the term. The
splendid common-sense of the movement is seen in the
records of Livingstone's travels. And in the early missionary
movement, schools and works of relief, the wants of the body
as well as of the soul, came within the range of Evangelical
sympathy. The fierce commercial exploitation had, of course,
to be encountered. The cheap sneer that the rum and the missionary went together is made in the face of the fact that the
rum was going whether the missionary went or not, and that
the rum without the missionary would have been simply un-
mitigated hell.

The influence of the Moravian Missions upon the Evangelical efforts is a still inadequately written chapter. It was in
many ways a most fortunate circumstance that the early leaders of the Evangelical movement were well acquainted with
Moravian methods, by which men were trained in trades and
useful arts for their work as missionaries. To build houses,
and make wheels, to be able to repair simple machinery and
to understand the processes of husbandry; these things were
as important in the early stages of missionary work as the
literary culture which too often is the sole equipment. The
early zeal of Evangelical Missions was wisely guided by Moravian experience, and the practical philanthropic character
has, happily, never been lost.

In a certain sense the movement was dogmatic, and even narrowly dogmatic. That is to say, a somewhat rough-and-ready dogmatic ground-work in theology was assumed to be the teaching of the Bible and was rather unreflectingly accepted by nearly all. At the same time, as at home so on the mission field a certain quite refreshing freedom marks the early leaders. The real interest of the movement was evangelical and not theologically dogmatic. The real heart of the great missionary uprising whose climax has not yet been reached was its loving and religious humanitarianism. Its aim was practical, its ambition was the world-wide proclamation of loving brotherhood as a religious experience, and the redemption of the sons of God from the chains of sin, disease, ignorance and misery. This religious experience had given reality to the work at home, and now the work in foreign lands had a softening and elevating influence in turn upon the Churches at home. The missionaries told of hospitals and schools they founded for the natives of far off lands, and pity and compassion were the springs for moving to ever-wider generosity.[1]

The true spirit of Christian mission is always born out of a revival of religion. Toward the end of the eighteenth, and in the early years of the nineteenth century not only did missions receive the impulse they needed but the antislavery movement under William Wilberforce, prison reform under John Howard, the founding of the Bible societies, the beginning of the Sunday School movement under Robert Raikes— all testified to the reality of a new current of religious life which followed in the wake of the revival. It was William Carey who touched the new missionary movement into activity. A most interesting feature of his approach was the necessity he felt to overcome the inertia caused by the theory which had held Protestantism bound for so long—the theory that since the work of missions was God's concern it was not for us human beings to interfere. In 1792 he published his celebrated pamphlet entitled *Enquiry into the Obligation of Christians to Use Means for the Conversion of the Heathens.* The significant word in this title, which sounds a bit queer to us today, is "means." Christians were not to sit idly by waiting for God to act but were to "use means" to carry the gospel to the "heathens." The Methodist emphasis on human freedom also made its contribution as well as the growing Arminianism in the Church of England. From this time the Protestant churches began to accept their responsibility and there has been no drawing back. The one query is: Why was it delayed so long? The missionary movement must have a solid theological foundation, yes: but, as we have seen, there are theologies and theological foundation viewpoints which effectively block the missionary impulse and make it impossible for the missionary spirit to grow into active expression. So much of an explanation we may confidently make.

A new missionary agency came into operation in Protestantism, namely, the missionary society. In the beginning it was usually a voluntary organization, and in a number of cases it was interdenominational. Its philosophy was very simple. William Carey said to his friend Andrew Fuller, "I will go down into the well if you will hold the rope at the top." In other denominations with a more central organization the society became a part of the official programme. But whatever the form of organization, the idea of the responsibility of the church at home for the support of those going to foreign countries was fully accepted . . . in accepting their responsibility the Protestant denominations have worked out a vast organization which is intended to reach every individual church and every member.[2]

A Program for Foreign Missionaries

The number of missionaries now residing at Serampore amounted to eight, and Mr. Carey and his colleagues were anxious to establish subordinate stations in the country. Previous to the adoption of this plan, however, they considered it important to place on record the leading principles on which they thought it their duty to act in the work of evangelising the heathen. This document embodies the experience of six years of ardent and unremitting exertion in the missionary field, and is interesting, not merely from the strong illustration it affords of their devotedness to the work, but also from the sound and practical views of missionary labour which it exhibits. It will be necessary, therefore, to present a rather copious analysis of its contents. They considered it necessary, in order to gain the attention of the heathen, that the missionary should be fully acquainted with the current of thought which prevailed among them, with their habits, their propensities, their antipathies, and the mode in which they reasoned about God, sin, holiness, the way of salvation, and a future state; and that he should not forget the humiliating character of their idolatrous worship, feasts, and songs. They considered it necessary to abstain from whatever would tend to increase the repugnance of the natives to the Gospel, to keep out of sight those English peculiarities which were offensive to their feelings, and at the same time to avoid any attack on their prejudices by exhibiting any degree of acrimony against the sins of their gods, and on no account to do violence to their images, or to interrupt their worship—"the real conquests of the Gospel being those of love." "It becomes us," they remark, "to watch all opportunities of doing-good, to carry on conversations with the natives almost every hour in the day, to go from village to village, from market to market, from one assembly to another, and to be instant in season and out of season; this is the life to which we are called in this country." Regarding the style of their addresses to the heathen, they notice the necessity of adhering to the example of the Apostle Paul and making the subject of their preaching, "Christ the crucified." "The doctrine of Christ's expiatory death and all sufficient merits has been, and ever must remain, the grand means of salvation." They deemed it important that the natives should repose the most entire confidence in the missionary, and feel at home in his company, and that in order to gain this confidence he should be willing to listen to their complaints, to give them the kindest advice, and to decided on everything brought before him in the most open, upright, and impartial manner. "We ought to form them to habits of industry, and to exercise much tenderness and forbearance, knowing that industrious habits are formed with difficulty in all heathen nations. We ought also to remember that they have no common sacrifices to make in renouncing their connections, their homes, their former situations, and means of support, and that it will be difficult for them to procure employment with heathen masters." Regarding their conduct towards the Government, the missionaries observe that it was their duty to honour the civil magistrate, and in every state and country to render him the readiest obedience, whether persecuted or protected, and that it became them to instruct their native brethren in the same principles.

Among the means of diffusing Christian truth in India they considered the training of native preachers as the most important. "Another part of our work is the forming of our native brethren to usefulness, fostering every kind of genius, and cherishing every gift and grace in them: in this respect, we can scarcely be too lavish of our attention to their improvement. It is only by means of native preachers we can hope for the universal spread of the Gospel through this immense continent. Europeans are too few, and their subsistence costs too much"—even upon their scale of allowances—"for us ever to hope that they can possibly be the instruments of the universal diffusion of the Word among so many millions." And it was mainly in reference to the establishment of native churches, with native pastors, that their attention was fixed on the necessity of improving the talents of native converts. "The different native churches will, in that case, also, naturally learn to care and provide for their ministers, for their church expenses, and the raising places of worship; and the whole administration will assume a native aspect, by which means the inhabitants will more readily identify the cause as belonging to their own nation. If under the divine blessing, in the course of a few years, a number of churches be thus established, from them the Word of God may sound out even to the extremities of India, and numbers of preachers being raised up and sent forth may form a body of native missionaries, inured to the climate, acquainted with the customs, languages, modes of speech and reasoning of the people, able to become perfectly familiar with them, to enter their house, to live on their food, to sleep with them, or under a tree, and who may travel from one end of the country to another, almost without any expense." The document then refers, in strong language, to the duty of promoting translations of the Sacred Scriptures into the languages of Hindoostan, and of distributing religious tracts as extensively as possible, well as of establishing native free schools; and it closes with the following disinterested and animating exhortation, written in Mr. Ward's own fervid style—the paper was drawn up by him. "Finally, let us give ourselves up unreservedly to this glorious cause. Let us never think that our time, our gifts, our strength, our families, or even the clothes we wear, are our own. Let us sanctify them all to God and His cause. Oh, that He may sanctify us for this work! Let us for ever shut out the idea of laying up a dowrie for ourselves or our children. If we give up the resolution which was formed on the subject of private trade, when we first united at Serampore, the Mission is from that hour a lost cause. A worldly spirit, quarrels and every evil work will succeed the moment it is admitted that each brother may do something on his own account."[3]

The Purpose and Methods of Foreign Missions: The Changing View

Just as at home, so abroad also the emphasis falls less entirely than it formerly did on the individual, and is being more laid upon the society. We are recognising that the individual does not, and cannot be considered by himself, as his inheritance, physical or social, from the past, as well as his present environment, is a potent factor in making him what he is. We must in dealing with any man in the interests of morality or religion take due account of his evil or good, his helpful or hurtful surroundings.

Accordingly the purpose of Foreign Missions is seen to be not the snatching of a few brands from the burning, but the Christianising of the civilisation, culture, morals, and manners of whole nations. Industry must be substituted for war as the dominant interest of savage peoples. Education must lay hold of the young so that the Christian influences may mould the conscience and character when the personality is most flexible. Prejudice and hostility must be overcome by philanthropy, the outer boons of the Gospel must prepare a welcome for its inner blessings. Medical relief is a necessary auxiliary of evangelical appeal.

It is true that this argument is sometimes carried too far. Social amelioration cannot be substituted, either at home or abroad, for individual conversion. India cannot be Christianised unless we make each Hindu a Christian. Mass movements, while they make the change from heathendom to Christianity easier for the individual, always involve the risk that the alteration as a whole will be superficial. It might be a question of temporary tactics whether a missionary should devote his energy to getting such an influence over a whole society as to prepare gradually for a general Christian confession rather than to securing immediately individual conversions but it can never be the resolve of permanent policy to allow individual conversions to fall into the background in the missionary outlook. The condition of Christendom to-day in Europe is a warning against the attempt to make nations as a whole Christian without making sure that the men and women composing them are fully and thoroughly converted. When Jesus compares the Kingdom of God to the leaven which changes the lump He does justify the endeavour to make Christianity a pervasive influence in any human society; and it is not loss but gain that this aspect of mission work is today receiving fuller recognition than ever before.[4]

Our altered religious thought in the West, and our altered knowledge of the East, not only necessitate a restatement of the case for Missions, they make such a restatement possible. The newer thought can appreciate the newer knowledge, and the newer knowledge can find its place in the newer thought. Christian Evangelisation, in the truest sense, is no longer the forlorn hope of plucking a few brands from the burning; it is the building of an empire, into which are incorporated all the kingdoms of the world. The mission of Christianity is not to destroy but to fulfill the religious aspirations of men. The Church does not impoverish herself in giving of her best to the world, but enriches herself. In the religious realm the kings of the East have yet to bring their treasure into her storehouse. The religious preparation of India has been within and not outside the scope of God's providential dealing with the race. The Church however must realise that she must work in truest cooperation with the Spirit, and not in opposition. In the work of redemption the Spirit has preceded the Church in India, and we must follow with due regard to Him who has preceded us.

It is of supreme importance that we should recognize that the missionary motive abides the same under the newer as under the older thought. To the newer thought the faith and hope have changed, but the love abides; and its constraining power is still the motive force which compels it to seek and save that which is lost. The newer thought may have altered the terms in which it seeks to express its conception of the person of Christ, but it speaks with no less emphasis of that chief constituent of His personality, His deathless and unquenchable love. . . . It may have doubts as to the authority of what is called His great commission, but it has no doubt that it correctly conveys the Master's will. It no longer believes in everlasting punishment, from which a belief in any dogma can save men; but it believes more intensely in the eternal connection between sin and suffering, and that through Christ there comes the power which saves us from the life of self, and brings us unto harmony with the will of the Father. It sees in the love which loved even to the uttermost, the complete surrender of His life for the life of the world; and it believes, whoever may have written it, that if Christ so loved us, we ought also to love one another.

Under the older conception, missions to the heathen were regarded in the light of expeditions sent forth with the primary object of conquest. Other faiths and other ideals of life were to be destroyed, and the faith of the Church and the ideals of the West imposed upon the races which had first been subjugated. From this older standpoint it was not easy to regard other faiths in any other light than that of enemies, by whose extermination alone the land of promise could be possessed. There is a sense, of course, in which the destruction of some beliefs is the necessary precursor to the establishment of a truer conception of life. It is not, however, a ruthless destruction, a mere iconoclasm which defaces the image of the outer shrine, while the reverence within the worshipper's heart still remains. The idolater's faith must first be elevated before his idol can wisely be cast down. Under the newer conception therefore, the missionary enterprise is no longer an expedition for the subjugation of other faiths and the destruction of other ideals; it is an ambassage for the emancipation of subject races from the fetters with which they are bound, and their incorporation into the empire of Christ. The missionary goes forth not to impose a creed, but to evoke a richer faith; not to deny but to affirm; not to destroy but to fulfill. . . . The empire of Christ is not the destruction of those distinctive features in other faiths which have sustained and nourished the religious life, and the imposition of an alien creed promulgated from a Western seat of authority, but the incorporation of every religious thought and feeling which is vital and life-giving, into a union of loyal devotion to the eternal and universal Christ. Of necessity much will pass away that now holds captive the religious aspirations of the race . . . The kingdoms of the world will become the empire of our God and of His Christ and that empire will far surpass our most extravagant dreams.[5]

EVANGELISM

We have become so familiar with the idea of conversion as the characteristic of much of the popular Christianity of our own day, that we realize with difficulty that it was presented as a new truth in the last century—a thing so obnoxious to the common sense of the age that it seemed to defy all dignity and decency in religion. It is not easy to recall the prevailing tone of thought which explains why the doctrine of conversion was so obnoxious. One reason for its offensiveness lay in that which constituted its peculiar charm to those who had experienced it—that God came into direct contact with the soul. It was this conviction which underlay the great evangelical awakening, and that marks the movement as distinct in its kind from every other in history. It controverted the deistic conception of God, not by the reason, but by the experience. It declared that every man might be conscious of the action of Deity in the recesses of the spirit. It rested the reality of the religious life in sensations and emotions which were regarded as bearing witness to the presence of God.

The doctrine of conversion, as it was preached by Wesley and Whitefield, has another interest in the history of religious thought besides the change it indicates in the conception of Deity. It passed out of the narrow sphere in which it was first proclaimed among the Methodist or evangelical societies; it invaded, to some extent, the Church of England: it was accepted by Presbyterians, Congregationalists, and Baptists. It gave homogeneousness to the sects which date their birth in the seventeenth century, thus binding together in a common method bodies which had originated in antagonism to each other. It illustrates how when God is believed to be in immediate, and, as it were, tactual relationship with the soul there is no longer any inclination for priesthoods and sacramental agencies which usurp His place. As the idea extended that God Himself works the great change in man by which he is turned from sin to holiness, the last relics of the system of sacramental grace vanished from the popular mind.

Another distinctive feature of the evangelical awakening, whether in England, Germany, or America, was its social character. It did what the church was not doing—it bound men closely together in groups or societies, making them feel their close relationship to each other, by making them realize their relationship to God. Such was the origin of the Methodist movement in its germ at Oxford—a band of men associating themselves for a religious purpose. It was here that the evangelical movement began to correct the disintegrating tendencies of the age. Wherever it spread it carried with it the spirit of coterie. The charm of the movement in its earlier days in the Church of England, was the bond which united its adherents as in some mystic brotherhood. As in the ancient church, the scorn and contempt which they encountered only served to deepen the ties which bound its members together. Such may be called the first practical step toward dispelling the illusion that society was based upon some selfish contract, by which a check was put upon those natural tendencies of men which would otherwise tend to their destruction. The idea of the church was reappearing in its original beauty and simplicity, as a form of association growing out of the very necessities of the religious life—a prophecy of a regenerated society which has its being in God.

It is useless to look to the evangelical movement in any of its forms for any theologian who directly advanced the progress of Christian thought. The study of the evangelical theology is only interesting as showing what were the truths in the formal theology which appealed most strongly to the emotional moods. Methodists and Evangelicals were children of the feelings. In what they accepted or rejected they were guided by instinct, not by reason. As we examine the tenets to which they attached the highest importance, we can see that the motive which imparts to them their significance is the bearing they have upon the central truth of conversion. If they took up again the discredited doctrine of original sin, holding to it with surprising energy and tenacity, it was not so much, with Augustine or Calvin, as the cornerstone of a system of theology, but because it magnified, by contrast, the value of that work of redemption of which they were conscious as the work of God in the soul—a transformation which no human effort could accomplish. If the divinity of Christ became to them as an essential truth in the presence of an Arianizing tendency which hung like an atmosphere over the age, lowering the tone of Christian piety, it was because they felt it to be indispensable to their religious life, not because they had reasoned out its necessity or saw its speculative value in a system of theology. They returned to the Bible with an unqualified devotion because they found in its teaching that which corresponded to their experience and met the deepest wants of the soul. They did not stop to reason about prayer, or how a special Providence could be reconciled with general laws; they prayed because they found in prayer the vital principle of religion. In a word, it was a theology re-

posing upon the feelings as the only sure foundation when
every other support had given way.

. . . Attention should be called to the principle which divided the Evangelicals into two distinct schools, and which
has also made itself felt in the later history of theology. The
separation between Wesley and Whitefield involved a point of
primary importance. Wesley rejected the Augustinian or Calvinistic idea that the will had lost its freedom through Adam's
fall—a tenet which Whitefield retained. While with both conversion was a change, sudden, revolutionary, and complete,
with the one it was regarded as a process for which man
might prepare the way, with the other it was necessary to
wait until God chose to act. But while the assertion of Wesley,
that the will was free, might seem to be advance in theology—
a rejection of the Augustinian dogma of original sin, yet it
does not appear that Wesley grounded his belief in a truer
intellectual conception of the nature of God or of His relation
to man. It is a characteristic of Wesley as a religious re-
former, that he is disclosed to us in his earlier life as under-
taking a new search after God. How to find God, and how
to adjust one's relationship to Him, under the consciousness
of sin, are the uppermost questions in his mind. The one man
of the age who, above all others, may be said to have lived and
to have had his being consciously in God, was William Law,
a non-juring clergyman of the Church of England. To him
Wesley turned for assistance, but came away disappointed.
When, at last, he had reached a principle which seemed to
solve his difficulty, he reproached Law with not being a
Christian, nor understanding the true meaning of the work of
Christ. Wesley had accepted as the fundamental principle in
religion that which Law intelligently and determinately rejected. He had found peace with God through belief in a doctrine of the atonement such as Anselm or as Calvin had taught
it. The doctrine came to him through the Moravians, and
while it was essentially the old Latin doctrine in spirit, it had
assumed a grossness of form and statement which makes Anselm's view seem lofty by comparison. The effect of this belief
in Wesley's theology was to give an almost exclusive prominence to the person and work of Christ. As with the Mora-

vians, Christ takes the supreme place in Christian experience, while, if one may so speak, God is relegated to the background, as if a being from whom Christ had come to deliver us. Thus an element had entered again into the popular theology which affiliated it with the predominant characteristic of mediaeval religion, and which also explains the ease with which the transition has been so often made from the Protestant faith to the acceptance of Romanism.[6]

CHAPTER SIX

Protestantism and the Twentieth Century

Protestantism entered the twentieth century as a branch of Christianity world-wide in its influence. In its basic principles it had not changed, but practically every formulation of its beliefs and every understanding it had of itself had required much rethinking and restatement. We may say that through the years it had come to a much deeper awareness of itself and of the place to which God had called it within His continuing activity. In the minds of many within the Protestant churches there was a clear sense, held with the utmost seriousness, that their history had been a response to God's leading. A few would have claimed that in their responses, the churches had been fully faithful to God's will; by far the majority of churches, however, were aware of human fallibility. Nevertheless, there was a widespread feeling that in the course they had followed, in their thinking, inner life, and action in the world, the churches had given themselves responsibly to their understanding of God's leading.

Protestantism was much divided into denominations and sects and national churches. More than this: there were serious divisions among Protestants on theological grounds. In some cases those divisions cut across other divisions, so that church membership was not the sure indicator of the group within which people had found their most significant religious connection. A man might belong to a local congregation of a certain denomination, yet be meaningfully related to people and congregations outside his own denomination.

Men had begun to have some concern about this situation. They saw some of the evils—competition, jealousy, duplication of effort, weakness in carrying forward the work of the church—to which the divided state of Protestantism gave rise. And through meetings and conversations between men of different groups and corporate enterprises a measure of tolerance between denominations had grown. Few there were who at the beginning of this century would claim that their knowledge of the Gospel of Jesus Christ was the only full and complete knowledge, and fewer still were inclined to call groups other than their own non-Christian. While this change of attitude had taken place, the divisions of Protestantism were reasonably content within themselves and held that individually they were companies within which the truth of the faith was to be found.

When the century began, there were a few men in the Western world who began to draw attention to what they considered to be signs of danger for civilization. To the general public all seemed well. Peace had reigned among men for years; industry had increased in effectiveness, adding greater ease and comfort to life. Some of the obvious evils which had existed had been largely removed; and people moved with great freedom from one nation to another. Men felt that they were on the way to a more perfect society, and while there remained much to be done before that desired end was reached, the progress that had been registered appeared to indicate that the achievement was within human possibilities.

This understanding of the human situation had molded the thinking and the work of the Protestant churches. They saw more deeply, perhaps, into the power of the evil which remained to be overcome, and realized more clearly the amount of effort and time needed to realize the vision men saw before them. Yet they, too, were caught up in the widespread optimism of the period.

Protestantism, in general, was not aware of the world-shaking events through which it would have to pass. Here and there in the churches men caught glimpses of impending trouble, but those who spoke of their visions were not able to be very specific and their contemporaries were not ready to listen to them. Man the Protestant, believing as he does that he stands before God to live by faith, has had to face and deal with the events of the last half-century. And we have to ask, what has happened to Protestantism through that experience.

We turn, first of all, to brief descriptions of developments during the twentieth century as background for Protestant reactions.

As a result of the events of the past year we know that we live in a new age, an age which we do not yet understand but which arouses in us deep foreboding. There are many elements in the situation which are still unpredictable, but whatever events the next years may bring forth there are some characteristics of this new situation which will profoundly influence our lives. Those who speak about this new situation are usually classified as inhabitants of a dream world or as psychological victims of the war—so difficult is it to be or to seem objective in one's attitude to it. This new situation in which we live may be a better one in which to make Christianity seem true and relevant at least in those parts of the world where there is still freedom to teach a relevant form of Christianity at all; but Christianity will necessarily be taught with a different emphasis and to people who have lost faith in much that has been identified in their minds with the gospel.

The first of the underlying factors with which we must now reckon is the end of the spiritual unity of the Christian West, a unity based upon a combination of Christianity and humanism as the sources of the moral standards recognized by the conscience of the West.

We used to live in a world in which people generally realized that Christian standards had a claim upon them, in which minorities could speak freely and keep national life under judgment in the light of those standards, in which those who exercised power were at least inhibited by the scruples of their own or of other people's Christian conscience. Europe and America—the so-called West—belonged to that world, and we were conscious of membership in a common moral universe of discourse. It is the unity of that world that has been shattered and in most of its parts the authority of Christian standards is more seriously threatened than at any time since the days of Charlemagne. So long as we were able to take that kind of world for granted we thought little of it. Did we not find ourselves saying at times that good healthy paganism would be better than nominal Christianity? But we usually assumed that our healthy pagans would retain the Christian ethic.[1]

The war itself has shocked people into facing the grimmest of realities; but it is not in itself sufficient to promote an understanding of the forces that have brought on this world catastrophe. In its later phases, the war has caused people to accept unthinkable sacrifices: but they have yet to accept the hardest sacrifice of all, and that is, to give up their illusions about this civilization. Modern man is the victim of the very instruments he values most. Every gain in power, every mastery of natural forces, every scientific addition to knowledge, has proved potentially dangerous because it has not been accompanied by equal gains in self-understanding and self-discipline. We have sought to achieve perfection by eliminating the human element. Believing that power and knowledge were by nature beneficent or that man himself was inherently good when freed from external obligations to goodness, we have conjured up a genius capable of destroying our civilization. The disproportionate development of the sciences themselves only hastens this malign end.

The physical victory over the barbarian in war is no answer to the problem that the barbarian's existence has conjured up: it merely clears the way for an answer. Even if valour and skill in war give the democratic peoples a temporary military ascendancy, that in itself will not be sufficient either to secure a lasting peace or to raise up this battered civilization. For the disease that threatens us is an organic one: it is no localized infection that can be lanced, cleaned, bandaged; on the contrary, it requires a reorientation of our whole life, a change in occupation, a change in regimen, a change in personal relationships, not at least, a change in attitude and conscious direction: fundamentally, a change in religion, or total sense of the world and life and time. If we seek salvation more cheaply, we shall not be ready to undertake the heroic feats and sacrifices, the spiritual and practical efforts that will be necessary to create a life-sustaining community and a life-directed personality. To make use of our vitalities and energies—and potentially these were never greater—we must reassert once more the primacy of the person.[2]

Such experiences of the past years have imposed upon Protestantism the task of re-thinking its nature and role. The pressure of events has literally tested beliefs and structures and has made men review the temporal body in which their faith was cast. For to Protestants the body and flesh in which faith lives is not the object of faith itself, but is open to change when it proves itself unable to deal with the human needs made apparent by life. Inevitably, Protestantism, holding to the principle upon which it rests, produced a number of responses to the challenge of the present. And since the condition of disunity among the churches was one of the realities brought to focus by contemporary events, there came to be a strong effort to uncover the elements of unity in the churches. Out of this appeared a rather broad stream in Protestantism which is marked by wide areas of agreement. We shall let this broad stream speak for itself about its beliefs.

In order to do justice to all developments within Protestantism, however, we must note the work of those who stand outside the main stream. On one side are those who would hold fast to the extreme liberal insights of the Victorian Age: they have deepened those insights, explained and defended them more clearly, but insisted that the catastrophe of the twentieth century was nothing more than a challenge to them to become defenders of a faith wrought out of the Protestant heritage. On the other side are those who have continued to insist upon certain literal interpretations of the orthodox Reformation teachings in the face of the findings of science, the work of Biblical criticism and the studies of the theologians. To this group, also, the events of this century have been but the reason for a stronger avowal of their understanding of the Christian religion, and a more determined effort to maintain its purity and enlarge the number of its believers. Both these groups see in the present a time for the utmost loyalty to the definition of the Christian faith that had been reached during an earlier time. Both groups have been willing to restate and refine the positions they hold; but essentially they feel no call for any basic rethinking of their positions.

THE MODERN LIBERAL

An outstanding liberal stated the case for his position in an imagined conversation between Simmias and Cebes. The two ancient Greeks settle themselves in comfortable seats in the car of a train and talk of religion.

We were discussing the role of ideas in a world seemingly ruled by impersonal forces, said Cebes, and I gained last time the impression you were not wholly sure that it was by ideas or by the liberal's use of them that the world would be saved.

The remark does justice to your academic caution, replied Simmias. I should prefer to say that the appeal to reason, as a method and a philosophy, is all washed up.

Hobhouse once remarked, said Cebes, that although great changes are not caused by ideas alone, they do not come without ideas. I wonder whether you aren't a little confused as to the role that ideas and reason may be expected to play. Admitting the justice of much you have said and trying to use your own approach, I would still hold that the appeal to ideas and the attempt to keep them coherent is a basic human interest.

I want to try to make clear the role of reason in religion, he continued, because this is crucial for my whole point of view. We both agree that man's need is desperate. You say the need will be met by a glorious God of majesty. But who is this king of glory? The old answer, shouted by conquering armies amassed at the temple gate, their spears still dripping with blood, was: "Jahweh of hosts, the Lord mighty in battle." Yet I think that the writer came nearer to the truth a few verses earlier when he said that the man who may ascend to the hill of the Lord is the one who has clean hands and a pure heart. If God is really an object of worship, and if he is to act as God in human experience, he must be a God who knows what cleanness means. This is to say that he must be a God for whom values are of primary importance and his own power must be of the sort that values can exert. Now the liberal is the one who best understands what this signifies because, as I shall try to show, he has the right approach to a knowledge of what values are and how they work. Let me put the matter in this way. Religion is devoted and loyal commitment to the best that reason and insight can discover. The liberal understands what loyalty to the best means as the authoritarian never can.

On the contrary, almost any form of authoritarianism would seem to me more religious, said Simmias. Take the Roman Church, for instance. It has a dignified history, a supernational organization, a well-articulated philosophy, and a ritual that symbolizes in unparalleled form the cosmic drama of creation and regeneration. Further, in such devices as the confessional it shows that it understands what goes on in the human soul. Or, if you wish a tradition nearer your special background, take Calvinism. It has its own majesty and grandeur in its theory of the Sovereign Creator and Ruler of the world. And surely recent events have verified its low opinion of man.

So often I hear Calvinism praised by men of your type, broke in Cebes rather irritably. Yet I don't see that you go on to join and attend the Presbyterian Church. This is what we would believe, you say, if we believed anything. Well, who is dreamy now? I'd like to say. Who is playing with ideas and allowing them to be artificial instead of forcing them to meet the issues of life? As to its pretensions to authority—of course Calvinism claims to speak for God. But the same claim has been made by thousands of others who turned out to be false prophets. You spoke of its majesty and grandeur. Yet what do you mean except that, by your own confessedly fallible standards and in your own eyes, the Calvinistic God appears to be a Superior Being? The truth is that you simply can't escape the judgments of human reason and appreciation in religion or elsewhere. You may recall the old lady who at the age of eighty took up the study of Hebrew. When her friends asked why, she said it was so that she could talk to God in his own language. As a matter of fact, God has to talk our language if we are to understand him, and if we don't understand him I see no use in talking either with him or about him. But if he talks in language that we understand he must talk with words that are reasonable.

Don't you believe in revelation, then? asked Simmias.

Let me ask you this, said Cebes in reply. How do you know a revelation when you meet one?

Probably by its uniquely overpowering character, said Simmias.

Yet the psychopathic hospitals are full of people who have accepted revelations on that basis, said Cebes. My strong feeling that I am right does not make me right, nor, I regret to say, does yours justify you. There is a distinction, my friend, between psychological certitude and reasonable certainty, and too often it turns out to be the distinction between delusions and truth. Of course I'm not saying that every datum that insists powerfully on being heard must be false. I'm simply affirming that every datum, whether it comes forcefully or feebly, must be interpreted before we can know whether or not to accept it as true. As it comes it makes a knowledge claim. It is not actual knowledge until we have submitted it to the tests of coherence and found it to conform to fact and to be consistent with the rest of our reasonably established judgments. Every sense experience, value experience, or experience of God must be put through the critical mill, must so to speak become liberalized and, in a good sense rationalized, before it can take its place in the reasonable stream of thought.

Even the man who deliberately rejects this process makes use of it according to his lights, Cebes continued. The man who says "I have a revelation straight from God independent of my reasoning powers" is using his reasoning powers to accept the experience and label it revelation. In his own limited way he is reasonable and critical in spite of himself. This is why I just cannot understand my erstwhile liberal friends who have now gone over into neo-orthodoxy. They have had a taste of the liberal method and they know how inescapable it is, yet they pretend that they can bypass it. In the defense of their orthodoxy they actually use all the liberal arguments. This belief fits the facts of history, they say—it works well in human experience and is consistent with the best that human thought has produced, including the latest speculations of Eddington and Millikan. How they can affirm this in one breath and then go on in the next to talk of the complete unknowableness of God is what I cannot understand.[3]

The Liberal and Scripture

Most liberal theologians—one cannot, of course, tar them all with the same brush—try to evade this consequence by trying to take the Bible seriously as evidence of the historical evolution of religion, from a really primitive religiosity (anthropomorphic representations of God, human sacrifice, etc.) through the "moralistic" religion of the prophets, up to Jesus, the great "teacher" and "master," who profoundly deepened the ancient idea of God, so that his disciples "found in him God" (Christ's Sonship of God is interpreted thus), who teaches a new morality and speaks of forgiveness in such a way that it makes all ideas of sacrifice superfluous. After Jesus—so runs the opinion—the development becomes again retrogressive: Judaic—apocalyptic and Hellenistic influences obscure the picture of the master even in the later books of the New Testament—nay, even in the synoptic Gospels, out of which happily we can extract the form of the "Jesus of history."

From this fundamental view, common to liberal theology, different possible relations to the Bible emerge. This may serve as the typical liberal opinion, that one confines himself to presenting the life and especially the teaching of Jesus so clearly, that even our generation may be "followers of Jesus." On this view, metaphysics and dogmatics are ignored as far as possible, and the ethical side of Christianity is strongly emphasised. It cannot be overlooked that this was done with the greatest eagerness, and that it is still done with rather diminished zeal. Relations with the Bible remain fundamentally very loose, or indeed very "free." We must not be bound by the letter of the Bible. "We have the mind of Christ" becomes the confident slogan of Christian freedom. Anything that the Bible contains beyond the ethics of Jesus is regarded from this angle as antiquated scaffolding or as temporary and gloomy background: we have at most to go through all this in order to extract the bright light of the "teaching of Jesus." Where this is done, only parts of Scripture have any present-day meaning. Accordingly one does not trouble oneself radically to find one interpretation for (the whole of) Scripture. One does not on this view interpret: one selects.[4]

THE CONSERVATIVE

At the opposite extreme from the Liberals are the Fundamentalists. The title is unfortunate because of its various connotations. To those outside the group of Christians to which it refers, it carries a somewhat derogatory air, as though the Fundamentalists were rather unacceptable citizens; to those within the group, however, it becomes a fortress to be defended at all costs. Yet the characteristic marks of the group are clear. In contrast to the Liberal who asserts the supremacy of reason over all religious belief and doctrine, the Fundamentalist asserts the supremacy of particular interpretations of belief and doctrine over religious life. Both rest their positions on understandings that were reached in the previous century: and both insist, in the face of the challenge of the present, on the necessity of holding fast to that which was. In this respect both Liberal and Fundamentalist are thoroughgoing conservatives.

It is much easier to record the beliefs of the Fundamentalists than it was that of the Liberals for there is always a consistent orderliness to their writings. In the following passages the material is organized in accordance with the traditional Protestant pattern.

The Bible says, "God is." To believe this is the first requisite in finding God—"He that cometh unto God must believe that He is, and that He is a rewarder of them that diligently seek Him." It is to earnest and believing hearts that God manifests Himself.

God could reveal Himself to physical touch, but the manner of His revelation is to our spirits by the Holy Ghost.

Divine attributes are those qualities which belong to God. "Attributes are any qualities or properties which characterize and differentiate, by virtue of which the subject is what it is." Generally speaking the attributes are considered as "natural and moral," the natural being those which describe God's Being, such as His wisdom and power, the moral attributes being those which describe His character in relation to moral beings, such as holiness and love.[5]

Divine revelation is a supernatural communication of truth from God to man. "Supernatural" means beyond the light of nature or reason. Revelation means "the unveiling, or disclosing, of God's purpose to mankind." It includes every manifestation of God to human consciousness. While we recognize the Scriptures as God's revelation, the unfolding of God's Word and will may also be considered revelation.

While nature might be a means of revelation that God is, it is in the Scripture that we find the revelation as to the purpose of God, especially as such purpose relates to man.

When Jesus knew that He was soon to "go away," He foretold the coming of the Comforter, with the promise that He would guide unto all truth. Thus speaking Jesus gave assurance that, upon His departure, the Holy Spirit would be sent to the disciples and by His guidance they should be instructed in such manner as to be enabled to provide for future generations the infallible Scripture of the New Testament. It was necessary that they have the Holy Spirit in preparing the Scriptures. It is equally necessary that we have the same Holy Spirit that we might be guided in our understanding of them.

In the Scriptures we have the accumulated revelation of the mystery of God, the result of centuries during which God has been revealing Himself and His Word to man. If in the natural world one generation of men owe a debt to the accumulated wisdom of those who have gone before, in the Christian faith this should certainly not be less a truth. It takes faith for the natural man to believe the results of others. Faith is required also in the study of Divine truth.[6]

We are to declare that the entire Bible—the canonical Scriptures of the Old and the New Testaments—is the Word of God. Also, when we speak of the authority of Scripture we mean "that property by which it demands faith and obedience to all its declarations."

We must assert that all teaching and all truth and all doctrine must be tested in the light of the Scriptures. Here is God's revelation of Himself, given in parts and portions in the Old Testament with an increasing clarity and with a culminating finality, coming eventually "in the fulness of the times" to the perfect, absolute, final revelation in God the Son. He in turn enlightens and reveals His will and teaching to these apostles, endows them with a unique authority, fills them with the needed ability and power, and gives them the teaching that is essential to the well-being of the Church and God's people. We can build only upon this one, unique, authority.

The choice for us today is really as simple as it was for those first Christians in the early days. We either accept this authority or else we accept the authority of "modern knowledge," modern science, human understanding, human ability. It is one or the other. Let us not be confused by the modern argument about a changed position. We are still left where believers have always been left. It is still "Christ or the critics."

For us, for the reasons that I have tried to give, there is no real choice. On the one hand, trusting to human ability and understanding, everything is flux and change, uncertain and insecure, ever liable to collapse. On the other, there is not only "the impregnable Rock of Holy Scripture" but there is the Light of the world, the Word of God, the Truth itself.[7]

THE MAIN STREAM: THE PRINCIPLES

We shall ask the Commissions of the World Council of Churches to speak for the middle position of Protestantism. This is not to imply that the great majority of Protestants would agree unequivocally with all that follows, but it does imply that since the World Council is made up of the largest proportion of Protestant churches, and since the statements given here have been worked out by men belonging to divergent groups, they represent as nearly as anything can the positions reached by Protestantism. We shall use other sources in addition to those of the World Council, but they will be works of men who stand in the same general Protestant groupings.

God

The Christian conception of God has remained pretty constant through all the storms of controversy that have raged around other doctrines. It is based upon the Old Testament revelation of God as the Holy One of Israel, infinitely exalted above all the creatures he has made, yet caring for his creatures, ruling and overruling the events of history in justice and mercy, and promising eventual peace to mankind through Israel his specially chosen servant. In the New Testament, the God of Israel is further revealed as the God and Father of our Lord Jesus Christ, "God with us" (Immanuel) in a new and more intimate sense, God walking with us in the person of our Lord, God abiding in our midst through the activity of his Holy Spirit in the new community, the Church, which he has begun to gather from all nations to inherit his Kingdom.

In the Trinitarian and Christological controversies, the centrality of the new revelation in Christ was clearly established, without abandoning the old revelation in Israel or compromising its monotheism; and at the same time a point of contact was established between the Biblical idea of God as Creator and the Greek philosophic idea of God as the Absolute Being that endures beneath the multiplicity and transiency of the visible world. The consistency of this alliance between Hebrew and Greek monotheism has been seriously challenged in recent times, as we shall see; but for the classical schools of Christian theology, both Catholic and Protestant, it has held as firm as the alliance between the Old and New Testament revelations. Through all the schools of Christian thought runs the common conception of God as the creative Source and Ground of nature, the exalted Ruler of history, made man for our redemption in Jesus Christ, working on since Christ by his Spirit in the Church, toward the gathering of a City of God, a Kingdom of Justice and love.

The main issue now seriously under debate in this field is not an issue on which Catholics are divided from Protestants, or Calvinists from Arminians, or liberals from conservatives, but one which cuts across churches and parties in a most extraordinary way.

A balanced concept of God is so hard to maintain that each approach to it needs to be checked and controlled by other approaches: the central revelation in Christ by other stages of revelation within the Bible; the Biblical revelation as a whole, rich in concrete imagery, by the abstract researches of philosophic theology into structure of being. Throughout the history of Christian thought, as we have seen, a balance of this sort has been fairly well maintained between the metaphysical and moral, communicable and incommunicable attributes of God. . . . If a purely metaphysical God is a cold abstraction, a wholly unmetaphysical God is a finite idol, whose worship violates the First Commandment.[8]

For the personal relation to God which gives all its meaning and worth to religion, God must be conceived as at least personal, although the mystery of His Being may not be fully manifested in personality, and even reverence may lead us to concede that He is *supra-personal*. Reason in interpreting the significance and value of nature and man lends support to, and does not challenge this conception of God.

While God may be spoken of as personal, He should not be called a person, one among many, an individual separated as well as distinguished from others; for He is the all-embracing, all-sustaining, all directing reality, without whom neither nature nor man would have any reality, and in whom alone they possess such reality as is granted them.

Hence His relation is not external, as is that of one human individual to another at least as embodied; and although in spirit there can be a community, which transcends differences, yet we must speak of persons, conscious of their individuality. The defect of the deistic tendency is that it represents God as a person thus externally related to nature and man.

Such constant dependence of nature and man on God having been asserted against deism, we must against pantheism no less maintain that within that dependence God gives to His world a derived and limited independence; so that we can speak of an order of nature and a course of history which seems to us autonomous in its unity and continuity. Relative to it God's continuous activity is conditioned; what will be by what has been and still is. The man of science as such is justified in investigating the order of nature without any *deus ex machina*, and so is the historian the course of history. Philosophy in interpreting the world cannot leave out, without loss of adequacy, God as ultimate cause, final purpose, and directive presence. The order of nature and the course of history bear witness, not to divine caprice, but to divine constancy.[9]

The Knowledge of God

As against all theology of the religious consciousness, or of ethical or mystical experience, or of philosophical reflection and speculation, Karl Barth's is a theology of the Word.

What is God's Word? It has a three-fold meaning. It is, first, the Word as preached. As such, it has an imperative character. God's Word is not simply a communication or an objective statement, but a positive command which does not permit man to assume the attitude of a spectator or to enjoy mere disinterested research. It is a motive which is not given as a datum of consciousness or of any human experience whatsoever. It is not subject to our power, but is effective whenever, wherever and however it wills.

The second form of God's Word is the written Word, the Holy Scripture. This is God's Word in that it is a memory of a past revelation of God and an expectation of future revelation. The Church possesses a written Word, a canon of Holy Scripture, but the autonomy and independence of the Word of God in relationship to the Church is not thereby jeopardized. God's Word remains a free power and a living revelation of what God has done and will do. This prevents the Church from identifying itself, its experience and its tradition, with God's Word. It forbids the Church from claiming to be herself the Word of God. It keeps her in the position of one who is addressed by an external and superior authority.[10]

We concur in affirming that the Word of God is ever living and dynamic and inseparable from God's activity. "In the beginning was the Word, and the Word was with God, and the Word was God." God reveals Himself to us by what He does, by that activity by which He has wrought the salvation of men and is working for their restoration to personal fellowship with Himself. . . .

We are at one in asserting the uniqueness and supremacy of the revelation given in Christ, in whose Name alone salvation is offered to the world. But when we turn from this to the question whether we can come to know God through other and partial revelations we find differences which demand further study and discussion. None of us holds that there is a revelation outside Christ which can be put on the same level as the revelation in Christ. But while some are prepared to recognise a *praeparatio evangelica* not only in Hebrew but also in other religions, and believe that God makes Himself known in nature and in history, others hold that the only revelation which the Church can know and to which it should witness is the revelation in Jesus Christ, as contained in the Old and New Testaments.[11]

Doctrine of Man

When man thus reflects upon himself, he recognizes that as subject, knowing, feeling and willing, as conscious of himself as well as the world, he has a significance and value greater than any of the objects known. Vast as is the physical reality around him in space and time, small as he in his habitation earth and in his duration as a race may appear, size is no measure of meaning and worth. The telescope of observation with which he sweeps the heavens does not disclose greater wonders than the microscope of reflexion with which he scans himself. For in himself he not only discovers facts to be apprehended as in the world around, but also ideals to be realized, values to be appreciated and to be appropriated—truth, beauty, goodness, and a voice of authority within which bids him become what he can and ought to be.

The mind that can know the world's vastness and man's smallness in terms of space and time is greater than that world which is not aware of itself. Moral law within, which commands and can be obeyed or disobeyed, has value greater than the natural laws which describe necessary processes. The spirit in man, whose reach exceeds its grasp, and so rises above things seen and temporal to things unseen and eternal, from world and self to God, is more significant than this "passing show of things."

However unworthy man makes himself by his folly and his sin, his worth as rational, aesthetic, moral and religious personality, is not thereby annulled; and a reactionary theology which talks about "a fallen world" as if man were always and only vile is irreverent and ungrateful to the Creator, who has endowed His creature men as He has done, and who is preserving man from the utter ruin that sin unrestrained by His wisdom and goodness might inflict. With this tragedy of human history man's need of redemption and the sufficiency of Christ alone to redeem will be affirmed.[12]

As the creature of God the Creator, man is finite and mortal, like other mere creatures, and belongs to the order of nature; but he bears the image of his Creator in a special sense. Other creatures may mirror the glory of their Creator unconsciously in their structure; but man, as Brunner puts it, is a "responsible" creature, a person capable of personal confrontation with God, and conscious "response" to God. In this basic fact, man's "chief end" is already indicated; he is made for fellowship with God.

In the sight of God his Judge, man is a sinner. It has somehow become second nature for him to oppose the will of God, and thereby to fall into contradiction with his fellow men, with himself and with the world. This is not a condition to which God has fatally condemned mankind, but a perversion of the nature and destiny of man as God created him, for which man himself is responsible. It is a misuse of the great powers with which God has endowed man, so that he dishonors his Maker instead of glorifying him, hates and oppresses his fellows instead of loving and serving them, is inwardly at war with himself, and becomes the slave of those natural and temporal forces he was meant to dominate. So long as man remains impenitently in this condition, he remains under the condemnation of God his Judge.

There is thus a considerable agreement among Christians concerning the position of man in God's world, the fact that he tends tragically to miss his high calling, and the centrality of sin among the imprisoning forces from which he needs deliverance, if he is to be restored to his true destiny.[13]

God and Man's Salvation

God in His free outgoing love justifies and sanctifies us through Christ, and His grace thus manifested is appropriated by faith, which itself is the gift of God.

Justification and Sanctification are two inseparable aspects of God's gracious action in dealing with sinful man.

Justification is the act of God, whereby He forgives our sins and brings us into fellowship with Himself, who in Jesus Christ, and by His death upon the Cross, has condemned sin and manifested His love to sinners, reconciling the world to Himself.

Sanctification is the work of God, whereby through the

Holy Spirit He continually renews us and the whole Church, delivering us from the power of sin, giving us increase in holiness, and transforming us into the likeness of His Son through participation in His death and in His risen life. This renewal, inspiring us to continual spiritual activity and conflict with evil, remains throughout the gift of God. Whatever our growth in holiness may be, our fellowship with God is always based upon God's forgiving grace.

Faith is more than intellectual acceptance of the revelation in Jesus Christ; it is whole-hearted trust in God and His promises, and committal of ourselves to Jesus Christ as Saviour and Lord.[14]

In classic Protestantism, the doctrine of "justification by faith" contains the same two elements, but in inverse proportion. The gracious act of God in Christ, forgiving our sins, is the objective ground of our salvation; but since this is already done once for all, the main emphasis now falls on the individual Christian's act of faith (trust) which seizes hold of this assurance, feels gratitude and penitence commensurate with the grace received, and finally brings forth fruit "meet for repentance," but does not consider these "good works" as any essential part of the process of salvation.

The Christian's own faith and prayer came now to be numbered among the decisive means of grace, alongside of the Word, the sacraments and—as the Calvinists would add—Church discipline. . . .

For Christian faith, sin and grace are not two single and separate items, but correlated facts. Grace exists only for the sinner, and we only speak of sin in respect of grace, which is the central meaning of the principal dogma of the Reformation, justification by faith. This dogma declares that the sinner is justified by a sovereign act of God through the sacrifice of Jesus Christ. He is saved by a decree of God's judgment alone and not by any merit or synergistic co-operation of man, or by subsequent sanctification. It is the sinner who is justified—*simul justus et peccator*, as Luther says. The process is not that a man by his moral effort and an act of grace

ceases to be a *peccator* and becomes justified. This is not
only the Catholic conception, but also the temptation to which
Arminian Methodism is exposed. The Christian is justified
before God as a sinner and must accept this paradox in his
faith—a paradox which finds its parallel in the dialectic
method of Barthian theology.[15]

In these beliefs the Protestantism of this age reaffirms
the principles upon which the Reformation rested in its
origin. Clearly, a new depth of understanding has been
added to each. This was inevitable, if Protestantism was
to remain true to itself and to wrestle with its beliefs as
the world posed questions. The answers reached, in so
far as they were adequate and satisfactory, were found
to be more profound statements of the reality to which
the beliefs themselves pointed.

But there are other elements in Protestantism in which
greater changes have taken place. Some elements, too,
have assumed great importance in church life, though
they were hardly discussed at all when Protestantism began. For example, in the early years the Reformers
asserted the place of the Holy Scriptures in the life of
Christian people; and they strove to make the Scriptures
available to the people in their own languages. But no
one asked how the Scriptures were to be used, where
their authority rested, and what meaning was to be given
to the words themselves; nor did the Reformers foresee
the development of Higher Criticism and its effect upon
man's understanding of the nature and formation of
Scripture. Similarly, while the Reformers were quite sure
of the reality and place of the church in Protestantism,
they did little thinking about it. And they had no way of
foreseeing what would happen to the church or the very
fundamental problem of its nature and structure and

purpose that has been created for the church by the passing years. The knowledge which Protestantism has had of the church has undergone a considerable change.

Understanding the Scriptures

It is no accident that today many Biblical scholars are among the first to raise the demand for a theological interpretation of Scripture. We have to see in this the consequence of a history of New Testament study that has been full of tension. Without going into details, we can set forth the final important stages on this road. It is to be understood of course that (unhappily) the development is not so direct and simple as in the description that follows.

The historico-literary investigations which began in the nineteenth century led to a long-continued process of analytical enquiry. In the course of this, almost all elements of the New Testament were dissolved into their component parts, and their genuineness called in question. Radical views, such as the denial of the historicity of Jesus, were not able to stand up against exact study. Others in the course of time were much modified. . . .

In respect of method, a new turning was reached with the technique of examining the genus to which texts belong, and the subsequent form-criticism. Here the question was: What led the authors of the New Testament to compose their writings? One began to enquire how for example the Gospels developed out of the apostolic preaching. This procedure is manifestly significant in a formal respect to begin with; but it also brought important theological consequences with it, which have by no means been fully worked out yet. . . .

The aim is here to unfold with an ever-fresh concern the fulness of that which Christ has committed to his Church; everything which has been thus unfolded during the centuries was, in its essence, already inherent in the message of the primitive Church and in Scripture. Just as Christ is present not only in Scripture, but also and chiefly in the Church, so the witness of the Church today is understood to be the direct

continuation of the witness that lies in Scripture. What need
can there be of escaping outside this? . . .

Recourse to Scripture takes place not because there is need
to hold on to what has been transmitted, but quite the other
way round: because all has become dubious, and because in
consequence the position of the preacher of the Gospel has
also become dubious. In this profound crisis, questions in the
foreground concerning the validity of single scriptural words
and so on lose more and more of their meaning, over against
the radical fact that the Bible is God's Word to men, that as
we deal with the Bible God speaks to us even today and that
he addresses precisely those that despair. The "Word of God"
here becomes not identical with the very letter of Scripture;
it is rather in a literal sense God's act of speaking with us,
his claim upon us, or as the Reformers used to say *viva vox
evangelii*. Not only the too precipitate systematisation of
ethics, but also the too precipitate systematisation of dogmatics, are sharply criticised here.

At the same time, the Bible is understood quite unambigu-
ously as a human word. Hence we must hear and reckon
with this human word, as it has been spoken, since it is of
prime importance that the message of the Bible be received.
The historical and literary work done on the Bible is fundamentally approved and regarded as part of the task of interpretation. Whenever we hear the Word of God in the human
word, the message of the Bible becomes no longer a message
out of the past, but an event in the present. It then happens
that God speaks and man hears, and this means that he
accepts the message of Jesus Christ. "The Bible becomes
clear where it becomes clear that it says this one thing—that
it proclaims the name of Jesus Christ and therewith God in
his riches and mercy and man in his need and helplessness"
(Karl Barth). The decisive demand of this theology is accordingly apparent in that justice is done to the message of Christ
as the centre of Scripture."[16]

The necessary theological presuppositions of Biblical interpretation are:

It is agreed that the Bible is our common starting point,

for there God's Word confronts us, a Word which humbles the hearers so that they are more ready to listen and to discuss than they are to assert their own opinions.

It is agreed that the primary message of the Bible concerns God's gracious and redemptive activity for the saving of sinful man that he might create in Jesus Christ a people for himself. In this, the Bible's central concern, an authoritative claim is placed upon man and he is called upon to respond in faith and obedience throughout the whole of his life and work. The law of love has always a binding and compelling hold upon us, and in it we encounter the inescapable will of God. On the other hand, in the more specific laws provided for the detailed organisation of the social life of a people who lived under conditions different from our own, we should through reverent and serious study seek to distinguish in the light of God's revelation in Christ the permanently binding from that of purely local and temporal significance.

It is agreed that the starting point of the Christian interpreter lies within the redeemed community of which by faith he is a member.

It is agreed that the centre and goal of the whole Bible is Jesus Christ. This gives the two Testaments a perspective in which Jesus Christ is seen both as the fulfilment and the end of the Law.

It is agreed that the unity of the Old and the New Testament is not to be found in any naturalistic development, or in any static identity, but in the ongoing redemptive activity of God in the history of one people, reaching its fulfilment in Christ. Accordingly it is of decisive importance for hermeneutical method to interpret the Old Testament in the light of the total revelation in the person of Jesus Christ, the Incarnate Word of God, from which arises the full Trinitarian faith of the Church.

It is agreed that allegorical interpretations which were not intended by the Biblical authors are arbitrary and their use may be a disservice to the proper recognition of Biblical authority. But Christian exegesis has been justified in recognising as divinely established a certain correspondence between some events and teachings of the Old and of the New Testament.

It is agreed that, although we may differ in the manner in which tradition, reason and natural law may be used in the interpretation of Scripture, any teaching that clearly contradicts the Biblical positions cannot be accepted as Christian.

It is agreed that if we are to receive the guidance of the Holy Spirit through the Scriptures, we must discover the degree to which our particular situation is similar to that which the Bible presents. It must be remembered that absolute identity of situation is never found, and therefore the problem of adaptation becomes acute. Nevertheless in each new situation we must allow ourselves to be guided by the Bible to a knowledge of the will of God.

It is agreed that the Bible speaks primarily to the Church, but it also speaks through the Church to the world inasmuch as the whole world is claimed by the Church's Lord. The Church can best speak to the world by becoming the Church remade by the Word of God.

It is agreed that in applying the Biblical message to our day, interpreters diverge because of differing doctrinal and ecclesiastical traditions, differing ethical, political, and cultural outlooks, differing geographical and sociological situations, differing temperaments and gifts. It is, however, an actual experience within the Ecumenical Movement, that when we meet together, with presuppositions of which we may be largely unconscious, and bring these presuppositions to the judgment of Scripture, some of the very difficulties are removed which prevent the Gospel from being heard. Thus the Bible itself leads us back to the living Word of God.[17]

The Church: Its Nature

We are at one in confessing belief in the Holy Catholic Church. We acknowledge that through Jesus Christ, particularly through the fact of His resurrection, of the gathering of His disciples round their crucified, risen, and victorious Lord, and of the coming of the Holy Spirit, God's almighty will constituted the Church on earth.

The Church is the people of the new covenant, fulfilling and transcending all that Israel under the old covenant foreshadowed. It is the household of God, the family in which the fatherhood of God and the brotherhood of man is to be realised in the children of His adoption. It is the body of Christ, whose members derive their life and oneness from their one living Head; and thus it is nothing apart from Him, but is in all things dependent upon the power of salvation which God has committed to His Son.

The presence of the ascended Lord in the Church, His Body, is effected by the power of the one Spirit, who conveys to the whole fellowship the gifts of the ascended Lord, dividing to every man severally as He will, guides it into all the truth and fills it unto all the fulness of God.

We all agree that Christ is present in His Church through the Holy Spirit as Prophet, Priest and King. As Prophet He reveals the divine will and purpose to the Church; as Priest He ever liveth to make intercession for us, and through the eternal sacrifice once offered for us on Calvary, He continually draws His people to the Most High; and as King He rules His Church and is ever establishing and extending His Kingdom.

Christ's presence in the Church has been perpetual from its foundation, and this presence He makes effective and evident in the preaching of the Word, in the faithful administration of the Sacraments, in prayer offered in His name, and through the newness of life whereby He enables the faithful to bear witness to Himself. Even though men often prove faithless, Christ will remain faithful to the promise of His presence, and will so continue till the consummation of all things.

In their apprehension of this Faith different persons lay a different emphasis on one or another aspect. Some lay greater stress on the perpetual and abiding Presence of Christ in His Body and with His people, while others lay greater stress on the fact that Christ is present only where His Word is truly preached and received by faith.[18]

The fundamental Protestant idea is that the Church is not above judgment, inerrant and "self-authenticating" as though she were God Himself; she is the servant of God's Word, and must perpetually be judged by her degree of conformity to that Word. The Reformers "put into the hands of their members a Book by whose standard even the Church may be weighed and judged . . . the Word had its being before the Church and is the foundation of it; there may be found the sure and infallible rule whereby may be tried whether the Church doth stagger or err, and whereunto all ecclesiastical doctrines have to be called to account."

The Church is to be reformed not just once but continually, by constant comparison with God's Word. . . .[19]

The position is, then, that we believe together that there is a Church in the churches, but that we cannot say together how and where it exists, or how and where it functions. For some, the marks of the Church are the traditional ones of acceptance of the creeds and the episcopal order; for others, they are in the exclusively Biblical purity of doctrine; for others, in the personal faith of the Church's membership; for others again, in complete freedom of doctrine and worship. It is therefore, humanly speaking, impossible to discover how out of these different approaches we may come to one common conviction as to what the Church in the churches really is, and how it should be concretely expressed in ecumenical form.[20]

The Church: Its Inner Life

The function of the Church is to glorify God in adoration and sacrificial service and to be God's missionary to the world. She is to bear witness to God's redeeming grace in Jesus Christ in her corporate life, to proclaim the good news to every creature and to make disciples of all nations, bringing Christ's commandments to communities as well as to individuals. In relation to those who belong to her fellowship or who are placed under her influence, the function of the

Church is through the ministry of the Word and the Sacraments, and through Christian education, to make them into convinced Christians conscious of the reality of salvation. The needs of individual souls call for pastoral care and for a fellowship in the things of the Spirit through which the members provoke one another to good works, and to walk worthily of their calling, by true friendship, mutual help and consolation, and the exercise of loving discipline. She is to intercede for all her members, especially for those who suffer for their faith, and for all mankind.

The Church must proclaim the righteousness of God as revealed in Jesus Christ and thus encourage and guide her members to promote justice, peace and goodwill among all men and through the whole extent of life. The Church is thus called to do battle against the powers of evil and to seek the glory of God in all things, looking to the day when His Kingdom shall come in the fulness of its powers.[21]

It is the common faith of Christians that the Church owes its existence to an act of God in history. It derives its being from God. It draws its nourishment and sustenance from God. Its primary functions, therefore, are those which relate to the divine source of its life—the acts by which it is ever anew constituted as a Church and takes fresh possession, so to speak, of the Reality which makes it what it is. These functions have a receptive and an active side. . . .

The acts of reception by which the Church ever anew constitutes itself a Church are the hearing of the Word and the receiving of the sacraments. To listen to the Word is to open the mind and heart to the message of the grace and truth that came by Jesus Christ. This truth enshrined in the Bible is made living and effectual by the Holy Spirit. Only by the continuous exposure of the whole being to its transfiguring influence can we fulfil the apostolic injunction not to be conformed to this world, but to be transformed by the renewing of our minds. It is not merely individual members of the Church, but the Church as a whole in the person of its teachers and leaders and rulers that has thus to listen to God's

Word that it may be progressively converted to the mind of Christ.

We misunderstand the significance of Christian worship if we think primarily of its subjective aspects. The central thing is not the elevation of the soul to God in pious thoughts, but the new orientation of life which follows from the acknowledgment of the reality of God, and from the deliverance through His redeeming grace from self-centredness, which is the essential, fundamental sin and evil and the corruption of all morality.

Corresponding to the receptive acts by which the Church is ever constituted afresh, there are the active functions in which, through its appointed officers, the Church mediates what it has received. These are, first, the proclamation of the Gospel—not merely in preaching and addresses, but in acts of worship and deeds of mercy and love that declare its central message—and, secondly, in the administration of the sacraments, with their unfailing witness to the objectivity and reality of God's redemption.

Without the exercise of these essential functions in which the Church renews its life, the Church would no longer be a Church in the Christian sense. But this is not to say that the preaching of the Gospel and the Sacraments are the only expression of the life of the Church. They are the source of a new life which is meant to manifest itself in new attitudes and behaviour and to bring about transformations in the life of society. . . .

Worship is not only the natural expression and language of the Christian soul, but the fountain and source of creative activities. Without continual reference to an ultimate standard and absolute judgment all work tends to lose its significance. The self becomes identified with the object of its pursuit. Our souls shrink to the dimensions of the things that we do. The witness of the Church draws reality and depth from its worship. . . .

The Church is the realization of true community. Its essential nature is fellowship between persons. It can be the manifestation of the true meaning of community because its life is rooted in the love of God. It is only the love of God which can deliver us from our self-centred isolation and set us free to love our fellow-men. The more we struggle to overcome our egocentricity the more egocentric we become. Only a love that comes to us from without and gives our lives a new centre in the One who loves us can break the fetters of our self-love. The Church is thus the sphere of free relations of mutual love and trust between persons, and is meant to be the witness to the world of the true relations of men with one another.

It is the task of the Church to interpret, both to its own members and to the world outside, the meaning and implications of the Gospel which it proclaims. The interpretation in thought of a truth which is inexhaustible can never be more than fragmentary. But the striving for an understanding that is clearer, deeper, and richer can never cease.

In the present crisis in which the Church finds itself the response to God's call must include the response of thought. The rival systems which claim men's allegiance make their appeal to men's understanding as well as to their feelings, and must be engaged and countered in both spheres. This is necessary not only for the sake of the witness of the Church to those who are without, but in order that its own members may be established and fortified in their faith. In the fulfilment of its task the Church must call to its aid the best minds that it can command. These will include laymen as well as theologians.

The clearer understanding of the significance of Christian faith for the actual life of our time which we desiderate is not primarily a matter of scholarship and learning. It is rather the fruit of spiritual insight and understanding, and we must never allow ourselves to forget that the realities of the spiritual world may be hidden from the wise and prudent and revealed to babes. The truth we are seeking may come through prophets raised up by God to serve the needs of our generation, or it may be silently born in the minds of multitudes of plain men and women, as they loyally endeavour to do the will of Christ in the ordinary circumstances of their lives, and spread from one to another till it becomes a common possession. What we have in view is not a body of doctrinal teaching imposed from above, but a widely shared, growing clarity in regard to the true ends of life, by the light of which ordinary men and women will be able more surely to direct their steps. But the truth thus apprehended, in order to do its full work in the world, must be thought out in all its implications and defined with increasing clearness in relation to the thought and problems of the age. The task of thought is to illuminate and strengthen Christian witness and action.[22]

The Church: Its Work in the World

All through the centuries the Church has steadily done three things. It has helped countless people to relate themselves to God, teaching them the truth about God revealed in Christ, bringing to them a sense of the meaning of their lives, mediating to them the divine forgiveness, giving to them hope in the hardest places of life. The gospel has been too big for the Church to hide. Also, the Church has done a vast amount to tame and to refine the human race, to preserve standards which were recognized even when they were not obeyed, to develop a common mind which was controlled in part by Christian insights. But most important of all, the Church has always nourished minorities which have more fully represented the mind of Christ. There have always been saints, mostly uncanonized, who have kept alive the vision of God and the understanding of man's true nature and possibilities. These minorities have sometimes been in cloisters. They have often been found among the revolutionary sects which the established Church of the time rejected, but which would never have existed apart from the background of the Church. These minorities have also been leaven within the Church, and have been represented among its thinkers and ecclesiastical leaders. (This is remarkably true of the contemporary Church). We see within the life of the Church a stream of true Christian devotion which has never stopped. In good times and in bad it has been present, exercising an influence all out of proportion to the numbers involved. There is a cumulative aspect of this minority movement within the Church because we today are the heirs of all the prophets and saints. For our own inspiration and guidance we can choose the best from every century.

A very significant reason for faith in the Church is to be found in the trends within the contemporary Church which seem to indicate that we are living in a period of its reformation. I have said that periodically the Church is reformed by the scourge of external circumstances and by the Spirit of God that is within it. We can see both factors at work today. The scourge of external circumstance is creating situations which suggest to many people the defeat of the Church, the restricting of its influence. I think that we must realize that the prestige and power of the Church in the past have been very much inflated. Our ancestors were in many situations converted by force and, until very recent times, the power of the state has bolstered up the institution of the Church. Today the Church must depend upon the adequacy of the Christian religion to meet the needs of men and upon the responsiveness of the world to the truth.[23]

The more we occupy ourselves with the problems of the social and political, and in particular of the international order, the plainer it becomes that one of the fundamental obstacles to a solution is the fact of complete disagreement in regard to the ultimate purposes of life. How is agreement possible in practical affairs among those who hold irreconcilable philosophies of life? The conditions prevailing in the social and political spheres are determined, in part at least, by the attitudes and decisions of persons. If the purpose of God is to be realized in these spheres, and if the Christian understanding of life is to influence social and political action, it must come about through a change in the attitudes and actions of persons. Those movements within the Church which insist on the primary necessity of a change of the heart and mind of individuals are striking at the root of social evil. Most emphatically the conversion of individuals is not all. For, in the first place, the individual in isolation is a pure abstraction; he is inseparable from the social context, by the ideas and institutions of which he is moulded, and in which he has to act. And, secondly, the significance of conversion lies in the ends to which men are converted and the content and quality of the new life to which they commit themselves. None the less it remains true that repentance and conversion are the starting-point of the Christian life. To be a Christian is to undergo a complete change of mind. The Christian purpose in the social and political spheres can be achieved only by those who have been converted to the Christian understanding of life. While this conversion of the heart and mind is only the beginning, it is the indispensable beginning. In proportion as the Church is in earnest about its responsibilities in the social and political spheres it must address itself with renewed energy to the task of evangelism. The social order can be improved only by persons whose lives have found a new orientation. To ignore this in thought, in policy, or in practice, is to evade the realities of life and to escape into a dream-world of fanciful imaginations and empty hopes. . . .

While services to the sick, the poor, and the unfortunate, which were initiated and for long undertaken by the Church, are now to a large extent provided by the State, there remains, and will always remain, an extensive and important sphere for the specifically Christian ministry. The needs of the outcasts, whom society despises and rejects, and of neglected classes whose wants most people are too preoccupied with their own concerns to perceive and remember, will always make a claim on Christian charity. Even among those for whom adequate material provision is made by the State there exist a multitude of individual needs which no large-scale administrative system can reach, and above all the need for personal understanding, sympathy, and friendship which no organization can supply, but must always be the gift of man to man.

The service of the Church is rendered to men. But it is not the world of which the Church is the servant. It can serve the world only as it is free from bondage to the world. The service which it renders is not a service of its own choosing, or that which the world desires, but that to which the Church is commissioned by Christ.

The witness of the Church is to the manifestation of a new reality—the grace and truth that came by Jesus Christ—and to the coming Kingdom of God. It is directed not merely to individuals, in order that they may believe and be saved, but to the total life of the community. The beliefs and practices of society must be set in the light of the truth that has been revealed. The Church can fully serve men only as it helps them to see the whole of their life and all their activities in relation to the purpose of God. The Church has a responsibility to the community or nation as well as to the individual.

The manner in which the Church is called to discharge this function will vary with the circumstances of the age. The Church has different tasks to fulfil in different conditions of social and political life. Where it has been recently planted in a new soil, and is still young and small in numbers, its influence in the general life of the community is necessarily restricted. Its primary task is to win fresh adherents to the faith; though sometimes, as the history of the mission field shows, the freshness of its message and the contrast between it and the prevailing ideas enable the Church to exert an influence on the general thought and practice out of all proportion to its numbers. Sometimes, again, under autocratic and hostile Governments severe restraints may be placed on the freedom of the Church. It may have to content itself with keeping alive the torch of faith in the hearts of a small handful of believers and waiting in patience for the day of God's deliverance. It may be compelled, as in the early centuries, to seek refuge in the catacombs. Under other conditions the Church may have full liberty to proclaim its own understanding of the truth and to express a judgment on public policy and social practice.[24]

The Church: The Challenge to Its Dividedness

The International Missionary Council at its enlarged meeting at Jerusalem in 1928 did not assemble for the purpose of considering Christian unity. It met to confer on "The Christian Life and Message in relation to Non-Christian Systems." Yet because the subject of the Meeting was the primary question confronting Christianity, the crippling results of disunion were seen as a spectre dominating the background of every proposal for effective advance. Christian unity was the one great practical question which emerged from this conference, in which the native leaders of the younger Churches were present for the first time in representative strength. Moreover, in the call to unity which was adopted by the Meeting, representing as it did fifty nations and almost all the reformed Churches of the world, the authentic voice of the younger Churches of Christendom is heard:

> It is fully recognised that it is not the function of the International Missionary Council to pronounce upon questions of ecclesiastical polity. At the same time, the Council is only performing an inescapable duty when it appeals to the older Churches to adopt a sympathetic attitude towards the longings expressed by the younger Churches for a more rapid advance in Christian reunion.
> We appeal also to the older Churches to encourage and support the younger Churches in facing the challenging task of evangelising the non-Christian world, and to take steps, according to their ability, to solve what perhaps is the greatest problem of the Universal Church of Christ.

. . . The younger Churches of the world are in their creative period. There has been in the last two decades a rapid increase of Church-consciousness among the Christian groups in the mission field. With this consciousness is also the determination to achieve unity for many urgent reasons.

Owing to the divisions within the Christian Church, Christianity has been taken overseas by numerous Churches, societies, and sects. At the present time some 120 distinct Christian organisations, many of them mutually exclusive, are endeavouring to present some form of Christianity to China. In many instances, not only in China, but throughout the whole foreign field, all sorts of peculiar tenets and extravagances, from Seventh Day Adventism to prohibition, are in the forefront of the programmes of some of these agencies. In India some 158 different bodies are at work, and about 134 in Africa. All the divisions of Western Christendom, all the half faiths that claim to be Christian, have been transplanted to foreign soil. Some sort of comity has more recently been followed with regard to spheres of activities, but the results have been appalling. Apart from the fact that in some areas various missions compete side by side for converts, it happens, frequently in the case of "single-society spheres," that Christian converts find themselves separated by questions of Western origin from their fellow Christians in another area a few miles away. Not rarely the bitter antagonism, the mutual fear and distrust of Churches in the West has appeared in the mission field also. That, in spite of what has happened overseas in the last hundred years, Christianity has made such headway as it has done, may be taken as proof of its supernatural character and the essential sameness of Jesus Christ yesterday, to-day and for ever. . . .

The disunited condition of the Church shocks those who are recapturing afresh from the Source the fellowship of the Spirit. Native Christians desire and intend to have fellowship with each other, in spite of the attempt of groups of foreign Christians to keep them apart. We at home are so case-hardened that we cannot understand the impatience of, say, an Indian Christian in the face of the sub-divisions of the Church in his land. We certainly cannot readily appreciate the difference that his acceptance of Christ makes to the whole of his life. Two illustrations given by Indian Christians will serve to make the position clear. First as to the difference which Christianity makes. Father Nehemiah Goreh says: "The difference between a Hindu who worships a cow and an Indian Christian who has ceased to do so is so great that any theological differences there may be between Indian Christians makes no impression upon us." Bishop Azariah, speaking at the Lausanne Conference, showed how great is the scandal of the divided Church in the case of those for whom the acceptance of Christ means social ostracism. "In the non-Christian world . . . the Church's message . . . united in so far as it speaks of the Kingdom of God, realised in Jesus Christ, loses its distinctness when we pass on to ask the convert to separate himself from his past fellowship and enter the fellowship of Jesus Christ. We have no united answer to the questions: Should a man join the Church, and, if so, what Church? Should he be baptised, and, if so, by what baptism? India has a great admiration for Christ, but we fail to carry it further, because over against the anti-Christian divisions of caste we have no true Christian unity into which the Christian can pass."

It is on this sort of situation that Bishop Palmer comments: "The more thoughtful know that division has for centuries been the ruin of their own country and the cruellest divisions are the result of the caste. They dread the possibility of different Christian Churches becoming caste-Churches." And with words which are true at least of the younger native Church leaders throughout many parts of Africa and the Far East as well as in India, he continues: "They are indignant when they reflect that the divisions in which they find themselves imprisoned had their origin in the controversies of foreigners in distant lands, in which they had no part and have no interest." It is doubtful if any convincing reasons were forthcoming for the Chinese Christian student who asked a missionary: "Why should I be a member of the Dutch Reformed Church in China?"[25]

CHAPTER SEVEN

Protestantism: The Challenge of Present and Future

There can be no resting place for Protestantism. The basic concept of the Protestant churches is clear: it is the belief that God actively continues His work for the salvation of all mankind and that He works through the Living Christ and the Church. But this basic belief needs interpretation. Such interpretation is worked out in the life of man as he lives by his beliefs; and since the circumstances in which man lives are forever changing, the way man understands his beliefs necessarily changes also.

We have been reviewing the changes in the Protestant Church which have taken place in the past. Professor Paul Tillich has suggested that the Protestant era is coming to its end. We are not concerned with passing judgment upon the correctness of that suggestion, but in it there are two implications which bear upon the study we are making.

First, the suggestion implies a relationship between Protestantism and the democratic process in government and industry. Since Protestantism is an expression of man's freedom in the religious sphere, that same freedom must also be expressed in other aspects of man's living. Protestantism has been the form of Christianity to be found primarily in the nations that have conducted their affairs by the consent of the governed, that consent known through the unhindered expression of free men. And in Protestant lands those churches which are essentially authoritarian in belief and practice have undergone a modification in the direction of freedom. Living-by-freedom and Protestant Christianity have in general been bound together.

Second, the suggestion implies that, since all across the world there are restrictions upon the actions of men—in free countries as well as in those governed by totalitarian regimes, man is no longer safely to be trusted to manage his affairs in freedom. If that is what is taking place there are bound to follow changes in the form in which the Christian faith appears. In this sense one can say that the end of the Protestant era is in sight.

Or, we can put this in another way. Protestantism began, as we have said, with the onset of the modern age. Protestantism was part of the great upsurge of man's spirit which gave rise to the entire development of Western civilization, its extension across the world, its science, its establishment of democratic political institutions and independent agencies for varied purposes, its inventions, its scheme of education, its art and literature, and all the rest. Underlying these was man's insistence upon his right to be free and to act according to the dictates of his own conscience. Protestantism was the religious expression of that self-assertion. But now humanity has run into trouble. And that trouble has infected all aspects of living. Some people, in facing the situation, have seen in it evidence that man's attempt to live by freedom has been a false enterprise; its falsity is shown by its failure. Such people return to some kind of an authoritarian existence justifying their action in any one of a number of ways. Other people, however, see in the present evidence that man has erred in working out his freedom, that at some point he has failed to find where the true relationship between freedom and authority lies. Such people now undertake readjustments in human institutions and practices and try to create new patterns for society which will serve the newer insights which they have gained.

Protestantism, as the branch of Christianity which belongs in a unique way to the age of freedom, is involved in this time of readjustment. And within it there are those who respond to the present by establishing some authority over the faith they hold. This authority may be a tradition which has come down from the past or an organizational structure which had an historical origin or a formal doctrine which has been turned into a test of the faith itself. When such a stand is taken wholly on the ground that what has been must ever continue to be, then Protestantism ceases to exist, and the Protestant age has come to an end. For Protestantism, in principle, must deal with every changing circumstance in freedom and under the guidance of Jesus Christ by faith. Protestantism as it now exists may well disappear, but that will be of little consequence, for it will not necessarily show that the Protestant faith has been lost. Protestantism will continue as long as its adherents persevere in their God-given task of living completely in the freedom of the spirit.

Thus, today, Protestantism has been driven to take serious account of what it is, of the faith it holds, of the organizations through which it lives and of the work it is doing. The rapidly changing face of human society, of man's knowledge, and of the relationships between people force Protestants to be consciously aware of themselves and to subject themselves to the test of their own adequacy to live in the presence of God and under His will in the circumstances of the present time. There is a broad stream within the churches that shows a deep concern over the condition of the faith. These men would hold fast to the basic beliefs of Protestantism and then would seek to understand what those beliefs involve now. Moreover, since those beliefs have been expressed in actions of various kinds, they also must be subjected to careful examination to determine whether they are valid forms for the Christian faith. It does not follow that because they were once valid they have remained so. Thus, Protestantism, while carrying on its work, is in a state of considerable ferment. We will take up some of the issues that are considered to be of contemporary importance.

A GENERAL STATEMENT OF THE SITUATION

The task of the church is an unfinished task, and always will be. This affirmation is made not on the basis of any theological presupposition, but simply in recognition of the fact that the church exists in history, and that history is the scene of perpetual change. Some religious systems disregard history or deny its importance. Not so the Bible. The Bible teaches that history is the sphere, the medium, in and through which God has chosen to carry out His purposes in the world, and that therefore He can achieve those purposes only in certain ways and not in others. We are in the church, and we are in history. We are called to take a hand in the fulfillment of the purposes of God. It will help us, if we can come to a right understanding of the conditions under which those purposes are coming to fruition.[1]

THE ISSUE OF AUTHORITY

Protestants have been firm in their insistence upon their right to order their religious lives as they thought right. But hidden away beneath that insistence, often quite unrecognized, has been some authority upon which they have depended. Men are justified by faith, but in their living they must depend upon the guidance of God mediated through the Scriptures or the Church or some prophetic voice. In that way the Scriptures or the Church or the voice became an authority. Now men have been led to investigate more carefully and more directly the whole matter of the authorities under which they live in their Christian lives. And while there has been no agreement as to the authority that ought to be acknowledged there has been a clarification of the authorities that are now being accepted.

Although all members of the committee accept the general principles of historical study in the treatment of the Bible, the type of authority assigned to its testimony is very different.

First of all, it is necessary to have a clear understanding of what we mean by authority. This calls for a distinction between the ultimate source of authority and the one to whom authority might be delegated. The latter possesses only a derived authority. One must also recognize channels through which authoritative teaching and discipline pass.

Again, there is a clear distinction between authority in teaching and authority in rule. We designate as an authority one who knows what has been learned in a given field to date. On the other hand, we describe as authorities those persons or institutions which assert the right to command and possess the means to enforce that claim. In the first case, authority does not rest upon any assertion of power but on the inherent witness of the truth. In the latter, there is power to enforce decisions irrespective of their validity. When this distinction is applied to the field of the Church, one is a strictly religious authority; the other is ecclesiastical and can be exercised only through an organized institution.

In the field of religion, we are all agreed that God and only God is the ultimate authority. He has the right to command absolute obedience; on Him all life is dependent. Some desire to add that Jesus is an ultimate authority. With the spirit of this assertion all would concur, but when it is carefully examined it raises many difficult problems. Just what part of the tradition is to be accepted as literally from Him? On what subjects are words of Jesus final? In practice, even the most biblically minded select what is authoritative for them. In the New Testament, Jesus is the revealer of God and the redeemer of men, but it is much less clear in what sense this belief solves the problem of authority. To raise the question of the authority of Jesus, as a matter of fact, throws us back on the channels of information about Him: (1) the earliest Christian writings, the New Testament, (2) the Church which produced and preserved them, and (3) the continuing guidance of the Holy Spirit.

Instead of speaking of channels of authority, many would prefer to use the phrase "source of guidance" as a more accurate description of their function. Among the sources of guidance are Scripture, the Church, and the interior witness of the Holy Spirit. Yet the relative importance assigned to them varies greatly and depends upon a man's total interpretation of Christianity. One does not function in isolation from the others, but men lay greater stress on one or another.

For some, the seat of authority and the rule of faith, life and worship is the Bible as the written Word of God read in the light of its fundamental message, the grace of God in Jesus Christ. Christian preaching, (1) as bound to this Word, (2) as centred in God reconciling the world unto Himself in Christ, and (3) as applied by the Holy Spirit, is a primary mark of the Church. In so far as the Church lives by the Word and Spirit, it has authority to proclaim, interpret and enforce the law of Christ, the King, in so far as given in Scripture.

Others who lay emphasis on the centrality of the Word of God do not identify this with a book, but with the message of God's creative and redemptive acts. The Bible is itself a product of the saving activity of God and is not an authority apart from the Spirit and the Church. These are necessary to save us from literalism on the one hand and individualism upon the other. The authority of the New Testament is absolute in so far as it brings us the Word of God and His grace. This message is found by the guidance of the Spirit and normally within the fellowship of the Church. But there is no binding authority in any of the institutions which the New Testament presupposes. These have only a functional value, and are always relative to particular times and circumstances.

Others would lay emphasis upon the Church itself as the channel of authority. It is historically more basic than the New Testament, because the first generation of Christians had not so much as heard that there could be a New Testament. Since the New Testament documents were written in and for the Church and their acceptance as a sacred canon rests upon the decision of the Church, it is correct to say that the Church was normative for the New Testament. The reversal of this historic position is not only untenable, but has proved the source of controversy, division and confusion. The Church is the living and continuous channel of authority, able to bring forth out of its treasure things new and old. If it could bring forth authoritatively the New Testament, it could with equal authority bring forth the creed and the ministry.

Still others would lay the primary emphasis on the ever present guidance of the Spirit. They believe that it is a misapprehension of Christian truth to identify it with a solid body of doctrine which needs an infallible earthly interpreter. Fixed statements of ideas and institutions are historical expressions which have only instrumental value. The living God is not to be thought of in terms of a dualistic supernaturalism in which revelation is infallible and unchangeable. On the contrary God reveals Himself to us within the limitations of the empirical, human and historical. Hence to seek an external authority of any kind is to look for what does not exist. Agreement cannot be brought about among adherents of discrepant absolutes until they come to admit that these have all been brought forth in an historical movement in which there is much that is relative along with the abiding. This does not mean an anarchy of values or individual caprice, but it does recognize the authority of God who is of the eternal and living Spirit.[2]

THE ISSUE OF UNITY

Protestantism has produced a great number of separate organizations: denominations and sects. No one really knows how many of these varied groups there are; nor would it do any good to attempt to count them because before the task was completed new groups would have formed and some of the existing groups would have disappeared. Such a state of affairs has been inherent in Protestant principles. Man's loyalty has been to his understanding of his faith. Now men have been made aware that there is evil in their dividedness. In this matter there has been much careful study to try to understand the basis upon which the divisions rest. This is part of the effort to re-establish the unity of the church which, men now realize, is urgently needed.

The other direction in which advance may be looked for has relation to the life of the Church as a whole. While Christians differ deeply about the nature of the Church, they all believe that there is, and can be, only one universal society acknowledging Jesus Christ as Lord. Yet to-day the Church is divided, not only in organization and government, but in the understanding of the Gospel and of its implications for conduct. The Church cannot hope in such a condition to meet the demands of the present situation. It is a vital question how advance may be made towards a large unity.[3]

It is the call of Christ which arrests us. What He said then with human voice He repeats now through His indwelling Spirit. The general need of unity is set down by Him in a proverbial saying—"Every kingdom divided against itself is brought to desolation; every city or house divided against itself cannot stand." This is as true to-day as when it was first uttered. It has been accepted by the world of men as applying to every department of life in its separate groupings, political, intellectual, scientific, social. In increasingly wide circles men are striving for unity. Lying at the centre of all and providing the only enduring cement is religious unity.[4]

We find that the obstacles most difficult to overcome consist of elements of "faith" and "order" combined, as when some form of Church government or worship is considered a part of the faith.

But we are led to the conclusion that behind all particular statements of the problem of corporate union lie deeply divergent conceptions of the Church. For the want of any more accurate terms this divergence might be described as the contrast between "authoritarian" and "personal" types of Church.

We have, on the one hand, an insistence upon a divine givenness in the Scriptures, in orders, in creeds, in worship.

We have, on the other hand, an equally strong insistence upon the individual experience of divine grace, as the ruling principle of the gathered Church, in which freedom is both enjoyed as a religious right and enjoined as a religious duty.

We are aware that between these extremes many variations exist, expressed as well in doctrine as in organization, worship, and types of piety. These variations are combinations of the two contrasted types of Church to which we have referred.

But what are the obstacles in the way of unity?

Obstacles which are, in part, theological or ecclesiastical, and, in equal part, sociological or political.

Such obstacles are met in the case of a national Church which hallows the common life of a given people, but is at the same time exposed to the perils of an exclusive provincialism or of domination by a secular state.

Obstacles which are due mainly to historical factors. We have, in Western Christendom, many separations which are the result of the divided secular history of Europe.

We have, in the Near and Middle East, certain conspicuous examples of religiously isolated communities, whose isolation is primarily due to their loyalty to an ancient heritage which goes back to earliest Christian times and often to lands far off from those in which they now exist.

Obstacles which are of "cultural" origin. In Churches which already enjoy substantial agreement upon matters of faith and order, and which may be said to stand upon common ground as representatives of one or other of the two contrasted types of Church, the prospect of corporate union is by no means clear or assured.

These Churches are not conscious of any obstacles to such union because of mutually exclusive doctrines. They are, however, kept apart by barriers of nationality, race, class, general culture, and more particularly by slothful self-content and self-sufficiency.[5]

THE MISSION OF THE CHURCH

The missionary enterprise of the Church, that work of sending men to various parts of the world to preach and teach the Gospel of Christ, was part of the expansion of Western civilization. Whether missionaries or traders landed in a foreign country first is an incidental question of no basic significance. The West moved as a whole, economically, politically, religiously. Church people were Western spokesmen, whatever else they were, and the response that was made to their efforts produced Christian churches that were, in part, Churches of the West. Now the relationship between the West and the rest of the world is undergoing a profound change. Non-Western people have established their own governments and are in control of their own affairs. The West has not withdrawn within its borders, it cannot do that, but its dealings with other people are now on a different basis than formerly. In face of this the Church has had to re-assess its missionary enterprise and has had to come to a clearer understanding of its responsibility toward non-Christian people.

No longer is the right of the Christian Churches to carry on missionary operations in the non-Christian world taken as something in itself self-evident. "The question whether we have in all circumstances the right to meet the non-Christian religious systems with the claim that we, and we alone, possess the truth, is one that must be settled not a priori but in the light of a penetrating study of the actual facts of the situation." Behind this formulation one can trace the influences of the "comparative religion" school of thought. Is Christian faith, perhaps, only one particular form of the mystical experience of the divine which is the common groundwork of all religion? Should not Jesus, Buddha, Confucius, Mohammed and the rest be considered as different branches on the single tree of the religious experience of mankind? Are the differences between the various religions perhaps only relative differences between a more perfect or a less perfect stage of evolution?

The Gospel is to be preached to all men. Can it be so preached in our generation? To preach to men is not the same as to convert them. God alone can command success, and it is always open to men to resist His will. Yet, when we consider the present extension of the Church, and the divine and human resources available, we dare to believe it possible that, before the present generation has passed away, the Gospel should be preached to almost all the inhabitants of the world in such a way as to make clear to them the issue of faith or disbelief in Jesus Christ. If this is possible it is the task of the Church to see that it is done.[6]

Unlike the great missionary gatherings in the succession of which we stand, we meet amidst the sobering actualities of failure and opportunity. However long or short it may be, however convinced we are that the present situation is transitional, the compelling fact is that the missionary movement of the Church is confronted by the contagion and the power of rival and revolutionary faiths. Not since the seventh century, when the missionary expansion of the church stood before the ominous threat of Islam, have the message and the strategy of the Christian mission been so searchingly tested and tried. It will not do to say the same old things in the same old way. Nor are we called upon to supply the missionary movement with a fully elaborated missionary theology. We have only to say what we must say to the Church and to the world about the missionary responsibility of the Church in this convulsive time.

Our word is not one of retreat but of advance; not one of discouragement but of confidence. Our God is the Lord, let the people rejoice; the Lord is King, be the people never so impatient. It is open to us to do again what our brethren thirteen centuries before us set their hearts and hands to. We must take up the cutting edge of our confidence and our commitment and, with urgency and intensity, seek to bring the world to acknowledge and serve the Kingship under which we stand. The conflict is on between Him whom God in His almighty purpose has raised up and made both Lord and Christ and the rival loyalties and commitments which govern the hearts and the minds of men in our time. The missionary task of the Church is to make its obedience to the Lordship of Jesus Christ plain and persuasive wherever this Lordship is still unknown and still unacknowledged. In the providence of our God who is King, the present paradoxical situation of the missionary movement is this: that at the moment when dark and forbidding curtains have abruptly altered missionary manoeuvre-ability and advance, the missionary movement is being judged for its failures and called to repent. At the same time, the opportunities which open out before the Christian mission are gifts of God which call for fresh obedience.

God sends forth the Church to carry out His work to the ends of the earth, to all the nations and to the completion of time. By the terms of the Church's charter it is given responsibility for:

(1) Every inhabited area of the world. No place is too far or too near for the exercise of the mission. Every group of Christians in the world today is surrounded by people who deny or do not know the Christian message; and that group of Christians, because it is the Church sent by God, has an immediate responsibility to them. But because the Church represents the cosmic Christ, King of kings and Saviour of all mankind, the responsibility of that group of Christians is not limited to its immediate situation. The command "Go forth" requires the Church to exercise its mission both in the actual area where the Church is already established and in an area where it is not yet established.

(2) Every social, political and religious grouping of mankind. This means that the Church must direct its mission to those places and societies where men are living by a faith which denies or rebels against the faith of Christ, whatever form that faith may take. It also means that the Church, in its mission, must come to grips with the actual social, political and cultural life of the people for whom it is concerned. This gives any group of Christians an immediate responsibility for the society in which they live. But because the Church is sent to all nations and because Christ is the one Lord of all, the responsibility of that group of Christians is not limited to its immediate situation. Nor is it limited by weakness, persecution and closed doors, for these are the conditions which the Church has been told to expect and with which it must do battle.

(3) Every time of opportunity. This means that the mission of the Church forbids it the temptation to drift helplessly

before the events of our time and denies it the possibility of
fleeing before them. At one and the same moment opportunities for advancing the mission of the Church lie alongside
the catastrophic destruction of that mission. Because the
Church is sent forth to do its work until the completion of
time, and because Christ is the only one sent forth to judge
and redeem the life of man, the Church is bidden in its mission to seek out the moments of opportunity and to interpret
the catastrophes as the judgements of God which are the other
side of His mercy.[7]

THE CHURCH AND THE WORLD

We have seen in previous pages the problem that was
raised for Protestantism in the relationship of the Church
to the common life of man. And while the problem was
especially acute for Protestantism because of its break
with the Roman Church, it was raised for Christianity
as a whole because with the onset of the modern age
men began to take full authority for their institutions.
Instead of looking to the Church for guidance, men
worked through their own wisdom and their own interests to direct matters as suited them. This resulted in
vast inequalities of opportunities and rewards among
men; and it produced much suffering, injustice, exploitation, and hardship. Some individuals within Protestantism
became aware of these conditions and undertook efforts
to change them. Gradually society itself took the situation in hand and brought about a more orderly arrangement of human affairs. By that time the Church had
grown aware of its responsibilities for the welfare of
mankind. But now, when governments everywhere are
concerned for their citizens, the Church finds it necessary

to think clearly about the responsibility it has for humanity and the way it must carry out that responsibility.

Christian social responsibility is grounded in the mighty act of God, who is revealed in Jesus Christ our Lord. He has created the world, and all time is embraced within His eternal purpose. He moves and acts within history as the ever-living God. The centre of world history is the earthly life, the cross, and the resurrection of Jesus Christ.

He has established with men a living relationship of promise and commandment in which they are called to live in faithful obedience to His purpose. The promise is the gift of abundant life as children of God for those who hear and follow the divine call. The commandment is that men should love God and their neighbours. In the call to responsible social action, the promise and the commandment of the righteous and loving God require us to recognize that in every human being Christ Himself comes to claim our service. Responding to God's love in Christ and being aware of His final judgement, Christians will act responsibly. The call to social righteousness is sustained by the sure hope that the victory is with God, who in Christ has vanquished the powers of evil and in His own day will make this victory fully manifest in Christ.

Man and all the powers of this world are under the sovereignty of their Maker who calls men in families, societies, nations and all human groups to responsibilities under Him. From Christ men receive the direction for their service, the obligation to share heartily in the world's work and daily tasks, and the responsibility to seek a better social and political life. Our hope in Christ enables us to know that there are limitations set upon every human ideal and achievement, so that we never make an idol out of any social cause, institution or system. Moreover, because our hope is in Christ, we are saved from frustration where our efforts to influence public opinion or social action are seemingly in vain and we are saved from despair when all human hopes collapse.

The first Assembly of the World Council of Churches coined the term "The Responsible Society." It was stated that the responsible society is a society "where freedom is the freedom of men who acknowledge responsibility to justice and public order and where those who hold political authority or economic power are responsible for its exercise to God and to the people whose welfare is affected by it."

"Responsible Society" is not an alternative social or political system, but a criterion by which we judge all existing social orders and at the same time a standard to guide us in specific choices we have to make. Christians are called to live responsibly, to live in response to God's act of redemption in Christ, in any society, even within the most unfavourable social structures.[8]

THE MINISTRY OF THE LAITY

The Reformers spoke about "the priesthood of all believers," meaning that each individual was both a priest for himself and for his fellow man. That is, every individual was able to deal directly with God, or God would deal directly with him without the mediation of any earthly organization. But, while always repeating the Reformers' phrase and priding itself on the fact that in the Church all were equally laymen, Protestantism has done little to clarify what the phrase means. Today, the question of the structure of the Church has been raised and that has pushed to the forefront the allied question of the role of the layman in the life of the Church.

The Reformers, in returning to the Bible and finding there that the Lord Jesus Christ is the only true Head of the Church, ruling the whole Church by His Holy Spirit and by His grace and forgiveness, eliminating all gradation of powers, rights and authority, were determined to have done with the system of hierarchical gradation and the identification of the Church with the priestly-sacramental clergy. The Church was a body of believers and forgiven sinners. But in organizing or re-organizing the Church their attention was mainly turned to the avoidance and elimination of the flagrant abuses and corruptions of the dominant ssytem. The Reformers' thinking on the Church did not become fully Biblical, because quite understandably in the stress and heat of battle it was strongly determined by protest and polemics. Moreover, Luther's defiant words, that every baptized Christian had the power which the Pope, bishops and priests had, hid some pitfalls.

The Reformation coupled with its radical distinction between "clergy" and "laity" a vehement stress on the pre-eminence of the preaching office. This vehement stress on correct, "pure" preaching as the sustaining nourishment, required a specially qualified group of bearers of this office. The right administration of the Sacraments, which was also emphatically proclaimed as one of the essential marks of the Church, did not, however, in many Churches, particularly in regard to the Eucharist, obtain the same position as the "pure preaching of the Word." Its administration was reserved for the "ministry." Although this development had many good reasons, it kept an inner ambiguity in the whole conception of the "ministry," because on the one hand it tended toward a re-establishment of a kind of clergy, whereas on the other hand the abolition of the distinction between "clergy" and "laity" was, at least in principle, maintained. Ordination to the status of *rite vocatus,* which had become the wall of separation between "clergy" and "laity" in the early Church, became in fact again a sort of dividing line. As already observed, it was motivated by the argument that this distinction happened for the sake of order. In light of the principle of "the universal priesthood of all believers" and what was meant by it, this is of course the only right motivation. It wanted to express, in answer to the priestly-sacramental conception of the past, a definite adieu to the idea of the indelible character of the "clergy" as existing in elevated isolation from the laity. Yet in fact, contrary to the theory of fundamental non-distinction, it encouraged the practical recognition of a secondary status of the "laity" in comparison with the ministry, the breeding of an attitude of passivity in the laity as a whole, the accentuation of the significance of "office" and its leadership.

This trend of development was strengthened by the fact that the ministers, whose main work was considered to be the right preaching of the Word, appeared more and more as the "theologians," the "knowers," and in the existing framework of social stratification and honour they represented the "spiritual status" by profession. The counter-effect was that the laity gradually got into and, generally speaking, accepted the position of the "ignorant," the spiritually non-adult. It has led to the situation which is at present still prominent, that there is in all Churches a clear division between the leading office bearers and the laity, functioning on the tacitly accepted assumption that, properly speaking, the Church is essentially the concern of the ministry.

The general conclusion that can be drawn is that for the greater part of its history the Church has provided little place in its thinking for expressing the meaning of the laity in the divine economy of salvation of the world and in the economy of the Church. At best the laity was the flock; always it was object, never subject in its own calling and responsibility. When, as with the Reformation, in principle a strong vindication of the laity as *subject* and not merely *object* was made, the plea in concrete reality broke down on the general inaptitude of the laity to function as a subject in the Biblical sense, and on the enormous preoccupation with the raising and implementing of the ministry. This ministry, though not in theological theory, yet certainly in the realities of the sociological structure and psychological apprehension, became in many respects a metamorphosis of the former "clergy." The priestly-sacramental notions related to the "clergy" were of course largely eliminated and reinterpreted in a religious moral sense; but in actual fact the "standing" and "apartness" of the new-born ministry were in many respects similar to those of the former "clergy."[9]

Clergy and laity belong in the Church together; if the Church is to perform her mission in the world, they need each other. The growing emphasis in many parts of the world upon the function of the laity is not to be understood as an attempt to secure for the laity some larger place or recognition in the Church, nor yet as merely a means to supplement an overburdened and understaffed ordained ministry. It springs from the rediscovery of the true nature of the Church as the People of God. The word "laity must not be understood in a merely negative way as meaning those Church members who are not the clergy. Though not yet fully articulated, a more positive understanding of the ministry of the laity is gaining acceptance. The phrase "the ministry of the laity" expresses the privilege of the whole Church to share in Christ's ministry to the world. We must understand anew the implications of the fact that we are all baptized, that, as Christ came to minister, so must all Christians become ministers of His saving purpose according to the particular gift of the Spirit which each has received, as messengers of the hope revealed in Christ. Therefore in daily living and work the laity are not mere fragments of the Church who are scattered about the world and who come together for worship, instruction and specifically Christian fellowship on Sundays. They are the Church's representatives, no matter where they are. It is the laity who draw together work and worship; it is they who bridge the gulf between the Church and the world, and it is they who manifest in word and action the Lordship of Christ over that world which claims so much of their time and energy and labour. This, and not some new order or organization, is the ministry of the laity. They are called to it because they belong to the Church, although many do not yet know that they are thus called.[10]

References

References

Chapter I

THE RISE OF PROTESTANT CHRISTIANITY

1. Susanna Dobson, *The Life of Petrarch*. Collected from *Mémoires pour la vie de Pétrarque*, 2 vols. (London: Associated Booksellers, 1797), p. 20.
2. *Ibid.*, Bk. 1, pp. 165–66.
3. *Ibid.*, p. 151.
4. H. B. Workman, *The Dawn of the Reformation* (London: Epworth Press, 1933), Vol. I, p. 38.
5. *Ibid.*, Vol. II, p. 76.
6. *Ibid.*, p. 121.
7. Frederic Seebohm, *The Oxford Reformers* (London: Longmans, Green & Co., 1896), pp. 74–75.
8. *Ibid.*, pp. 330–331.
9. *Ibid.*, pp. 129–131.
10. *Ibid.*, p. 326.
11. Matthew Tindal, *A Pathway into the Holy Scriptures in the Writings of Tindal* (London: Religious Tract Society, n.d.), pp. 76–78.

Chapter II

THE PRINCIPLES OF THE REFORMATION

1. Martin Luther, *First Principles of the Reformation* (London: John Murray, 1883), pp. 104–108, 113, 118, 119, 121–123, 125, 129, 132, 135–137.

2. *Ibid.*, pp. 21–23.

3. *Ibid.*, pp. 116–117.

4. *Ibid.*, pp. 162–164.

5. *Ibid.*, pp. 165–166.

6. John Calvin, *Institutes of the Christian Religion* (London: Thomas Tegg, 1844), Vol. I, p. 36.

7. *Ibid.*, p. 56.

8. *Ibid.*, pp. 59, 63.

9. *Ibid.*, p. 191.

10. *Ibid.*, p. 211.

11. *Ibid.*, pp. 392–396.

12. *Ibid.*, pp. 432–434.

13. *Ibid.*, pp. 478–479.

14. *Ibid.*, pp. 543–545.

15. *Ibid.*, Vol. II, pp. 54–56.

16. *Ibid.*, p. 62.

17. *Ibid.*, p. 201.

18. *Ibid.*, pp. 227–229.

19. *Ibid.*, pp. 561–562.

20. R. Christoffel, "The Achetcles," *Zwingli* (Edinburgh: T. T. Clark, 1858), p. 19.

21. *Ibid.*, "Circular Letter of 1525," p. 183.

22. M. A. Curtes, *History of Creeds and Confessions of Faith* (Edinburgh: T. T. Clark, 1911), pp. 143–146.

23. Philip Schaff, *The Creeds of Christendom* (New York: Harper and Brothers, 1890), Vol. I, pp. 396–399, 400–409, 410–413, 420.

24. *Ibid.*, p. 216.

25. G. C. Richardson, *The Church Through the Centuries* (London: Religious Book Club, 1938), pp. 177–178, 180.

26. Willeston Walker, *Creeds and Platforms of Congregationalism* (New York: Charles Scribner's Sons, 1893), pp. 4–5.

27. *Writings of Rev. Dr. Thomas Cranmer* (London: Religious Tract Society; no date, no author), p. 11.

28. *Ibid.*, pp. 14, 40, 268.

29. *The Book of Common Prayer* (London: S.P.C.K., 1905).

Chapter III

PROTESTANTISM: ITS INNER LIFE

1. Frederic Temple, "The Education of the World," *Essays and Reviews* (London: John W. Parker and Sons, 1860), pp. 40–44.

2. *The Denominational Reason Why* (no author given) (London: Houston and Sons, 1890), pp. 279–283.

3. Philip Schaff, *The Creeds of Christendom* (New York: Harper and Brothers, 1890), p. 866.

4. Henry Carter, *The Methodist Heritage* (London: Epworth Press, 1951), pp. 163–170.

5. Schaff, *op. cit.*, p. 900.

6. *Ibid.*, pp. 886–887.

7. F. D. Maurice, *The Kingdom of Christ* (London: S.C.M. Press Ltd., 1958), Vol. I, p. 144.

8. Schaff, *op. cit.*, p. 828.

9. Willeston Walker, *Creeds and Platforms of Congregationalism* (New York: Charles Scribner's Sons, 1893), pp. 4–5.

10. Schaff, *op. cit.*, p. 609.

11. J. H. Newman, *Apologia pro vita sua* (London: Longmans, Green, Reader and Dyer, 1874), pp. 31–32.

12. Mark Pattison, "Tendencies in Religious Thought in England, 1688–1750," *Essays and Reviews* (London: John W. Parker and Sons, 1860), pp. 257–258, 267–269.

13. Matthew Tindal, "Christianity as Old as Creation," in J. M. Creed and J. S. Boys Smith, eds., *Religious Thought in the Eighteenth Century* (Cambridge: Cambridge University Press, 1934), pp. 31–34.

14. Baden Powell, "On the Study of Evidences of Christianity," in *Essays and Reviews*, pp. 102–103.

15. Charles Leslie, "The Certainty of the Christian Religion Proved by Four Rules," in Creed and Boys Smith, eds., *op. cit.*, p. 52.

16. Powell, *op. cit.*, pp. 127–128.

17. J. Graham Machen, *Christianity and Liberalism* (New York: The Macmillan Company, 1934), pp. 2–7.

18. Maurice, *op. cit.*, Vol. I, p. 71.

19. Horace Bushnell, *Nature and the Supernatural* (Edinburgh: Alexander Strahan & Co., 1861), p. 298.

20. William Cunningham, "The Christian Standpoint," in Henry B. Swete, ed., *Essays on Some Theological Questions of the Day* (London: Macmillan and Company, Ltd., 1905), p. 28.

21. J. K. S. Reid, *The Authority of Scripture* (New York: Harper and Brothers, n.d.), pp. 71, 92.

22. Richard Brook, "The Bible," in B. H. Streeter, ed., *Foundations* (London: Macmillan and Company, Ltd., 1912), pp. 27–31.

23. Frederic Chase, "The Gospels in the Light of Historical Criticism," in Swete, ed., *op. cit.*, pp. 415–417.

24. Charles Gore, "The Holy Spirit and Inspiration," in Gore, ed., *Lux Mundi* (London: John Murray, 1889), pp. 357–361.

25. Sydney Cave, *The Doctrine of the Person of Christ* (London: Duckworth, 1925), pp. 139–142.

26. W. R. Inge, "The Person of Christ," *Contentio Veritatis* (London: John Murray, 1916), pp. 91-94.

27. Swete, *op. cit.*, pp. 517–523.

28. Cave, *op. cit.*, pp. 218–220.

Chapter IV

PROTESTANTISM AND THE WORLD

1. Frederick John Foakes-Jackson, "Christ in the Church: The Testimony of History," in Swete, *op. cit.*, pp. 508-13.

2. Walter Rauschenbusch, *Christianity and the Social Crisis* (New York: The Macmillan Co., 1908), pp. 332–333.

3. Henry Townsend, *The Claims of the Free Churches* (London: Hodder and Stoughton, Ltd., 1949), pp. 255–262.

4. John Oman, *The Church and the Divine Order* (London: Hodder and Stoughton, Ltd., 1949), pp. 238–279.

5. Walter Hobhouse, *The Church and the World* (London: Macmillan and Co., Ltd., 1910), pp. 259–261.

6. Henry Carter, *The Methodist Heritage* (London: Epworth Press, 1951), pp. 111–123.

7. Ernst Troeltsch, *The Social Teachings of the Christian Church* (London: George Allen & Unwin Ltd., 1931), Vol. II, pp. 575, 646–650.

8. W. J. H. Campion, "Christianity and Politics," in Gore, *op. cit.,* p. 438.

9. Walter Rauschenbusch, *op. cit.,* pp. 308–317.

10. Ernst Troeltsch, *op. cit.,* pp. 1010–1013.

Chapter V

PROTESTANT AND EVANGELISM

1. J. P. Paton, P. W. Butting, and A. E. Garvie, eds., *Christ and Civilization* (London: National Council of Evangelical Free Churches, 1912), pp. 393–395.

2. Edmund D. Soper, *The Philosophy of the Christian World Mission* (New York: Abingdon-Cokesbury Press, 1943), pp. 117–124.

3. John Clark Marshman, *The Life and Times of Carey, Marshman and Ward* (London: Longman, Brown, Green, Longmans and Bros., 1859), pp. 227–230.

4. Alfred E. Garvie, *The Missionary Obligation* (London: Hodder and Stoughton, 1914), pp. 110–113.

5. Bernard Lucas, *The Empire of Christ* (London: Macmillan and Co., Ltd., 1908), pp. 20, 27–28, 32–34.

6. A. V. G. Allen, *The Continuity of Christian Thought* (Boston: Houghton, Mifflin and Co., 1897), pp. 374–379.

Chapter VI

PROTESTANTISM AND THE TWENTIETH CENTURY

1. John C. Bennett, *Christian Realism* (New York: Charles Scribner's Sons, 1941), pp. 1–2.

2. Lewis Mumford, *The Condition of Man* (New York: Harcourt, Brace and Co., 1944), p. 393.

3. Julius Seeley Bixler, *Conversations with an Unrepentant Liberal* (New Haven: Yale University Press, 1946), p. 44.

4. Alan Richardson and W. Schweitzer, eds., *Biblical Authority for Today* (London: S. C. M. Press, 1951), p. 143.

5. E. S. Williams, *Systematic Theology* (Springfield, Missouri: Gospel Publishing House, n. d.), pp. 165–191, *passim.*

6. *Ibid.,* pp. 43–46.

7. D. Martin Lloyd-Jones, *Authority* (London: Inter-Varsity Fellowship, 1958), pp. 33–60, *passim*.

8. Walter M. Horton, *Christian Theology* (New York: Harper and Brothers, 1955), pp. 85–102.

9. Alfred E. Garvie, *The Christian Faith* (London: Duckworth, 1936), pp. 98–100.

10. Adolph Keller, *Religion and the European Mind* (London: The Lutterworth Press, 1934), p. 56.

11. Leonard Hodgson, ed., *The Second World Conference on Faith and Order* (New York: The Macmillan Co., 1938), p. 228.

12. Horton, *op. cit.*, pp. 147–161.

13. Hodgson, *op. cit.*, p. 224.

14. Horton, *op. cit.*, p. 238.

15. Keller, *op. cit.*, p. 63.

16. Richardson and Schweitzer, *op. cit.*, pp. 131–148.

17. *Ibid.*, pp. 240–243.

18. Hodgson, *op. cit.*, p. 230.

19. Horton, *op. cit.*, pp. 209–240.

20. W. A. Visser 't Hooft and J. H. Oldham, *The Church and Its Function in Society* (London: George Allen and Unwin Ltd., 1937), pp. 94–95.

21. Hodgson, *op. cit.*, pp. 233–234.

22. 't Hooft and Oldham, *op. cit.*, pp. 154–166.

23. Bennett, *op. cit.*, pp. 143–144.

24. 't Hooft and Oldham, *op. cit.*, pp. 168–173.

25. V. F. Storr and G. H. Harris, ed., *The Call for Christian Unity* (London: Hodder and Stoughton Ltd., 1930), pp. 15–23.

Chapter VII

PROTESTANTISM: THE CHALLENGE OF PRESENT AND FUTURE

1. Stephen Neill, *The Unfinished Task* (London: Edinburgh House Press, 1957), p. 7.

2. R. Newton Flew, ed., *The Nature of the Church* (London: S. C. M. Press, 1952), pp. 239–242.

3. W. A. Visser 't Hooft and J. H. Oldham, *The Church and Its Function in Society* (London: George Allen Unwin Ltd., 1937), p. 251.

4. H. N. Bate, *Faith and Order: World Conference,* 1924 (New York: Doubleday, Doran and Co., 1928), pp. 4–5.

5. Leonard Hodgson, ed., *The Second World Conference on Faith and Order* (New York: The Macmillan Co., 1938), pp. 257–259.

6. Neill, *op. cit.,* p. 151.

7. Norman Goodall, ed., *Missions under the Cross* (London: Edinburgh House Press, 1953), pp. 238–243.

8. W. A. Visser 't Hooft, ed., *The Evanston Report* (London: S.C.M. Press, Ltd., 1955) pp. 112–113.

9. Hendrik Kraemer, *A Theology of the Laity* (London: Lutterworth Press, 1958), pp. 64–66, 72–73.

10. 't Hooft, ed., *The Evanston Report, op. cit.,* p. 161.